How Companies Can Create Game-Changing Ventures at Startup Speed

Linda K. Yates

HARVARD BUSINESS REVIEW PRESS

Boston, Massachusetts

The Unicorn Within

HBR Press Quantity Sales Discounts

Harvard Business Review Press titles are available at significant quantity discounts when purchased in bulk for client gifts, sales promotions, and premiums. Special editions, including books with corporate logos, customized covers, and letters from the company or CEO printed in the front matter, as well as excerpts of existing books, can also be created in large quantities for special needs.

For details and discount information for both print and ebook formats, contact booksales@harvardbusiness.org, tel. 800-988-0886, or www.hbr.org/bulksales.

Copyright 2022 Linda K. Yates
Unless otherwise specified, all tools, exercises, and methodologies are copyright Mach49.

All rights reserved
Printed in Gopsons Papers Pvt. Ltd.
10 9 8 7 6 5 4 3 2

No part of this publication may be reproduced, stored in or introduced into a retrieval system, or transmitted, in any form, or by any means (electronic, mechanical, photocopying, recording, or otherwise), without the prior permission of the publisher. Requests for permission should be directed to permissions@harvardbusiness.org, or mailed to Permissions, Harvard Business School Publishing, 60 Harvard Way, Boston, Massachusetts 02163.

The web addresses referenced in this book were live and correct at the time of the book's publication but may be subject to change.

Library of Congress Cataloging-in-Publication Data
Names: Yates, Linda (Linda K.), author.
Title: The unicorn within : how companies can create game-changing ventures at startup speed / Linda Yates.
Description: Boston, Massachusetts : Harvard Business Review Press, [2022] | Includes index.
Identifiers: LCCN 2021046690 (print) | LCCN 2021046691 (ebook) | ISBN 9781633698680 (paperback) | ISBN 9781633698697 (epub)
Subjects: LCSH: Success in business--Handbooks, manuals, etc. | Business enterprises--Handbooks, manuals, etc. | Entrepreneurship--Handbooks, manuals, etc.
Classification: LCC HF5386 .Y347 2022 (print) | LCC HF5386 (ebook) | DDC 650.1--dc23/eng/20220103
LC record available at https://lccn.loc.gov/2021046690
LC ebook record available at https://lccn.loc.gov/2021046691

*For Paul, you are my wonderful, my happy place, my laughter, my joy—
you are my best friend and true love always and forever.*

*For Kylie, Devon, and Piper, each a great gift to us and the world.
Be happy, be healthy, be hopeful, and always know
I love you soooo much.*

Introduction

Beyond the Myth
Unleashing the Unicorn Within

6

Part 01

Getting Started

Chapter 01 *Before You Start* 24
Preconditions for Success

Chapter 02 *People* 34
Selecting, Recruiting, and Onboarding the Team

Chapter 03 *Preparing to Incubate* 50
The Nuts and Bolts

Part 02

Building Ventures

Chapter 04 *Ideate* 66
Getting to New Ventures You Can Incubate

Chapter 05 *Incubate Phase I: Customer* 110
Does Anybody Want It?

Chapter 06 *Incubate Phase II: Product, Service, Solution* 150
What Should We Build? Can We Build It?

Chapter 07 *Incubate Phase III: Business* 176
How Do We Make Money? What's Our Plan?

Chapter 08 *Accelerate* 206
Moving Ventures from Funding to Product-Market Fit and First Revenue

Part 03   Institutionalizing Growth

Chapter 09 Building Your Own Venture Factory　228
Institutionalizing Growth for Decades to Come

Chapter 10 Driving the New Venture Growth Engine　262
The Role of the C-Suite and Senior Executives

Conclusion   Unleashing the Unicorn Within   298
The Ten Principles for Driving Growth and
Beating Startups at Their Own Game

Notes   305
Index   307
Gratitude   315
About the Author   323

Introduction

Beyond the Myth

Unleashing the Unicorn Within

Every mature company in every industry in every part of the world is at risk from outside disruptors—and every large business in the world knows it.

In the face of this danger, senior executives often feel helpless. They have watched as one industry after another has been overrun by smart, agile, new companies armed with the latest technology, tons of venture capital, and radically new business models.

They have seen great companies stumble, or disappear, when they failed to adequately respond. And they have had to explain to shareholders why they have left billions of dollars of market value on the table that should rightfully have been theirs.

For two years in a row, Jamie Dimon, chair of JPMorgan Chase, sent a letter to his shareholders in the company's annual report saying that what is keeping him up at night is the fear that "Silicon Valley is coming and they all want to eat our lunch."[1] Akio Toyoda, head of mighty Toyota, announced that his company now is in a "life-or-death struggle because the rules have changed."[2] And veteran Silicon Valley insider John Chambers, retired CEO and chair of Cisco, conducted a farewell tour around the world ranting to roomfuls of fellow CEOs that 40 percent of them are going to be out of business in ten years—because "70 percent of you are going to attempt to embrace digital transformation, but only 30 percent are going to succeed."[3]

The doleful message is that the future is bleak. It doesn't matter what industry you are in. Hospitality? Look at what Airbnb is doing to traditional hotels. Look at what Joby Aviation is doing to all forms of transportation—planes, trains, and automobiles. Amazon, to retailing and now health care. Rocket Mortgage, Chime Bank, and Stripe to every player in the financial services industry.

Perhaps most unsettling is that even when you identify what it will take to survive—much less thrive—*you can't get there from here*. Innovation transformation? How many companies have tried that over the last few decades? And how many succeeded? You can count them on one hand. How many have tried new venture creation? Even fewer, and those that did successfully start new internal businesses often see them get crushed through envy, corporate politics, conscious neglect, and all the other manifestations of corporate antibodies, inertia, and orthodoxies that typically kill good ideas or, at best, starve them of oxygen.

No, better to just enjoy the good times now and await the inevitable. After all, only 12 percent of the companies in the *Fortune* 500 fifty years ago still exist today—and that mortality rate keeps increasing.

The average life of *Fortune* 500 companies a half-century ago was seventy-five years. Today, it's only fifteen years and falling.

As of this writing, CB Insights reports that there are 1,135 Unicorns in the world valued at over $3.8 trillion, many—if not *all*—of which could have easily been founded by a Global 1000 company.[4]

But, hey, why fight the inevitable? Because it *isn't* inevitable. We are here to tell you that it doesn't have to be this way, you aren't going to go out of business, you don't have to be leaving so much money on the table, and you don't need to keep losing your best and your brightest to some startup that, frankly, has a lot less likelihood of succeeding than the ventures you produce.

Here's the truth:

- You can succeed against clever new startups and *beat* them at their own game.
- You can disrupt from within and generate meaningful growth, and you can do that forever by building your own incubator and accelerator, your own Growth Engine.
- You have advantages that new startups can never hope to match—as long as you don't get in your own way and fail to leverage those advantages. You have ideas, talent, capital, brand, technology, channels, and best of all, you have customers, often millions of them.

→ You Can Unleash the Unicorns Within

Silicon Valley doesn't run on some arcane alchemy; rather, it operates on a few simple rules repeated thousands of times each day. Understand customer pain, marry that with the art of the possible—the technology and trends currently available to solve that pain—and place a series of small bets. It's not wizardry. Put it all together and you'll find a handful of basic, easily replicable activities that, yes, mere mortals can accomplish.

In this book, we'll offer a learnable, repeatable, scalable process for disrupting from the inside out—helping you create, build, and launch a pipeline and portfolio of new ventures generated from within to drive meaningful growth. And just like a real Silicon Valley venture capital portfolio, some of those ventures you will kill, some will be singles, some doubles, others triples, and yes, you, too, *will* produce Unicorns. As the well-regarded founder of Cowboy Ventures, Aileen Lee, noted when she coined the term in 2013, and Dan Primack and Erin Griffith further defined in a *Fortune* cover story in 2015, "A Unicorn is a privately-held startup valued at $1 billion or more."[5]

Imagine what a valuation like that would do to your market capitalization.

It's time to embrace your internal entrepreneurs. It is time to leverage your core competencies, assets, and customers. It's time to believe in your ability to launch new ventures, as they represent your best chance of beating the disruptors knocking down your walls.

We've proven that great companies from all over the world in all industry sectors—from banking to energy, consumer packaged goods, industrial, insurance, consulting, engineering, media, health care, and more—with all kinds of competitive challenges can create, build, and launch new ventures.

Whether you are the CEO, a member of the C-suite, or an internal entrepreneur, this book is meant to create a virtual immersion into Venture Building, striving to get as close as we can to simulating the actual experience between two covers.

Of course, it won't have all our on-site, personal interaction and day-to-day guidance and mentoring from our experienced team of successful operating executives, venture capitalists (VCs), serial entrepreneurs, and specialists, but it will give you an overview of the whole process.* If nothing else, it will show you the best path to escaping your doldrums and getting back into the fight, to once again become the opponent your competitors—and startups—most fear.

→ What Will You Get Out of Reading This Book?

First, we will provide you with a systematic process for generating new business initiatives and new ventures with the greatest chance of success, all while preparing the parent company—the Mothership—to deal with the presence of these new enterprises within its operations.

---

* Though I'm the sole author of this book, the methodologies, activities, templates, and tools have been collaboratively developed and forged by a wonderful team of extraordinary colleagues at my company, Mach49. To honor the spirit of our work together, I'll be using "we" throughout the book.

We will include insights and activities related to the full spectrum of venture creation, including:

1. **Ideate.** Generating, prioritizing, and winnowing out good ideas for potential ventures.

2. **Incubate.** Finding customer pain, developing product or service solutions to solve that pain, and exploring business models able to generate significant growth (viable ventures with prepared teams and actionable business and operating plans).

3. **Accelerate.** Launching new enterprises with a series of pilots and small bets to reduce risk, find ultimate product-market fit, and generate revenue (scalable businesses).

4. **Scale.** Seizing the Mothership Advantage to ensure the ventures can reach escape velocity and outrun their startup or peer company competitors. Leveraging the Mothership's assets and overcoming its inertia will ensure your ventures can beat even the most well-funded startups.

Ultimately, the goal is for Venture Building to become a repeatable, scalable activity for your company so that you can establish a pipeline and portfolio of new ventures to drive growth—and recruit and retain talented employees who will be eager to populate these new enterprises—for years to come. Building a perpetual Growth Engine in the form of a Venture Factory to launch multiple ventures is far less expensive than getting disrupted and going out of business, and far more effective than having to buy that pesky startup competitor at a ridiculous valuation and deal with all the headaches that come with acquisitions and post-merger integrations.

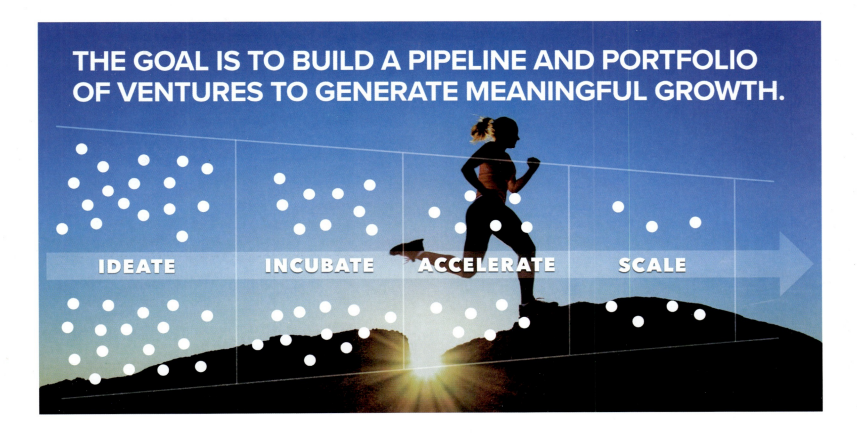

Repeat after me: you can without a doubt *incubate growth*. With a team of employees and just three months of dedicated work, that team can create a new business initiative—including a robust operating and execution plan to run it—as innovative and customer driven as anything seen in Silicon Valley. And at the end of twelve weeks, you can have a new venture ready to launch, with:

- A passionate set of founders
- A powerful product or service solving real customer pain—including a minimum viable product (MVP) and a product road map to roll out the much larger opportunity
- Customers excited to be part of the first pilots
- An initial go-to-market plan to test

- Identified risks and a series of experiments and small bets to launch to mitigate those risks, including a set of metrics and milestones that ensure the removal of the greatest risk on the least amount of capital
- A parent company that has been trained to support the new venture
- Champions at the executive level of the parent company to protect the new venture

Silicon Valley will not eat your lunch. Your company has built-in advantages in terms of ideas, capital, intellectual property, customers, brand, goodwill, global reach, and homegrown talent. *You just need to unleash those advantages.*

→ It's Not That Hard— It's Also Not Fairy Dust

We know what we say is true because of years and years of experience and evidence.

First, we live and work in Silicon Valley; many of us grew up here. For example, I am a Silicon Valley native. I was born in San Francisco and was lucky enough to grow up with the people who founded the venture capital industry. Those pioneers were all friends of my family, so I have been deeply rooted and connected in Silicon Valley my entire life. I am even married to my best friend and thirty-year veteran of Silicon Valley Paul Holland—a twice successful entrepreneur with two IPOs in his operating career (Pure Software founded by Reed Hastings, and Kana Communications founded by Mark Gainey and Michael Horvath) and a top-tier venture capitalist with the extremely successful Silicon Valley venture firm Foundation Capital for twenty years.

However, much of my professional career has been in the boardrooms and C-suites of the Global 500, so I am blessed to be truly bilingual in these two worlds. I have worked in global strategy, driving innovation for almost thirty years. I was the cofounder and CEO of Stratagos with Gary Hamel, who, with C. K. Prahalad, wrote the first game-changing business book ever written on corporate innovation, *Competing for the Future*—giving me a front-row seat to the dawning paradigm shift in the focus of global corporations from generic strategy and operations improvement to innovation. In addition, I sat on the board of directors of Sybase, a New York Stock Exchange, *Fortune* 500 company, for ten years until it was sold to SAP, and I have been doing private investing and board work for startups for years. Meanwhile, most of my friends, neighbors, and Mach49 teammates are fellow Silicon Valley entrepreneurs. Our three daughters are entrepreneurs, each starting companies or major projects by the time they were fifteen. In other words, Silicon Valley entrepreneurialism and risk taking flow in our blood. We know *how* this place really works—truly better than any outsider ever could—and we know *what* works.

In their careers, the team at Mach49 has worked with, and frankly been, those entrepreneurs and venture capitalists that keep the titans of industry sleepless at night. We know how smart these entrepreneurs are, but we also know that they aren't as prescient as the popular press makes them out to be. And they certainly aren't invincible. On the contrary, every day we see the mistakes they make and their vulnerabilities. We know the statistics; each year, the average VC hears about two thousand new companies, may investigate about two hundred, will invest in twenty, and perhaps two will really make those big returns you hear about. (What happens to the rest of them? Shhh, don't ask.)

We understand that many successful companies are so only because their established competitors let them succeed. Agility, speed, a relentless focus on customer pain, and a sense of urgency are why startups win and become Unicorns. The "Dinosaurs," as people who don't know better like to call our beloved global enterprises, cede the game even before it begins.

Second, as much as we love Silicon Valley and startups, we have an objective view of the Valley myth. We know that the process may look like magic, but I'll say it again, *it isn't that hard*.

→ Why *Your* Unicorns Should Win

If done properly, corporate ventures should have a higher success rate than their independent counterparts. Their destiny is to *succeed*, not fail—and the only reason for their high mortality rate is a failure of execution.

Independent startup teams typically don't have a robust mechanism to ideate—their ventures are already the result of someone's or some team's preexisting idea. Often, one or more of the founders independently comes up with a clever idea and then recruits others to join the venture by selling them on the dream. They haven't the money, the experience, or the bandwidth to come up with a dozen new venture ideas to sort through and test to see which ones will work. As a result, the actual sifting process that a corporate Venture Factory can go through to assess which ventures solve real customer pain, which solutions can actually be built, and which ideas are likely to make a lot of money with little sacrifice is instead a life-or-death event for a startup team: if its idea isn't workable or fails to find product-market fit, it burns through cash and shuts down. Hence, the mortality rate of startups of 90 percent or more, even in a supporting environment like Silicon Valley.

Here are some of the latest statistics:[6]

- Ninety percent of new startups fail.
- Seventy-five percent of venture-backed startups fail.
- Under 50 percent of businesses make it to their fifth year.
- Thirty-three percent of startups make it to the ten-year mark.
- Only 40 percent of startups actually turn a profit.
- Eighty-two percent of businesses that fail do so because of cash flow problems, which means they didn't find product-market fit fast enough.
- The highest failure rate occurs in the information industry (63 percent).

A second advantage is that most independent startups are unable or unwilling to do much market and customer testing, and if they do, they have no rigorous and robust model for conducting those interviews to ensure their findings are accurate. One reason is that they are often engineers with a technology-first mindset versus a customer pain–first mindset, so they end up being a technology in search of a market. The other issue is that they have no customers yet to query, whereas big companies often have millions of them.

Too often, startups build the product first, at which point, the entrepreneurs aren't really interested in whether customers have pain; they just want to know what you like or don't like about the product. The problem is, research demonstrates that once you have a product that looks anywhere near complete, your interviewees feel sorry for you and won't tell you the truth. They might tell you what they like or don't like but are frankly too polite to admit that they didn't want the product in the first place, so as good as it looks, they'll never buy it.

Finally, startups have neither the years of experience nor the data every corporation is sitting on. So, instead, they rely on gut feel. Sometimes they get it right (Steve Jobs's realization that people wanted personal computers), but most of the time, judging by the statistics, they get it wrong. Fatally so. The advantage of an internal startup is that the parent company already has a customer base that, if leveraged well, can provide the fledgling venture with a base of people to interview and a great way to look for pain.

As for accelerating and scaling, the differences here are even more obvious. The independent startup has to find enough capital to underwrite going to full scale—fast. How fast? In the modern digital economy, it means reaching millions of customers in a matter of months (particularly so with a software app or service), and funding that can consume vast sums of capital for customer acquisition, production, sales, staffing, and so on. That's why only two or three emerge at the other end of the venture investment process as Unicorn companies with tens of millions in investment and a valuation of a billion dollars or more.

By comparison, internal ventures can develop inside enterprises that are *already* at scale—that have long since implemented the tools and processes related to marketing, production, manufacturing, distribution, service, support, and so on to deal with a giant customer base. And if they can't build, they can often also use the cash on their balance sheets to buy, partner, or invest, which enables them to grow without impacting their expenses.

The worst part of being in an independent startup is having to regularly go hat in hand to beg for money from investors, nearly all of which will turn you down. The company is perpetually at risk because each step requires an even greater commitment from those investors. If you don't meet your targets, that money source can dry up overnight—or you will find yourself as the founder but no longer the CEO. That's why so many interesting startups disappear. By comparison, an internal startup, if it has the full commitment of senior management, can devote its efforts to actually building the enterprise and meeting its goals, with the knowledge that the next round of funding is waiting, assuming it hits its metrics and milestones.

Ultimately, the independent startup process is incredibly wasteful. And a lot of man-years of talented work by all those teams of ardent entrepreneurs are tossed away, not because VCs don't care about entrepreneurs—most of the good ones indeed *have* been entrepreneurs—but because their job is to return three to ten times the funds to their Limited Partners (LPs). So they need to focus on those with the most potential. Also, while many VCs have experience and networks to share with their startups, they don't have a methodology, so most entrepreneurs just wing it.

By comparison, large companies are disciplined enough to implement a repeatable, scalable model to incubate their ventures. They are also incentivized to kill ideas early, whereas a VC may prefer to keep any one venture alive—often longer than it makes sense—as that may provide enough time for another venture to have a positive return to offset the potential loss. The VCs succeed or fail in raising subsequent funds by having enough startups with positive results that they can minimize their limited partners' focus on the walking dead or failed. By implementing methodology and metrics from the start that may scream "this venture has no future," large companies will find they are killing off ideas, rather than companies. As a result, the corporations can conserve capital and talent. And we can avoid the human damage as team members aren't thrown out on the street but can remain valued employees of the company, often even more prepared and experienced to incubate the next venture or drive customer-driven change in the core business.

Put this way, internal entrepreneurship and new venture creation, rather than being a poor shadow of its garage startup counterpart, actually presents a much more appealing business strategy. And that is exactly what we have found through our decades of experience. It is that understanding—along with a detailed road map focused on execution—that we are offering to you in this playbook.

Done right, that is, following the opportunity pipeline from identifying customer pain to marrying that pain with the art of the possible in terms of the technology and trends available to solve that pain, then testing the reality of the solution in the marketplace by making small bets on the best opportunities—rigorously selecting the winners along the way—it is possible to achieve far greater odds of success than is ever found in the world of independent startups. (We know this is true because even our VC friends are beginning to come and ask us for help.) And then, as the best candidates for growth are found, the parent company can bring to bear all of its unique advantages, from capital to infrastructure to customers to, perhaps most important of all, *patience* (though not too much of that) to create an environment for success that can never be matched in the world of venture capital.

In other words, given all the factors at work, there is a better chance for an internally generated and incubated new startup to succeed than an independent one.

→ Managing the Mothership

So, why isn't more internal incubation occurring? Or rather, why do big companies *believe* that internal ventures are doomed to fail? Because the statistics aren't so great. Sifted, the new innovation media platform for the *Financial Times*, recently reported statistics from Alex Mahr of Stryber that "traditional startups have an 11% success rate, that increases to 12% if the venture had been part of a Silicon-Valley-like accelerator (think Y Combinator, Techstars, or 500 startups) but the number decreases to 8% if the venture was part of a corporate incubator/accelerator."[7]

Sifted asked me to explain why those statistics were so bad, and I highlighted three main reasons.[8]

No Methodology

Corporations keep trying traditional VC and startup incubator models—money and mentors. That model doesn't work for large corporations, as VCs and incubators like Y Combinator can afford large failure rates because just one or two successes can return their funds. Corporations need much higher success rates, which come with a customer-driven, repeatable, and scalable methodology for venture creation.

Mothership Friction

Companies have the ideas, talent, assets, competencies, capital, and customers to create ventures and drive growth. Seizing the Mothership advantage for your ventures helps you beat the startups at their own game, but companies also have inertia, antibodies, and orthodoxies that have to be overcome.

Corporate incubators and accelerator teams often fail to engage the Mothership to make the from-to shifts in metrics, compensation, procurement, policies, politics, and so on to ensure their ventures reach escape velocity and thrive.

Executive Decision-Makers Fail to Grow

Senior executives must get out of a management review board mindset and adopt the discipline and perspective of top-tier VCs by:

- Thinking in terms of a portfolio strategy; building many, not one (seed fund your ventures; please don't overspend too early).

- Focusing on option value, not net present value.

- Recognizing that customer acquisition and revenue, not short-term profit, are appropriate KPIs for a startup.

- Removing the greatest amount of risk on the least amount of capital. Embrace placing a series of small bets and building to validate, then automate, and then grow.

- Having the discipline to kill ventures along the way. If they can't find customer pain, the product or solution isn't feasible to build, or if the business can't move the needle for the Mothership, the venture isn't viable.

Often internal startups fail because *senior* managers simply don't know what to do with them. They try to run new ventures like they run their core and legacy businesses. They fail to think about option value versus net present value. They wear a management review hat instead of a venture capital hat. Executives placed in charge of these programs don't set the right benchmarks and goals, make the right financial commitments, understand how to mitigate risk, or see the effort through.

Worst of all, too many companies spend too much money on the *one big thing*, which, when it fails, convinces them not to try another venture for another decade. They also lack *imagination*. They need to understand that in a successful and established company, any new venture is initially going to be little more than a rounding error compared to all the company's other operations. As our Mach49 faculty partner, John Danner, a Princeton and UC Berkeley business school professor and noted author, cleverly noted to me in a recent conversation, often Global 1000 companies suffer from the "Tyranny of the Large Denominator—chances are good that even their own original business (the one that made them so great to begin with) would not survive their current impatient new venture screening gauntlet. In other words, the G1000 is quite likely to eat its own young."

As a result, too often the new venture is treated as something less than, like a novelty, a side project, a hobby, not as the germ of something that may one day become a major source of company revenues. So, when it hits a bump or momentarily stalls, the new venture is abandoned or left to wither away. And when that happens, management refuses to recognize its own contribution to the failure, but instead shrugs and swears that it has learned its lesson and isn't going to try that new venture thing again.

But imagine if Marriott or Hilton had founded Airbnb (which pitched to forty VCs before it was funded), or Toyota or GM had launched Uber (really, a taxi-hailing app; how big could that be?), or Blockbuster had created Netflix (rather than spend millions of dollars on consultants to tell it Netflix would never be a threat).

The C-suite executives have to own their responsibility to incubate growth. That's why, almost uniquely, we spend a lot of time working with what we call the New Venture Board, those senior executives who must meet four criteria:

- Make go/no-go decisions on the new venture and provide funding to launch and accelerate the new venture once you have made the decision to launch
- Provide access to customers, channels, and markets
- Provide access to the Mothership's core competencies, assets, expertise, or capabilities the new venture may need
- Remove friction that may prevent the new venture from reaching escape velocity

We will show you in the pages ahead why it is just as important to manage the expectations and behavior of the parent company as it is to create a strong startup. That, we demonstrate, is the role of the Mothership's senior management and the New Venture Board. We teach these groups how to frame challenges they believe new ventures can address, how to do a Portfolio Review if they have an abundance of ideas, how to select their founding Intrapreneurs, how to write the specs for the types of specialists the teams may need to access, how to manage startup teams, and what expectations to set and how high the bar should be for new ventures to pass from stage to stage. We also lay out the types of from-to shifts the Mothership will likely have to make to ensure new ventures can succeed, and what it must give to the venture as a form of leverage in return for the expected return on its investment.

Most of all, this book teaches the C-suite and other senior executives how to overcome prejudices and to believe that their company is absolutely capable of creating, building, and launching game-changing new ventures—yes, including its own Unicorns—and beating the startups at their own game. Ultimately, our message is that you must disrupt from the inside out, including ultimately building your own internal incubator and accelerator—your own Venture Factory—so you can do that in perpetuity.

→ Your Road Map

In the pages that follow, we are going to give you a step-by-step guide for disrupting inside out and unleashing the Unicorns within—including a repeatable, scalable process for incubating those ventures in just twelve weeks, which includes more than managing the Mothership. It includes seizing the Mothership advantage.

In part 1, "Getting Started," we walk you through everything you need in advance of actually beginning to incubate your new ventures with a focus on preconditions for success, people, and preparation. We will include tips for recruiting and assessing New Venture Team members and New Venture Board members, and others who you may need to rely on in your Venture Building activities. We will also provide you with a Preparing to Incubate guide that will include ideas for setting up your space (whether physical or virtual), acquiring the necessary materials, and implementing the technology tools you need to make the twelve weeks work efficiently and effectively.

Part 2, "Building Ventures," gives you options for generating great ideas you can start to incubate and a step-by-step guide to incubating your new ventures. Part 2 covers the spectrum of new venture creation, including Ideate, Incubate, and Accelerate. We will break down the twelve weeks of incubation into three very practical phases: Customer, Product, and Business, providing methodology, templates, and tools throughout. And we will break the Accelerate phase into its three stages as well: Build to Validate, Build to Automate, and Build to Grow.

In part 3, "Institutionalizing Growth," we want to speak directly to the C-suite and senior executives who need to drive these ventures and help them reach escape velocity as members of the New Venture Board. We will provide explicit processes and practices to protect and nurture new ventures to enable them to succeed. We teach senior executives and the Mothership to do the hard work right alongside the internal entrepreneurs—to remove the behaviors and orthodoxies that typically starve new ideas of oxygen, at best, and at worst, kill them. When we are talking to the C-suite executives, we discuss New Venture Advocates and the need to build the internal ecosystem that will help your ventures seize the Mothership advantage—all those things that create the competitive advantage over even the most well-funded startups.

We will also provide you with our client-tested and -validated framework for building your own Venture Factory, including key questions you need to answer as part of the design work. Organic Venture Building through your own incubator and accelerator—your own Venture Factory—is *critical* to developing a thriving Growth Engine; corporate venture investing, strategic partnering, and tactical M&A are the other three arrows you need in your Growth Engine quiver, but we will leave those topics for another day (or the next book).

You won't need to break the bank to do any of the activities we lay out in the book. You won't have to gut your company, though you will likely have to change some attitudes. You won't have to do some massive innovation transformation, though there may be some investments you will want to make to create that group of New Venture Advocates who become innovators inside the company's core functions. And you won't have to rob your company of its key talent; on the contrary, you'll increase your chances of keeping those people and recruiting a new class of disruptors.

We promise you the worst that can happen is that your New Venture Team members and New Venture Board will have learned valuable lessons about finding customer pain that you can use in your core and legacy businesses. At best, you will create, build, and launch not just one new venture, but a pipeline and portfolio of new ventures—generated from within, ultimately in your own Venture Factory and founded by your own talent—that will restore your company to a level of competitiveness it hasn't known in years, one that will provide a powerful source of new revenue and will defend against outside disruption. That will transform the market's perception of your company as a value stock to a growth stock. And it will enjoy a native advantage in future competition with disruptors. Indeed, your company will become the disruptor; *you will build the Unicorns.*

→ We Need You; Get to Work

Large corporations must develop an autonomic, repeatable, scalable ability to create and innovate, not least because many of the large, complex problems the world faces—poverty, disease, climate change, water, racism, education, and others—cannot be solved by dysfunctional governments. Nor can they be solved by nongovernmental organizations (NGOs) on their own, because as wonderful, well meaning, and dedicated as NGOs are, they don't have the experience or resources to solve problems at global scale. Large companies do; and if they lean in and believe they can change themselves, they can also change the world for the better.

That's why we wrote this book; we want to share what we have learned helping established companies become young and disruptive again. We want to give people in those companies meaningful, purposeful, creative work. And we don't just mean the millennials: disruptors come in every age, gender, race, sexual orientation, geography, learning difference, or any other category you want to define. We want to foster as much positive innovation and growth as possible. And to do that, we are hoping to share our playbook in as portable and cogent a way as possible.

If you can tap into and cultivate your advantages, if you can become more agile and innovative, not only can big companies survive, but the impact on society overall will be historic—in a positive way. There is no reason why the next generation of Unicorn companies must come out of Silicon Valley; they should come from everywhere. They can come from your organization. Indeed, we promise you do have Unicorns within. There is no inherent upper limit on how many multibillion-dollar companies there can be in the world, nor on the potential amount of human creativity and innovation that they can unleash.

Are you up for the journey?

Good. Let's begin.

Part 01

Getting Started

Chapter 01
Before You Start

Preconditions for Success

Every company can be successful creating ventures and building its own Venture Factory—its own Growth Engine.

Every company has the ideas, talent, core competencies, capabilities, assets, channels, and customers to drive meaningful growth. Period.

However, before you interview your first New Venture Team member, source your first great idea, or buy that first pack of physical or virtual sticky notes, you need to understand the big picture in terms of the philosophical underpinnings of the methodology you are about to step through.

In addition, there are certain preconditions for success your company must understand and commit to if you want to create, build, and launch successful ventures. These are not onerous, but they are necessary; they are a lot less difficult than getting disrupted, losing market share, or telling shareholders why the new venture that someone else took public in your space wasn't yours.

→ The Foundational Elements of Success

Your success is contingent on four things. The best Silicon Valley startups do three of these things exceedingly and obsessively well: understanding customer pain, marrying that pain with the art of the possible, and placing small bets. You'll need to do the same. But that's the easy part. The fourth element—managing the Mothership so you can seize the Mothership *advantage*—is unique to corporate ventures. Unlike startup founders, as an Intrapreneur you must manage the powers that are inside your company. You can excel at the first three things, but, if you mismanage the fourth, you're in deep trouble.

Understand Customer Pain

If there is one thing you take away from our book, we hope it is a conviction that you must be obsessed with talking to customers. If you are an internal entrepreneur and have a great product idea and you didn't start by talking to customers, stop reading and return this book. There have been thousands of startups in Silicon Valley that never went anywhere because the super-smart engineers who founded the company had products first and then went searching for pain as opposed to finding pain and then building the solution. Too many thought they had all the answers and never bothered to actually interview a customer.

Why VCs do not make a minimum of a hundred to two hundred rigorously executed and robustly documented customer interviews a precondition for funding we will never understand. Your team (not some outsourced agency) must conduct the interviews in person. Face to face, phone, video all count; surveys, at least in these earliest phases, do not. I tell every large-company CEO on the planet that surveys are statistically significant, but strategically irrelevant, because all you have done is outsource your visceral understanding and empathy for the customer to someone else who will just repackage those insights and sell them to the next company.

No one knew they wanted a DVR, a microwave oven, or a minivan, but what they could tell you was their pain: they weren't getting home in time to watch their favorite show; they didn't have time to cook a healthy meal; and they were having to cart an ever-increasing number of kids, dogs, and sporting equipment to myriad places. In other words, customers can tell you their pain; they just can't tell you the solution. That is your job.

The best startups—whether they are VC-backed or Global 1000–generated—interview customers, hundreds of them, directly. If there is no pain, then you must be disciplined and kill the venture, itself a very valuable skill to learn. The other option is to pivot the venture to respond to the pain you do find. In the end, as our great friend and early Mach49 colleague Drew Harman quipped early in the development of our methodology, "Customer insights are the currency for credibility; everything else is uninformed opinion." To the board members and CEOs reading this book: When was the last time *you* interviewed a customer? You better step up—or step back and listen—because by the time we are finished, your Intrapreneurs are going to become far more expert on customer pain than you are. (We will dive deeply into how you uncover customer pain in chapter 5.)

Marry Customer Pain with the Art of the Possible

What are the current trends and technology you can employ to solve that customer pain you've discovered? For example, Uber does not get created if we don't have mobile phones, GPS, and real-time payments.

One of the biggest problems large companies have is that they are not current and have no way to keep up with the nonlinear pace of change. Yesterday it was virtual reality, today it is augmented reality; yesterday it was electronic payments, today it is cryptocurrencies. And by the time you read this book, even those will be either outdated or further up the curve. Startups born out of one of the ecosystems of innovation worldwide, whether Silicon Valley, Tel Aviv, Berlin, Singapore, London, or beyond, *bathe* in the art of the possible every single day. They hang out at the universities, go to meetups, attend demo days, read twenty tech blogs, collaborate with colleagues, and engage with their VC investors, their staff, and their global network of subject-matter experts.

Large companies are often particularly challenged because they are run by people who are not digital natives, which is fine as long as those leaders invest in their own learning and strive to stay current, or they are willing to abdicate critical venture decisions to those who are. One way for a large company to stay current is to build a world-class corporate venture fund because it will constantly be scanning the world in search of deal flow, sorting through hundreds of startups, and learning a ton it can share (if well-designed and well-managed) with its Mothership. A top-tier corporate venture capital (CVC) fund and a world-class Venture Factory are the yin and yang of each other where corporate growth is concerned.

While a CVC constantly sensing and responding to activity outside the four walls of the Mothership through its investing, partnering, and targeted M&A activities is highly effective, there are many other ways to ensure venture teams and Motherships stay current.

One way is to conduct inspiration and subject-matter expert interviews during the Incubate phase; another is to have great product people (sourced from either inside or outside the company) on your founding team who, by their very nature, are creatives scanning the environment for the next disruption. Another way is to partner with universities, from sponsoring research to attending events to building an affiliates program you can rotate leaders or future leaders through, as we do with Mach49's joint program with Stanford's Center for Sustainable Development and Global Competitiveness, where faculty, undergraduates, and graduate students can provide access to the future.

Sometimes companies set up outposts and build sensor networks that beam information back home or fund university labs to stay close to the cutting-edge research driving new trends and technologies. Intellectual curiosity and a growth mindset are key characteristics of the best investors, the best board members, and the best entrepreneurs.

> **We use the word "product" throughout the book as the catchall word to describe what your venture will produce; however, your product could be related to an actual physical or hardware product, or it could be a digital product, platform, or marketplace. It might be a service, solution, or experience; a new genre of food; or any other definition of the solution you are delivering to customers to solve their pain.**

Make Small Bets

Andy Rachleff, cofounder of Benchmark Capital, one of the most successful venture firms in Silicon Valley, once said, "Funding in Silicon Valley is like an onion, every layer of the onion is a layer of risk. It could be market, technical, or financial."[1] (We'd add, in the case of large-company-spawned new ventures, another risk could be governance; the Mothership either loves the venture to death or starves it of oxygen.)

The best startups and entrepreneurs know how to remove the greatest amount of risk on the least amount of capital. They know how to identify the risks and run experiments or pilots—place small bets—to demonstrate they can mitigate those risks. They identify the metrics and milestones that will tell them they have eliminated those risks. Only then do they unlock the next round of funding.

Most large companies don't know how to place small bets, many want-to-be internal entrepreneurs don't know how to preserve their cash, nor do they know how to iterate rapidly and pivot smartly. Too often, big companies demand too much perfection (and spend too much money) before going to market to learn from the only person whose opinion and behavior actually matters—the customer. (We talk specifically about placing small bets and risks in chapter 7 where we discuss building the business and execution plan, and again in chapter 8 where we discuss the Accelerate phase.)

Managing the Mothership

The fourth foundational element that you need to acknowledge before you begin—perhaps the biggest driver of large-company new venture success and failure, especially as a venture starts to scale—is the art of both *managing the Mothership and seizing the Mothership advantage*.

There really is no reason that any of the large hotel chains couldn't have created Airbnb; no law of physics prevented the major car companies from launching Uber, and ultimately, no established market leader ever had a logical excuse to surrender market share to an upstart new company. Don't misunderstand; the orthodoxies, inertia, and antibodies that exist in large companies can and will slow, impede, or kill Venture Building activities. Maybe your company has tried and failed before because it couldn't manage the Mothership. But it can be done, so don't give up. Don't be in denial either; embrace the reality from the start and prepare, with our guidance shared throughout the book, to actively address the challenge of managing the Mothership and reaping the benefits of doing so for years to come.

→ The Five Preconditions for Success

All the methodology, process, tools, and tactics we share with you rest on the foundation created from understanding these five fundamental elements. If these all make sense, then you are *almost* ready to begin.

There is one other exercise you want to conduct before building your venture, and that is to review our checklist of the five preconditions for success that we go through with every potential client. I say "potential client" because we are only as good as the last company we helped create, build, and launch ventures, so we won't work with a company if it can't fulfill these five preconditions for success because we know it can't be successful. And if it can't be successful, then we can't be successful. These preconditions are like holding up a mirror to the organization to see how serious it is.

I was talking to a senior executive from one of our big industrial clients about what we do. About two minutes in, I said, "You need to understand, we have five preconditions for success or we won't work with you because we won't take your money knowing you are likely to fail." He looked at me and said, "That's the most refreshing thing I have ever heard, because I have asked everyone we have talked to what the prerequisites are and they just keep patting me on the shoulder saying, 'Don't worry, we'll take you where you are.'"

No. If you want to succeed, if you want your ventures to succeed, and most of all, if you want your venture team members to succeed, then you must meet these preconditions. No exceptions.

Precondition 1: Build a Full-Time Team

You can't do innovation part-time. The biggest challenge for big companies is rarely cash. Have you seen their balance sheets? They can afford to seed fund their venture creations (and yes, we mean seed fund; we don't mean spending ridiculous amounts of money on consultants who have never built a successful startup). Rather, the biggest challenge they face is freeing up their own people.

To that, we say BS: if you are a multibillion-dollar company that can't free up four to six people full-time for twelve weeks, then you aren't serious about innovation. You are just checking the box for your board of directors.

That said, you *can* augment your internal team with outsiders to round out the skills portfolio of the internal New Venture Team, but to avoid the not-invented-here problem, you must have at least a few of your own internal entrepreneurs working on the new venture.

Precondition 2:
Choose a Team Lead

The team lead will serve as the venture's interim CEO/GM and must be someone the executive sponsors trust. In some cases, that interim CEO will continue on as the venture's CEO once launched; in other cases, that person may step aside for someone with more experience or different skills. But even then, they will usually continue to play a key founder role in the newly launched venture.

Precondition 3:
Identify the Source (or Sources) of Funding

Independent startups fund themselves initially with friends and family (pre-seed) and then venture capital (seed, series A, and beyond) to reach the point where they can generate revenue and, ultimately, self-sustaining cash. There's no point incubating a new venture if you don't have funds to launch them. The worst scenario is having a new venture that has developed a robust and rigorous business and execution plan with twenty pilots ready to go at the end of the Incubate phase, and now you are scrambling around to find the seed funding necessary to launch those pilots. (Hint: the customers eager to be part of your pilot won't wait.)

Precondition 4:
Assemble an Engaged New Venture Board

In essence, these senior executives will serve as the new venture's internal venture capitalists. The New Venture Board (NVB) can include the CEO and other C-suite members, but at the very least it must be fully supportive and fully empowered. New ventures are fragile things, more liable to be destroyed by in-house politics than a lack of market acceptance. They need powerful advocates in the corporation to protect them as they grow. (We discuss more on this topic later, including a whole chapter, chapter 10, dedicated to senior and C-suite executives.)

Precondition 5:
Prepare for the Accelerate Phase

Incubating is not enough; the best venture teams and the best NVBs will already be thinking about how, if funded, to rapidly move into the Accelerate phase—where the venture is launched and is running its pilots and experiments, continuing to learn so it ultimately can achieve product-market fit and its first real revenue.

You don't want to slow down after Pitch Day, because losing momentum means potentially losing those pilot customers you excited during the Incubate phase; they aren't going to sit around and wait for the company to get its act together.

When we work with clients, we hand them an agenda we call "Looking Forward to Accelerate." The agenda we have included on the following pages is the actual agenda we use for the executive session we run right after the team has made its final pitch at the end of Week 12. It covers all the additional decisions that a fund and launch decision triggers. We hand this agenda to clients on Week 0 and revisit it as a foreshadowing after the Check-in session around Week 8 or 9, so by Week 12, once they have made their decision to fund the venture, the NVB and New Venture Team are ready to act and launch Day 1 of the first week of the Accelerate phase. If you are reading this book because you want to launch new ventures, read the agenda now so you can familiarize yourself with the range of decisions that you need to make as you proceed. Working from the future backward is a muscle to develop soon.

Achieving all these preconditions doesn't mean that every idea you have will succeed. Indeed, learning to kill ideas is as important as learning how to ideate, incubate, accelerate, and scale them.

But if you understand the fundamentals and your teams are diligent, rigorous, and honest about starting with customer pain, any company can launch not just one, but a series of successful startups generated from within to drive meaningful growth for the company, for customers, for team members, and, as has been the case for many of our clients, for the world.

LOOKING FORWARD TO ACCELERATE

PREVIEW OF PITCH DAY DECISIONS ON THE HORIZON

- **Fund vs. No-Fund**
  - Do we have the right GM/business owner, product lead, and/or other critical roles in place to make maximum progress in the Build to Validate phase?
  - Do we have alignment on Build to Validate success milestones?
  - If future milestones are successfully met, what is the process to secure funding and what lead times are required?
  - Who else will have a voice in the fund/no-fund decision? Do they need to be prepped sooner rather than later?
  - Given that the venture will likely have customer pilots identified, are we prepared to launch the company immediately? If not, what is the likely timing?
    - Ideally, we can keep the team together and moving at Incubate pace.

- **Spin-In vs. Spin-Out**
  - What criteria will the New Venture Board/Mothership use to determine whether to spin in or spin out?
  - Who will own future investment/funding decisions in either case?
  - What will be the brand association?
  - If spun out, who are likely partners and when should they be approached?

- **Options for Execution (build, buy, partner, invest)**
  - Recommendations will be in the business and execution plan.

- **Future for Existing Team**
  - Immediate:
    - What is happening vis-à-vis their current compensation?
    - Assuming successful contribution to incubation, what type of company recognition will they or can they receive?
    - Have metrics been adjusted for the fact they will be working on something unique for three months that probably does not fit into their current performance plan?
  - Post–Pitch Day options for incubation team members:
    - For existing incubation members, will they be part of go-forward team?
      - Are they true founders or members of the team?
      - What role will each existing team member who stays play in the new venture?
    - If not part of the accelerating team:
      - Will they work on incubating the next new venture, either as a full-time or interim team member?
      - Will they help build the Venture Factory for the Mothership?
      - Will they move back to their former roles and share learnings with the home team?
    - Who will communicate roles and/or transitions to the team?

- **Team Composition Beyond Existing Team**
  - Accelerate will likely see additional hires plus outside development partners in early months.

- **Compensation**
  - Do we have an aligned incentive plan in place with the existing team and required new hires for Week 13 and beyond? Options may include:
    - Spin-In (either as a wholly owned subsidiary or as part of an existing business unit)
      - Careful consideration of additional hires needed from outside, if any.
      - Traditional compensation currently in place?
      - Salary plus bonus tied to results?
      - Salary plus synthetic or phantom equity tied to results?
    - Spin-Out
      - Careful consideration of additional hires needed from outside, if any.
      - What will it take to recruit required team members from the outside?
      - What will it take to have consistency for team members?
      - How can compensation structures appropriate for early-stage entrepreneurs be implemented?

- **Governance**
  - Will the venture be a new company, a new line of business, or part of an internal company Venture Factory?
  - Who will the new venture report to and/or who will be on the new venture's board?

LOOKING FORWARD TO ACCELERATE

- o Possibilities: C-suite executive, appropriate business-line executive sponsor, possible external funding source (traditional VCs or CVCs), experienced target market, industry and/or domain experts.

- **Legal**
  - Entity formation.
  - Pilot agreements.
  - Nondisclosure/invention assignments.

- **IT/Security Plan**
  - Maintaining continuity from Incubate to Accelerate.
  - How to set up infrastructure that allows the venture to be nimble.
  - How to set up security requirements that balance the need to protect the Mothership vs. the team's need to run fast and iterate.

- **Location of the New Venture**
  - Where will the new venture be headquartered?
  - Will team members have to move?
  - Who can be virtual?
  - What experience does the GM/business owner have in running virtual operations?

- **Will the venture be able to use external services, or will it use the shared services available at the Mothership?** (e.g., accounting, finance, communications, procurement, channels, etc.)
  - If shared services, have New Venture Advocates been appointed and trained to serve as the new venture's liaisons to ensure the new venture can maintain momentum?

- **Identification/Introduction**
  - Connect with partners who can help build the MVP and/or develop channels (partner, buy, invest).

- **Gives and Gets**
  - What will be the mechanism to manage the interaction with the Mothership to leverage the core assets, capabilities, competencies, channels, customers, networks, and brand to help the new venture accelerate faster?

LOOKING FORWARD TO ACCELERATE

- What from/to shifts does the Mothership need to make to provide incentives to core business leaders and/or management to ensure the new ventures can succeed? (e.g., metrics, comp., resourcing, procurement, governance, etc.)
- How will the Mothership gain benefit and realize value from the new venture?

- **Funding Launch and Accelerate**
  - What will be the Accelerate path forward? Options include:
    - o Team accelerates on its own.
    - o Team accelerates with specialist support (finance, go-to-market, product, customer success, HR, etc., until full-time hires are in place and the venture is fully functional and able to stand on its own).
    - o Team accelerates with a Board Member-in-Residence to mentor the team.

Chapter 02
People
Selecting, Recruiting, and Onboarding the Team

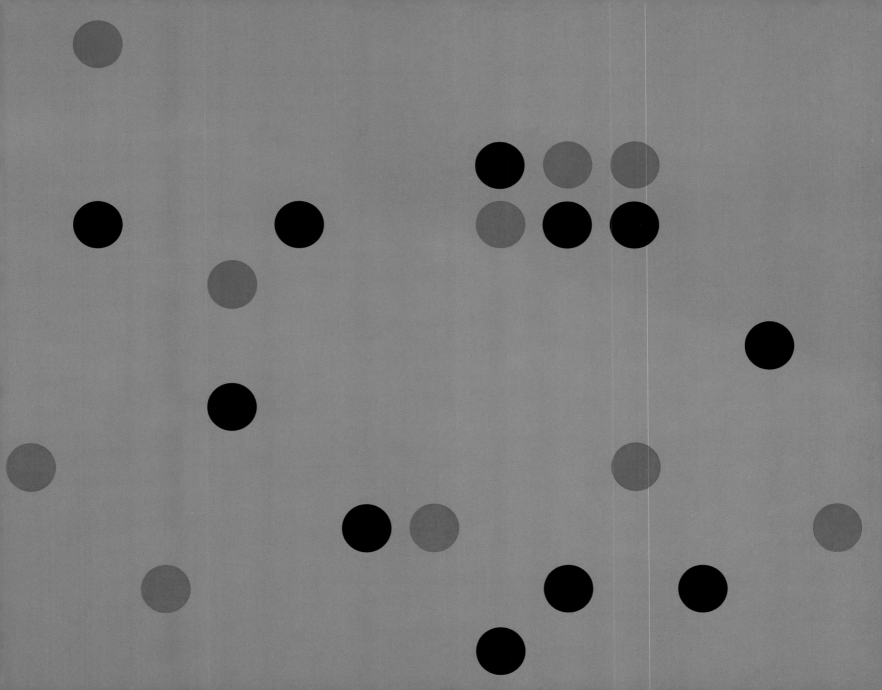

Any successful startup founder or VC will tell you that the most important indicator of success, besides finding customer pain, is a great team.

That's why as you make your way through the preparation phase, you should spend extra time selecting, recruiting, and onboarding team members.

Here are the roles to fill:

- New Venture Team (NVT) members form the founding team that will actually build the venture.

- New Venture Board (NVB) members are the senior executives who serve as the governing body for the new venture, your internal venture capitalists, if you will.

- Venture Factory Team members are those individuals who will become the "Mach49 Inside" team, ultimately taking on the process—serving as the guides and specialists the venture team may need if it hasn't built a company before.

- Advisory Board members are key influencers or company subject-matter experts the New Venture Team or the New Venture Board may want to be part of the process during the Ideate, Incubate, and Accelerate phases. They participate in all the activities the NVB members do; they just aren't the people making the fund or no-fund decision. If you worry that someone might block the venture because they weren't consulted, put them on the advisory board.

- New Venture Advocates are those members of various functions or departments who have been selected (and hopefully trained and empowered) to be liaisons to the New Venture Team when they need something from the Mothership, for example, marketing, human resources, sales, procurement, IT, legal, and so on.

While the New Venture Team and the New Venture Board are not optional—you need both to build ventures—Venture Factory Team members, Advisory Board members, and New Venture Advocates are optional. This chapter is going to focus on the NVT, with a short introduction to the NVB, as they go hand in hand.*

→ Selecting a Great New Venture Team

No two teams will ever look the same, and there is no one recipe for success as you choose your teams. What matters is that the members of your venture team represent a range of superpowers. Diversity in every manifestation of that word—whether how people present, how they think, how they learn and process information,

---

* More details on the New Venture Board will come in chapter 10, which is dedicated to the role of senior executives in the Venture Building process to drive growth. We'll cover New Venture Advocates in chapter 10 as well and the Venture Factory Team in chapter 9.

where they come from, their range of experiences, their education (or lack thereof sometimes), their networks—will make your venture better. The worst possible team is one where everyone looks, sounds, and thinks the same; good luck understanding the myriad customers you want to attract if everyone falls into a single category. The two things that really need to be consistent are that every person can handle being an entrepreneur—the lifestyle is not for everyone—*and* that they have a growth mindset and will listen to customers, colleagues, and sponsors. Teams with toxic members are doomed. Let us share what we have learned over the years regarding how to choose a New Venture Team.

Choosing What Type of Team to Form

There are typically three ways NVTs form inside large companies.

Self-organized teams. In some cases, say, if you've run a Venture Plan Competition for example, teams will be prepopulated and self-organized or recruited for the proposal they submitted for the competition.

Company-identified and company-organized teams. Often, before they seek our services, companies have a good idea of who they want to be team members, because these people have already been working on a particular problem, or they are high-potential, next-generation leaders. Usually parent companies make the right choices, but sometimes they can do better. For example, staffing someone because they have free time or are idle is highly problematic. The last thing you want is someone who looks at the project as just another tour of duty. Avoid the passionless founder at all costs.

Recruited teams. You may also choose to recruit talent. The recruits may come from both inside and outside the company, but don't generically target those who are looking for their next leadership opportunity. Instead, look for those who are especially skilled at the customer pain you've identified and/or the opportunity you've imagined. Ideally, they also can easily fit one of the roles we will outline later.

The number one rule to remember when forming teams is that not everyone is meant to be an entrepreneur. The character of your entrepreneurs is as important as their track records and skill sets.

Finding Talent

We usually work with top-notch employees—the recognized superstars. But high achievers in the established corporate setting are not the *only* people to build a new enterprise and, in fact, can sometimes be quite problematic, especially if they can't see several adjacencies outside your core and legacy business or are unwilling to break at least a few rules. You need a certain type of personality—one that may not fit well in a bureaucratic milieu; indeed, the best candidate may be the problem employee. At Strategos, we told clients that besides the obvious candidates, we wanted those new to the company, those on the geographic periphery, and even those considered on the "lunatic fringe."

Look at the history of Silicon Valley and its most famous entrepreneurs. You'll rarely see a bigger group of mavericks, troublemakers, egomaniacs, and rule breakers. This motley crew is not an accident. To build a new enterprise from the ground up, to handle the lack of structure and ambiguity, to have the resilience to deal with the twists and turns of the marketplace, and to fight to the death for that enterprise requires a personality that is willing to challenge the boundaries, take risks, and fight seemingly impossible odds. The person must *believe* with conviction that will not see them wither when the first know-it-all C-suite executive, who has never interviewed a customer, decides to play "devil's advocate."

In other words, the right person for your NVT may very well be that employee who is recognized as brilliant but missing out on promotions because they just don't know how to play the corporate game. Or the star employee who feels unfulfilled and is looking for employment elsewhere. Or is driving management crazy with endless new ideas—someone who seemingly suffers from an inability to stick to the assignment at hand.

It is easy to recruit your superstars for your NVT. Those individuals stand out from the rest of the staff and are easy to spot. And in a normal business setting, they are the perfect choice. You *know* they not only are going to deliver but will brilliantly navigate through the organization to get the resources and support their venture will need.

Those folks can be great advocates for your new venture program. But you also may be shocked to discover, because they are also great corporate politicians, that they actually may resist joining the program. Why? Because it takes them away from their comfort zone and more importantly, their career trajectory up the traditional organization chart. Moreover, the venture represents a higher degree of risk to the type of individual who usually works to minimize risk so they can present the perfect résumé. Finally, it requires perpetually thinking outside the box and dealing with the unexpected through improvisation—behaviors usually anathema to the smooth daily operation of a mature company.

What this means is that even before you begin, you may need to disrupt your own assumptions of who is a star. You may need to assume a risk that you never anticipated; you may need to populate your team with employees who make you nervous precisely because they are always asking "Why?" and putting the C-suite executives on the spot. These are the employees who hold up the mirror to the organization and ask if are you willing to walk the talk. They aren't shy in challenging you to see if you are forever going to be checking off boxes for the board and creating window dressing for your shareholders by talking about "innovation" and "disruption" but never actually *doing* anything.

The best team members are the ones you have tolerated in the past but are now going to trust with your new ventures, precisely because you *know* they are going to be able to deliver innovation and build new companies for you. Honestly, they are likely the ones standing between you and total complacency. You might never trust them with leadership of an internal company initiative, but if you want someone to take that hill, they are the first employees you turn to. Most of our senior executive clients come to realize they want teams filled with people who are *not like them*. They look for the ones taking a path that they and their other senior executives did not.

About now, if you are the senior executive reading this book, you may be sweating. If you are one of those internal entrepreneurs, you are jumping up and down saying, "Pick me, pick me!"

If you feel uncomfortable picking an NVT, get help. You no doubt have some senior managers or board members—or even trusted outside contractors—with past entrepreneurial experience. They can help you vet potential team candidates and, with luck, recognize their own past selves.

At Mach49 we are currently working with a number of heads of talent and human resources to help them reimagine their employee population as members of three different talent pools:

Intrapreneurs are the idea-a-minute people who are rarely satisfied with the status quo, but who understand customer pain, thrive on actually talking to customers, can handle a lack of structure, and love the ambiguity of a blank piece of paper.

Growth Geniuses don't like the ambiguity of the early startup phase but are incredible at taking something someone else started and growing it 15 percent, 20 percent, or 50 percent per year. They love the pace and the challenge. And they are great at putting in place the structure, systems, and processes necessary to turn a startup into a fully functioning, scalable global business.

Efficiency Experts are often currently running the core and legacy business. They have the experience, gravitas, and know-how to run a global enterprise. They know how to build in operating efficiencies, generate margins, and guarantee a return

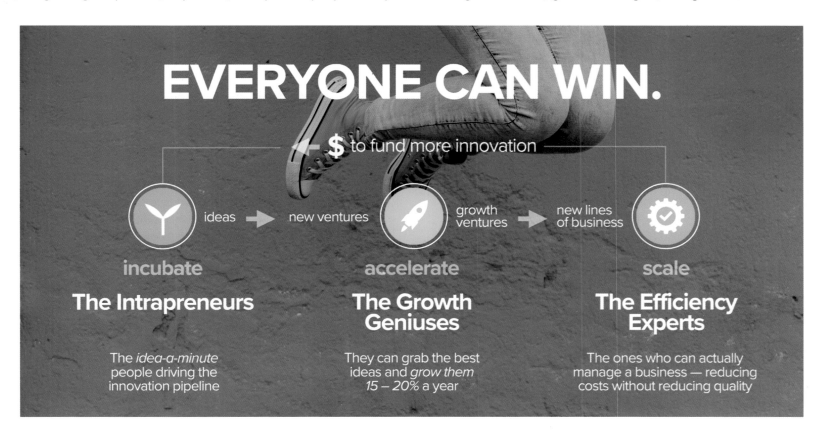

on investment. These individuals are likely not the entrepreneur with the idea. Rather, they stay focused on the current business at hand. They focus on putting in place the mechanisms to raise the cash needed to create new ventures that can become core and legacy businesses in the future.

Over time, a virtuous cycle forms.

Intrapreneurs create a pipeline and portfolio of new opportunities for the Mothership to truly solve real customer pain and innovate. Growth Geniuses make sure those ventures can scale. And Efficiency Experts create a long tail for those businesses and run them effectively and efficiently to spin off the cash to restart the cycle. All three types of people are equally valuable but just different. Companies that want to disrupt from the inside out need to celebrate, embrace, and reward those differences.

The biggest challenge is finding internal entrepreneurs, or Intrapreneurs. Your heads of talent, when recruiting new employees or conducting performance reviews, should look for those potential internal entrepreneurs and put them in a pool the company can draw on as new ventures are identified. We often say, think of yourselves as NASA and identify your astronauts. Not all of them are going to be part of the first mission, but they will be ready to go as you identify subsequent launches.

Focusing on Team Chemistry

Nothing impacts venture success more than team dynamics. The thing that will destroy a startup faster than any other challenge is toxicity. We see it all the time in Silicon Valley. So, putting some

IT'S NOT MILLENNIALS OR BUST

Disruptors in large companies come in every age, gender, race, sexual orientation, geography, or any other category you want to define. We often find greater diversity represented in our large-company NVTs than Silicon Valley startups; for example, three out of four of the technical ventures we have launched for a large industrial energy and automation solutions provider have had female CEOs leading them. As people progress through life, not everyone can afford to be part of a regular startup. Even though they might be just what a traditional, VC-backed startup needs, some extremely talented people can't afford the risk. However, internally incubated startups have options for compensating team members that allow individuals to manage their risk-reward equation, which opens the door for a much wider variety and diverse set of people to participate. Building ventures inside large companies is a way to democratize access to entrepreneurial opportunities, which has been an amazing benefit of the work we are doing. In chapter 10, we will discuss some compensation options that we have found attractive both to insiders currently working for the Mothership who join an NVT and to outsiders who you may need or want to recruit to fill a skill gap or role and who will likely be looking for more startup-like upside.

thought into not just the team members, but their interpersonal chemistry, is crucially important. As you put a team together, or if you are an internal entrepreneur looking for teammates, consider these additional issues.

Number of target customer or stakeholder segments. The number of interviews you need to conduct to cover all the players on the new venture's Stakeholder Map drives team size (on average, four to seven people).

- Multisided marketplaces need larger teams.
- Bigger is not better: balance diversity with alignment.

Comfort with uncertainty
- Incubation is about reducing risk over time.
- In Month 1, uncertainty is especially challenging.
- Not everyone is meant to be an entrepreneur.

Teams of peer cofounders
- High-potential team members need complementary skills and experience.
- Team members must be doers, not delegators.
- A facilitator-leader with a light touch is ideal.
- Members have to want to be entrepreneurs.

GREAT TEAM MEMBERS...	TOXIC TEAM MEMBERS...
Give credit	Blame others
Achieve optimal outcomes with high confidence	Achieve suboptimal outcomes with low confidence
Take ownership and behave as founders	Never take ownership
Believe in the rigor and discipline of the process	Doubt the need for a process; think startups should just wing it
Act with a sense of urgency, tenacity, and resilience	Act with no urgency, often focusing on effort, not outcome
Have complementary superpowers	Have no special skills or duplicate superpowers of others on the team
Challenge teammates to improve the outcome	Challenge teammates to dominate and paralyze
See incubating a new venture as a career-changing opportunity	See the twelve weeks of the Incubate phase as just a tour of duty

Personal characteristics
- Creativity and empathy are key traits.
- Visionaries need to explore the art of the possible.
- Members need the ability to develop hypotheses and imagine solutions. It's OK to fall in love with your own ideas but you must be willing to fall out of love with your ideas as well, letting go if your hypothesis is not customer validated.

→ New Venture Team Roles

Lead Roles
Typically, three primary roles represent the core of the team. One person can take on multiple roles.

Team lead. This person leads the team at startup speed and drives the strategy, story, and post-incubation Accelerate planning. They are the main interface with the NVB. They have the potential to become the CEO for the venture.

Customer development lead. This individual manages the customer and stakeholder interview pipeline, helps synthesize and document results, learns to design, and drives the product experimentation plans.

Product lead. This person ultimately drives and iterates the product vision, road map, minimum viable product (MVP), and technical feasibility assessment.

Supporting Players
Supporting roles can be filled either by a team member playing a primary role, additional team members added to the New Venture Team, or outside team members you decide to recruit.

The supporting roles required on a venture team typically include the following.

Program manager. This person coordinates and schedules the team's work, runs the team routines like daily stand-ups, nightly sit-downs, and weekly synthesis; manages the logistics for the team and the NVB; and works to resolve all blocks to the team's progress.

Subject-matter expert. The individual is the leading voice for the nuances of the industry and market, using deep domain knowledge. The team lead or product lead can play this role, or you can add an additional team member for this role from inside or outside the Mothership. Not all teams need subject-matter experts (SMEs). If you need them, you can bring them in for an hour, a day, a month, or for the entire incubation depending on the circumstance requiring an SME.

Designer or storyteller. Designers are specialists who support all areas requiring design, including storyboard and prototype development, plus the Check-in or Pitch narrative and visual imagery. Ideally one of the designers is also a storyteller. If you build your own Venture Factory, the storyteller can be a shared resource, but if the venture is stand-alone, someone needs to have a knack for telling the startup's story. Teams need to think about their pitch decks (really a business and execution plan) not as a PowerPoint with too many words on a page, but as a narrative. They should tell stories, not just report data. The storyteller/designer also makes sure the NVB actually feels the customers' pain, gets excited by the opportunity, and develops a sense of urgency.

Inevitably, team members play multiple roles. For example, everyone on the team has to work on customer development and interview customers. If you don't like talking to customers, then incubating a startup may not be for you (although we have found that some people who don't like playing the role of interviewer are skilled at other interview roles, such as synthesizing insights from interviews and detecting patterns, so don't think everyone on the team has to be an extravert).

The example in the following chart highlights some of the skills and traits you want the team members to represent as you move through the Incubate process. As you interview team members—or assess them if they were preselected—assign them a role and, using this checklist, make sure all the skills and traits you need to incubate your venture are covered somewhere on your team. Not everyone on the team needs to have all these skills and traits. You just want to make sure you don't have any gaps. If you fill out this checklist and find gaps, you have a good starting point to write the specifications to use to recruit the next person to the team.

Skills and Traits: Find Customer Pain

Month 1 Activities	GM/ Business Owner	Cofounder 2	Cofounder 3	Cofounder 4	External Resource
Source and set up interviews					
Relentless and tenacious	X	X		X	
Detail-oriented and organized		X			
Conduct interviews					
Extroverted and charming	X			X	
Confident, gently controls subject	X			X	
Document and synthesize interviews					
Thorough and reliable		X	X		
Sees the bigger picture			X		
Intellectually honest; no agenda		X	X	X	
Design and monitor interview plan					
Rigorous, organized, and scientific		X			

Skills and Traits: Create the Product

Month 2 Activities	GM/ Business Owner	Cofounder 2	Cofounder 3	Cofounder 4	External Resource
Generate product and feature ideas					
Empathetic and creative thinker		X	X		
Subject-matter expert				X	
Understands the "art of the possible"			X		
Create low/med/high-res UX stimuli					
Good visual design instincts			X		X
Assess desirability and feasibility risks					
Strategic: OK with difficult trade-offs				X	
Flexible/honest about rejected concepts				X	
Define product vision and MVP					
Drives big ideas down to details			X		
Primary product evangelist			X		
Primary technical contact			X		

Skills and Traits: Define the Business

Month 3 Activities	GM/Business Owner	Cofounder 2	Cofounder 3	Cofounder 4	External Resource
Define pricing model options					
Domain knowledge				X	
Estimate total available market					
Appropriately precise modeling		X		X	
Assess competitive landscape				X	
Generate go-to-market hypotheses					
Marketing and sales experience				X	
Digital marketing experience helpful				X	

Skills and Traits: Managing the Team and Mothership

GM/Business Owner	GM/Business Owner	Cofounder 2	Cofounder 3	Cofounder 4	External Resource
Lead team at startup speed	X				
Embrace Mach49's ways of working					
Maintain positive team energy					
Final arbiter (occasionally)					
Manage the Mothership	X				
Deep knowledge of the Mothership					
Respected by senior management					
Can extract Mothership resources ("gets")					
Own post-Incubate phase	X				

→ Don't Forget These Two Conditions

As you ponder the skills and traits you need, remember the five preconditions for success in chapter 1. Two of those relate to your team and are worth revisiting.

Precondition 1: Build a Full-Time Team

You must free the team from their day jobs to work full-time on the new venture for twelve weeks, with no exceptions. And, if the venture ends up launching, you want the team members to have the option of staying on as founding members and not go back to their former roles.

No matter how many consultants try to sell you on workshops and part-time venture creation, *you cannot do innovation part-time*. No independent startup ever is accepted into the Y Combinator, 500 Startups, or Techstars startup programs with team members who are working part-time. No VC is funding a venture team working two jobs.

If you are a multibillion-dollar, multinational company that can't free up four to six people to incubate a new venture for twelve weeks, then you aren't serious about innovation. The good news is that more and more of our clients already have some sort of rotation program that allows employees to take a temporary assignment for a period of time (usually three to six months) in the interests of leadership and professional development, without losing their position.

Precondition 2: Choose a Team Lead

You must designate a team lead, someone who serves as the venture's interim CEO or general manager. In some cases, the interim CEO continues on as the official CEO or GM once the venture launches. Or the NVB may determine that the new venture needs someone with more experience or different skills to be successful. In that case, the interim CEO or team lead, who has deep knowledge of your customers' pain, is still very valuable and ideally stays on as a founding team member, assuming another critical role.

As you begin to interview internal NVT members, you may find that, in some cases, they are missing skills or lacking areas of domain expertise that you feel are important to fully incubate the new venture. For example, a large automotive parts manufacturer, one of our clients, required 3D printing expertise and it didn't have any 3D printing experts to add to the team. So we reached out to our own network and recruited two subject-matter experts to join the team for twelve weeks. In other words, trust that you have internal entrepreneurs who can lead the effort but don't be afraid to go outside if you need to. One added advantage of having outsiders join the Incubate phase is that not only do you get great people to augment the capabilities of your team, but you also have an opportunity to try before you buy, as often you can hire them as a contractor for the Incubate phase without needing to offer them a full-time job that doesn't yet exist. Twelve weeks is a good amount of time to determine whether you want to make any of these people full-time job offers, should the venture launch.

→ Working from the Future Backward

What happens to the team members at the end of the twelve weeks? When we work with clients and recruit team members, we tell them that at the end of the Incubate phase, they will likely go in one of the following four directions:

- Stay with the new venture as part of the founding team and take it into the Accelerate phase
- Go back to their prior position (forever changed) at the parent company
- Participate in another incubation
- Become part of the inside team that will help their company build its own Venture Factory

The "Looking Forward to Accelerate" agenda in the last chapter includes this "future for the existing team" topic as a primary agenda item. We recommend that about three weeks before the final Pitch Day, the NVB member playing the role of sponsor should meet with each member of the team to understand what they want to do going forward. Do they want to stay with the team if it launches, and if so, what role are they interested in? Are they ready to go back to their home department or function? What can they teach their home teams? What kind of leadership role might they be able to play there with the new learning they have embraced? In some cases, team members loved the Venture Building activity, the topic wasn't one in which they were particularly interested or expert, but there is another venture they really want to incubate and can now lead. One team member learned a lot incubating a fleet-optimization venture for a large industrial client but was *really* excited to take that experience and incubate a venture around geospatial logistics.

If you are going to build your own Venture Factory to launch a portfolio of new ventures, there are no better guides for the next ventures than people on the team who have already been through an Incubate process. You just need to make sure that a subset of the team stays with the venture at least through the first phase of Accelerate.

That is usually an easy item to fulfill, however, because the reality is that 95 percent of the time the venture team members want to continue as full-time members, which means the NVB must ensure it has planned to backfill for those individuals, wherever in the organization they came from. The fastest way to kill Venture Building in your company is to make it a hardship for those left behind running your core and legacy businesses. Making Venture Building a win-win for everyone is a significant part of the Mothership management we discuss throughout the book.

Onboarding the New Venture Team

Once you've formed your team, your first impulse may be to jump right into Week 1. But even if your team has a strong willingness to tolerate ambiguity, starting too soon creates unnecessary anxiety. There's a good chance that most, if not all, members of your team have never been part of such an endeavor. A quick start may be disorienting.

In response to this initial confusion, we inaugurated what we call *Week 0* (which is, in fact, only about three days long). Week 0 is merely an overview of the twelve weeks of the Incubate phase that we cover in detail in chapters 4 through 7. All the material you need to conduct Week 0 is presented throughout the book. Feel free to improvise; there is no perfect agenda.

Besides helping the team see the end from the beginning, we also use Week 0 as a time when the team can practice a friendly customer interview and can work together to recruit the first set of customers to interview starting on Week 1. Week 0 is the time to make sure everyone has the tech stack they are going to use properly set up and to train those unfamiliar with the tools. Go over the calendar and any logistics (like vacations or holidays or time zone shifts) that may impact the team and agree on any norms team members might want to establish.

To summarize, there are several outcomes to seek during this Week 0 orientation.

Work Together for the First Time in a Low-Stress Environment

Often, team members do a personality profile before starting Week 0 so everyone can review them and understand each other's work and learning styles and differences. We use a publicly available tool called Predictive Index, but a simple and easily accessible Myers-Briggs Type Indicator can work just as well. These profiles help team members develop empathy for each other and are highly valuable for reference when or if team friction develops.

Learn How to Act Like High-Functioning Startups

Our New Venture Teams practice good startup hygiene throughout the Incubate phase by conducting:

- Daily stand-ups

- Nightly sit-downs

- Weekly syntheses (What did we learn this week and what do we need to learn next week?)

Get a Sense of the Entire Twelve Weeks of the Incubate Phase

In particular, how is the program laid out and what can the team expect as it moves through the customer development phase to the product or service opportunity and feasibility phase to the business viability phase?

Learn How to Recruit Customers to Interview

We share more on the customer development process in chapter 5. For now, the point is that the team members need this time to learn how to recruit customers. That way the team members can spend the next two to three weeks before the launch of the Incubate phase handing off or completing any outstanding work they need to finish from their old job, moving to the Venture Factory space (whether that is online or across the hall, the state, the country, or the world), and lining up interviews for the first week of the Incubate phase. One client came to the first day of the phase with ninety customer interviews already lined up. The bar doesn't have to be that high, but twenty to thirty is a good number to aim for.

The Role of the New Venture Board

Last, share with teams during Week 0 the role of their NVB and the expectations laid out for it. New venture creation is *not Shark Tank*, not in Silicon Valley, not in Tel Aviv, Berlin, London, Singapore, or any other startup ecosystem on the planet and definitely not in large, global enterprises. In real life, the best VCs are there to help their ventures, not sit in judgment. That is what every NVB is there to do as well. So who are they?

→ Selecting a Great NVB

Equally as important as selecting a great New Venture Team is curating a great NVB. Throughout the book, we add sidebars on the NVB's role, where relevant, throughout the incubation journey. We also devote chapter 10 to the C-suite and those senior executives with the ultimate responsibility to be the conductors of growth—building the pipeline and portfolio of new ventures and serving on the NVB as the new ventures' VCs. For now, however, an absolute requirement during the prep phase—and one of the critical preconditions for success—is to select and onboard an *engaged* NVB.

So, who are these board members and what do we mean by "engaged"?

While our primary focus in the Incubate phase is on the new venture, other work needs to happen at the corporate or leadership level to ensure the new venture can reach escape velocity and succeed.

The NVB is the decision-making body governing the new venture. In essence, members of the NVB are the startup's VCs. For that reason, the board must comprise leaders with the ability to do the following:

- Make the go/no-go decision on the new venture
- Provide funding to launch and accelerate the new venture once the Mothership has decided to launch
- Provide access to customers, channels, and markets, which is what differentiates your company from the well-funded startups out there potentially competing with you
- Provide access to the company's core competencies, assets, expertise, or capabilities the new venture may need
- Remove friction that may prevent the new venture from reaching escape velocity
- Determine the appropriate governance model to ensure the new venture can thrive
  - Spin-in. The venture joins an existing or new business unit, leveraging all or some of the support services from the Mothership or the Venture Factory (if your company has one).
  - Wholly owned subsidiary. The venture is set up as a wholly owned subsidiary, leveraging a mix of Mothership and outside support services.
  - Spin-out. The venture is spun out of the Mothership to become a stand-alone company that looks for outside funding in addition to whatever investment the Mothership decides to make.

The NVB members are usually senior executives from inside the company. If a company has a Venture Factory, a member of the Venture Factory Team would be on the NVB, as they have a portfolio view across all ventures currently being incubated and accelerated and the institutional memory of previous incubated ventures.

Depending on the nature of the venture, the Venture Factory Team member may join with other business unit or functional heads who generated the new venture idea or who are sponsoring the idea with either talent or funding.

Ideally one member of the NVB becomes the *Team Sponsor*. This individual is the main conduit between the team and the Mothership, and thus plays a more hands-on role by frequently attending the weekly synthesis sessions and providing a sounding board for the team as it prepares presentations for the Check-in and final Pitch Day sessions. The Team Sponsor also consults the team on what content and cadence is best for keeping the Mothership informed on the new venture and helps it develop an appropriate communication plan. Finally, the Team Sponsor drives the NVB to be ready to act so that the new venture does not lose momentum as it moves out of the Incubate phase and into the Accelerate phase, assuming it gets funded.

An *engaged* NVB commits to five touch points that are important for the success of the venture. Each of these is important, and we tell clients that the touch points are part of the preconditions for success they need to commit to or we won't work with them. We summarize the activities here; see chapter 10 for more details.

- New venture onboarding session (ninety minutes)
- NVB Day in the Life of the team (one half-day to full day; many NVB members learn so much they choose to return and join the team several times)
- Weekly synthesis (one hour per session; the team schedules this the same day, same time every week so the NVB members can attend as available; ideally, they should try to join at least twice during the twelve weeks)
- NVB Check-in presentation (the first formal presentation the team does for the NVB, typically three to four hours including an NVB executive session and feedback session for the team)
- Pitch Day (the final presentation of the business, execution, and operating plan the team gives to the NVB, again typically three to four hours including the NVB executive session)

All these engagement opportunities can be held either in person or virtually, depending on where the team is incubating. Recognizing that the team has a business to incubate in only twelve weeks, the NVB should be disciplined about *not* asking for interim presentations that take up the team's time that it can better spend interviewing customers. The NVB members are *always* welcome to join the team to experience firsthand what is happening. (You can find everything else you need to know about the NVB and the role of senior executives in chapter 10.)

Do you have all the people you need?

Great, let's help the team prepare to incubate.

Chapter 03

Preparing to Incubate

The Nuts and Bolts

Since this is a how-to guide, we are trying to leave no stone unturned. So, while the contents of this chapter may seem mundane and even obvious, as Ben Franklin noted, "To fail to prepare is to prepare to fail."

A successful Venture Building effort starts with collaborative preparation that roughly divides into three categories:

- General planning activities
- Team selection (chapter 2)
- Onboarding for teams (chapter 2)

We run through a how-to guide to Preparing to Incubate with every client on Day 1 of working together. Here are the topics and questions to address as you begin.

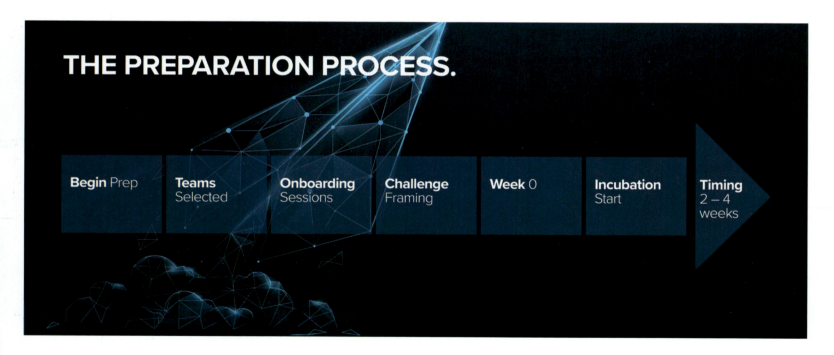

→ Incubation Mode and Venue

There are multiple options for incubating a venture: the New Venture Team can be physically together; the team can operate in a fully virtual mode; or the team members are together certain weeks and working remotely during the others, in a hybrid model. A lot of the process is the same regardless of what mode you are working in; for example, customer interviews are mostly by video conference or phone, but there are a few different categories to consider depending on which way you go.

100 Percent Virtual

If you go 100 percent virtual, the tools and technology are really important, as is calendar planning.

- People can handle only so many hours of screen time, so you need to determine the cadence. The team will be doing lots of customer interviews, which breaks things up throughout the days, but be conscious of how you organize the team's day.

- You also want to build in time for the team to become facile with the virtual tools they're using. For example, if the team is physically together, you can use whiteboards and sticky notes, but if the team is 100 percent virtual, it will still have the same functionality but using a technology tool the team members need to play with and adapt to. There is some breaking in to do, especially if you have people on your team who aren't digital natives.

- Another thing to think about is what hours the team will work. We often have team members in Silicon Valley and Singapore or Boston and London. We try to schedule the day so the team is together for core hours (and, yes, people do have to share the time-shifting requirements that are inevitable if you are doing a truly global venture, but hey, it is better than being on a plane all the time). Typically part of the team starts earlier and part of the team stays later. In some cases, when the time zones are diametrically opposed, the overlap between the teams comes in daily stand-ups and nightly sit-downs, which we do every day. So, one team's daily stand-up is the other team's nightly sit-down. Then we schedule other key meetings where the whole team needs to be together. It is important that at least two people are in the same time zone. No one interviews a customer on their own; it is too hard to listen, ask questions, take notes, glean insights, and stay honest on your own, so team members always interview in pairs and often three people. Make sure everyone has a buddy in a similar time zone so they can work together.

100 Percent Physical

If all your team members will be together somewhere in the world, then choosing the right place and setting up the space appropriately are incredibly important factors to ensure your New Venture Teams are extremely efficient and productive.

Step One: Get Out of the Building

Team members need to move out of the company's facilities and into a new place where they won't get swept away by the day-to-day flow of their former jobs. You can rent cheap warehouse space, take over an office that will fit the whole team at a coworking space (which has the added benefit of being surrounded by other startups and entrepreneurs with whom to build a community), or find a garage (it worked for Hewlett and Packard). You also can set up a war room at headquarters, but in that case, you need to find an isolated, open space with natural light where people can get outside to catch their breath. Wherever you pick, make sure it has good cell phone service and great Wi-Fi.

Step Two: Get Cozy

The stories of teams in Silicon Valley sitting in a garage on cardboard boxes around a folding table eating cold pizza are true. At least for the twelve weeks of our incubation program, team members work in one room—where all the artifacts of the new venture process (whiteboards, sheets of paper, Post-it notes) accumulate around them as testimony to their progress. Being together helps maintain the energy and pace and ensures constant communication. It also gets the team used to behaving like a startup. Even after it is funded, the team will still need to manage the burn rate—the amount of cash it is spending. Living like a startup versus maintaining the lifestyle supported by the Mothership is part of ensuring funding will last as long as needed to reach escape velocity. The incubation process is thus good preparation for the months ahead. The only thing needed in addition to the team space is access to at least one phone room because two teams will likely be doing interviews at the same time. Don't worry if it feels cramped: twelve weeks goes by very quickly.

Step Three: Decide Whether Home or Away

The last thing to determine is whether all the team members will move to the central location for twelve weeks or whether they will fly back and forth. If moving (and yes, we have had teams as far away as South Africa move to our Silicon Valley Venture Factory for twelve weeks), then you need to arrange people's housing and logistics prior to Week 1. We provide a concierge service to make that transition seamless for venture team members, complete with places to go, restaurants, grocery stores, and so on. If traveling back and forth, the team should agree to the travel plan. Typically our teams fly in on Monday morning and fly home Thursday afternoon and work remotely on Friday. Don't forget about visas if you are moving around international team members.

100% **Physical**

Hybrid

If you decide it's better for your teams to work virtually during certain weeks and come together other weeks, set up for both virtual and physical work. You also need to plan the calendar. Here is our sample calendar for our hybrid approach:

Once you have figured out the logistics, you should address the following topics.

→ Customer or Stakeholder Interview Approach

Teams need to conduct between 150 and 400 stakeholder or customer interviews over the course of the incubation. As a starting point, the team needs to know if the venture team can leverage the Mothership's customer contacts for interviews. If so, how does the team get access to those contacts, and who, from the Mothership, should own the logistics for managing the client database and providing access to the New Venture Team? (We cover this in detail in chapter 5.)

→ Project Budget

If you are in the planning stages of the Incubate phase, you have probably put aside the budget for the basics, people's time, tools, venue, and travel. However, at times the team may need funds for miscellaneous expenses, for example, customer interview recruiting, interview incentives, conferences, technology, or other miscellaneous expenses.

- Who should the New Venture Team work with to identify approved expenses and set a budget?
- What process should your venture team use to review and approve funds that might be needed?

→ Calendar

Venture teams move very quickly, and twelve weeks will go by in an instant. During the prep phase, build a calendar with dates preset, especially those dates when the New Venture Board needs to participate. In particular, the following dates are most important (we describe them in more detail as we get into the process):

- Week 0
- Official start date for the incubation
- Regular day and time for the weekly synthesis
- Check-in date
- Final Pitch Day date

Once we agree on the calendar and the dates, we try not to change them. Circumstances happen, but if you start to flex the schedule, make sure you have managed the New Venture Board's calendars, especially for the Check-in and Final Pitch dates, which can't be missed. Pay attention to local holidays (especially if you have a global team) and individual vacation plans.

→ New Venture Name

As one of their first bonding exercises, most New Venture Teams go through a new venture naming, branding, and logo exercise. We also set up a landing page or website for the venture; think of something very simple, with zero cost. We do this for a number of reasons. First, we want the team members to feel like they are a real startup, and we want customers we interview to know this is a real company worthy of their time—not just a project. Second, we want to test potential customers' reaction to the venture with and without the Mothership brand name attached (XYZ Company, powered by Mothership logo or XYZ Venture, a Mothership company) to see how those conditions impact the ratings for the venture. (It also sometimes makes sense to not use the Mothership logo at first if the Mothership wants to protect its brand in the early stages.) So, during the prep phase, you'll want to answer the following questions:

- How will members of the incubation team identify themselves to interviewees and other stakeholders (i.e., Mothership name, new venture NewCo name, NewCo name powered by Mothership)?

NEW VENTURES NEED A NAME AND A LOGO TO STAND OUT TO CUSTOMERS

AND A WEBSITE TO BUILD CREDIBILITY WITH CUSTOMERS

- What description will you use on your LinkedIn profiles?
- Who do you need to inform (but not involve; they will slow you down) about your name, logo, and website? Beware the marketing police.

→ Mothership Communication Plan

Often clients want to have the venture teams share their learning or activities with others in the organization. You can add communication to a regular company newsletter, a blog, or a short video.

- Do you want the team members to share their learning? How often? Using what medium?
- Who do we work with to design a Mothership communication plan?

→ Inspiration

Whether incubating physically or virtually, the team needs a space where lots of disruption is already happening. Silicon Valley and its sister ecosystems of innovation are successful because of the amount of collaboration and cooperation. Entrepreneurship is thick in the air.

If the team is together in a physical location, choose a place where there are universities with experts to tap into, startups to visit, VCs for coaching, or industry and domain experts to keep the team current on the art of the possible or help if it hits a snag. One of our client New Venture Teams was incubating in our Silicon Valley office. When it ran into a big data problem, we arranged for the team to have lunch with an expert at a hot local startup who solved the team's problem in sixty minutes. That's much faster than the six months it would have taken had the team been incubating at home with no state-of-the-art resources.

Oscar Wilde said, "Talent borrows, genius steals." Steve Jobs said, "Good artists copy, great artists steal." Simply put, being in an ecosystem of innovation gives you inspiration, ideas, analogs, and stories to apply to your own venture. Regardless of incubation mode (physical, virtual, or hybrid), look for opportunities for inspiration and networking. That could be a conference where potential customers may be convening, a demo day (physical or virtual), a regular online or in-person meetup, or a talk by a leading expert on a new technology.

- Looking at the calendar, what regular or special events might team members want to attend as a group or individually (and then share insights, learnings, contacts)?
- Where might the team find the type of people it wants to interview or network with?

→ Supplies

Remember when you went to camp or on a school trip and you were told what to pack? When New Venture Teams move into our space, we outfit the room with the following supplies. The team should have everything it needs for its twelve-week adventure. (Trust us: there is no time to go looking for the eraser or Post-it notes once you hit the Go button.)

- Post-it notes
- Whiteboards, dry erase markers, erasers
- Painter's tape and foam core boards
- Sharpies, pens, pencils, sharpener
- Stapler, tape, paper clips, binder clips, folders, scissors
- Tables, chairs, file cabinets
- Desktop monitors and access to a printer
- Extension cords, HDMI cables, computer connectors
- Storage or shelf unit
- Snacks and containers
- Watercooler
- Fridge and beverages
- Compostable paper products, plates, napkins, cups (for water and coffee), forks, knives, and spoons
- Coffeemaker, plus coffee, tea, honey, and sugar
- Recycling and garbage cans
- Cleaning supplies, tissues, basic first-aid kit
- Basic kitchen equipment so the team never has to leave the space

If the team is working in virtual or hybrid mode, especially if working from home, make sure folks are set up with what they need to be super productive throughout. Teams move just as fast working virtually as physically. Make sure your team members are set up for success.

→ Technology

For almost every one of our client teams, we need to buy computers. It seems crazy that our small firm serves as the bank for a *Fortune* 50 company, but IT departments are the tail wagging the dog when it comes to getting New Venture Teams up and running and fully functional from a technology standpoint.

In fairness, corporate IT shops have a mission to optimize and regulate—to make operations more efficient; 100,000 custom computers are impossible to maintain, and security takes precedence over functionality. In line with that philosophy, IT shops typically lock down computers or choose systems that they can control rather than tools that are functional. Nothing proved this more than when, during the pandemic, everyone moved to Zoom, which was easy to use, easy to share, and completely functional—instantly. Then people started freaking out over security and moved to other options—often clunky, impossible to share, no gallery view of the people you are meeting with, just terrible. We are not denying that security is an issue, but startups move with speed and agility, so your New Venture Teams need to be able to do so as well. A startup is in exploration mode and thus requires more freedom and a different set of digital tools. Twenty-five-year-old entrepreneurs often have easier access to the technology and communication tools they need than do New Venture Teams from giant multinational corporations. Such policies are growth limiting when it comes to new venture creation and ideally should be adapted.

New Venture Teams need technology, and they need tools. They also need the freedom to contemplate creating new platforms and digital environments, not be forced to adhere to the parent company's standards. Can you imagine if a VC in Silicon Valley funded a company and said, "Oh, we are happy to fund you as long as *all* of you work off this one platform." Not a chance. Faced with a new Venture Factory, the IT department of the Mothership needs to learn not to dictate this platform or that application; it must become more agile and adept at managing multiple platforms and programs. IT's job is to remove the friction and make sure New Venture Teams can move with the same speed as the little startups with which they are competing.

In line with our philosophy of make small bets and run lots of experiments, we are constantly trying out new tools. Ed Ross, Mach49 senior vice president of worldwide operations, who helps New Venture Factories get up and running, and Marvin Scaff, chief technology officer who keeps us current on the art of the possible (augmented reality is up next for us), put together the following list of the functionality every team requires.

Video Conferencing

Having a reliable video conferencing device that is mobile is key for teams. Our New Venture Teams are global, their New Venture Boards are global, and most importantly, their customers are global. Good video conferencing allows them to dial in remote team members for key discussions, interview customers face-to-face, and engage key influencers and NVB members from the larger Mothership, enabling them to participate at key moments. Using video also keeps travel costs down:

- Team. Teams need an easily movable, remote setup that simply plugs into members' computers and begins working instantly.
- Central hub. For the central hub of any office, a lean, but powerful setup allows teams to conduct their NVB presentations, should

any member be remote, and allows the internal team to conduct business development calls with customers with 100 percent reliability and clarity.

Speakerphone

An incubation team must have a mechanism that allows everyone to listen to customer interviews. A team Bluetooth-connected speakerphone allows calls with the entire team listening in from one room. The system should work from a team member's computer or smartphone.

TV

Each team room is fitted with a large-screen TV. The TV is a display for reviewing storyboards, wireframes, and prototypes; conducting script reviews for interviews; seeing the faces of remote participants on screen; and more. A key collaboration tool for teams, it allows everyone to watch interviews as they happen. It also enables the team to participate in group collaboration work.

Apple TV

An Apple TV allows teams to share to the TV directly through their computers via the Airplay functionality. Without using any cords, team members can share their computer screens with the rest of the team for easy collaboration.

Telepresence Robot

One day in an incubation can feel like one week in the real world. This pace is why remote team members should feel as connected as possible to the actions of the team room. Using a telepresence robot is the perfect tool to make remote team members feel as if they're right in the action with the team and allows NVB members to beam in whenever they have the chance.

Besides the equipment, we download the following tools onto the machine of every team member and teach them how to use them. Again, we get no referral or endorsement fees; these are just tools that we have found work every time, all the time.

Slack *(Problem being solved: seamless team communication)*

Teams use Slack for daily communication, planning, real-time communication during interviews, and more. We set up multiple channels with various purposes, such as questions during a test, where team members can "slack" each other in real time during an interview to give the moderator questions to ask. We also use Slack for events in which a bot automatically reminds team members (and the Mach49 team) any time they have a new event in the calendar.

Airtable *(Problem being solved: digital accounting and documentation of learning from customers throughout incubation. Airtable is a database that helps manage the venture. It becomes the institutional memory that allows a centralized database of all ventures incubated over time)*

Airtable (or an equivalent database) becomes the team's ultimate customer relationship management (CRM) tool. At the same time, it acts as an interview-capture mechanism. Rigorous documentation is a key success factor for every venture. We say if it isn't documented in Airtable, it didn't happen. For that reason, the teams rigorously document all user research in Airtable. Airtable stores all facts, assumptions, and history, along with the new ventures' ever-growing list of potential customers. The NVB also has access to the Airtable database, so it can keep up in real time with interviewees and the results of the interviews.

Some companies can't use Airtable, but they can use Google Sheets in the same manner. Documentation is especially important for companies that want to build a pipeline and portfolio of new ventures, as it provides critical institutional memory so the company doesn't reinvent the wheel with every venture and doesn't overuse any one particular customer.

Calendly *(Problem being solved: seamless ability for customers to schedule interviews with teams)*

This tool allows interviewees to self-schedule an interview slot. The team can skip the step of manually coordinating interview times. However, if your venture requires you to interview very senior executives, going through their executive assistants is the most effective approach.

Wordly *(Problem being solved: language barriers for multinational or multilingual ventures)*

Wordly is a language-on-demand service that we use when conducting interviews in foreign languages. It's a new real-time translation service for those on the team who don't speak the customer's language to follow the interview. Google Translate has also gotten very good.

Zoom *(Problem being solved: speaking with customers; testing stimulus; communicating with team members)*

Zoom is our go-to internal video and audio-conferencing tool, as well as the platform on which we conduct all user research. Whether conducting internal meetings or walking potential customers through prototypes, we do it all on Zoom. Zoom also doubles as one potential way of solving the remote team challenge, allowing team members to sit together in a team room and interact.

G Suite *(Problem being solved: shared tool set and detachment from the Mothership)*

G Suite encompasses many tools, but mostly it is the hub of productivity for teams and where the new team URL or domain lives.

Google Calendar *(Problem being solved: transparent, shared calendar. The team knows what is happening at all times)*

For an incubation team, we set up two calendars: a *customer or stakeholder interview calendar* and an *events calendar*. All customer interviews, once scheduled, go on a shared interviews calendar that every member of the team sees. Anything that is not an interview (meetings, out of office notices, etc.) goes on the events calendar. That way the team can operate with complete transparency and asynchronously as necessary.

Google Drive *(Problem being solved: need for shared repository of knowledge. Please don't allow Word docs to live on individual team members' machines)*

Google Drive houses all the team's materials. These materials range from interview guides to storyboards, opportunity frameworks on which the team is working, photos, important documents, and more. The team creates a structure and protocol for naming and storing files before incubation so that all team members know how to search for what they need.

Gmail *(Problem being solved: getting off corporate email; crafting a new identity)*
Each team member is issued a new email address before the Incubate phase. An email from the new venture's domain ensures the customers actually see it as a startup eager to solve their pain, not a big company trying to sell them something. It's not that the team won't introduce itself as a new venture that is part of the parent company (as that is usually a benefit, especially if it is a known and trusted brand), but the team members can operate as truly independent entrepreneurs in a new startup without the distraction of their Mothership email.

Google Slides *(Problem being solved: a shared area where all testing material lives and the ability to share it with customers)*
As part of the user research strategy called "storyboards," we often use the presentation software of Google Sheets to show remote participants the various value propositions of potential products and services that the teams can create. This tool allows teams to edit their concepts on the fly and work with user research teams worldwide in real time to generate feedback about concepts.

Website *(Problem being solved: digital front for the team to entice participants for customer interviews and enhance the legitimacy of the venture)*
From the first day we start incubating a new venture, designers work with the team members to come up with a name and a brand and set up a team website. This simple website allows prospective customers to understand what the venture does. It also gives the team a digital footprint to be proud of—a real startup, as opposed to a theoretical exercise. Most of the websites are set up in either Squarespace or Webflow.

Strikingly *(Problem being solved: landing pages to test stimulus with customers)*
Strikingly is a website builder that we have modified to run the storyboarding phase of a team's user research. It allows the team members to quickly modify visual tests they are running with users.

InVision *(Problem being solved: need to live test wireframes and concepts with customers)*
This tool enables teams to test their wireframes with users and provide product demos to their NVBs. InVision allows teams to take anything from low-resolution to completely realistic prototypes and run demos and tests quickly and effectively.

Sketch/Figma *(Problem being solved: demo high-resolution designs to customers and key stakeholders)*
These tools enable teams to create medium- to high-resolution prototypes and wireframes, design logos for teams or products, and bring visual frameworks to life. Design teams should have full mastery of these tools in order to create stunning visuals at a startup pace.

Balsamiq *(Problem being solved: testing low-resolution wireframes with customers)*
This go-to tool for low-resolution prototyping allows teams to quickly create digital wireframes that look hand drawn. Early tests should be low fidelity to allow the team to receive clean feedback about the concepts tested. If you put a polished product in front of

a customer in the early phases, when you are still trying to learn, you will receive false positive information; if it looks too good, the customer thinks you have put a lot of time into it and will feel sorry for you, so they often won't be brutally honest about how they feel about your product or solution. This tool enables teams to create prototypes quickly without having to draw them by hand.

Keynote *(Problem being solved: pixel-perfect design needed to demonstrate work done via presentation to stakeholders)*
Storytelling is key to the success of team presentations to their NVBs and other key influencers. We don't believe in traditional PowerPoint presentations. Instead, because design *really* matters, our teams create pixel-perfect presentations. With Keynote, the teams create artistically beautiful presentations at the speed of a startup.

Miro *(Problem being solved: digital freeform collaboration and whiteboards)*
Whiteboards, sticky notes, and drawing ideas are key activities to creating any venture. Miro gives the ability to do all of that virtually with teams working remotely. Teams can share unlimited sticky boards; digitally collaborate on presentations, storyboards, and prototypes; and engage virtually in other activities—never losing any of their work. Miro provides numerous application programming interfaces to bring harmony and connectedness to one shared digital whiteboard.

Tandem *(Problem being solved: lack of human feeling in remote work; lack of a consistent team room)*
In a fully digital environment, teams often miss the informal conversations and breakout opportunities that exist within an office. Tandem allows for ad hoc conversations, dedicated team rooms, and transparency of work for teams working fully remotely. In Tandem, team members can bump into each other in virtual hallways, quickly jump into a breakout room, and never deal with meeting links that get lost.

Otter.ai *(Problem being solved: lack of perfect note taking; spending hours hunting for specific quotes)*
A key part of note taking during interviews is to capture the voice of the customer; both quotes and actual audio can be incorporated into the Check-in and Pitch Day presentations. Otter.ai takes customer conversations and builds transcriptions with high accuracy in real time. There is no more hunting for quotes for a presentation or arguing about what a customer said in an interview—Otter.ai takes care of it.

OK, you have the people, the space, the training, the governance, the supplies, and the tech in place and ready to go.

Venture Building is next.

Part 02

Building Ventures

Chapter 04
Ideate

**Getting to New Ventures
You Can Incubate**

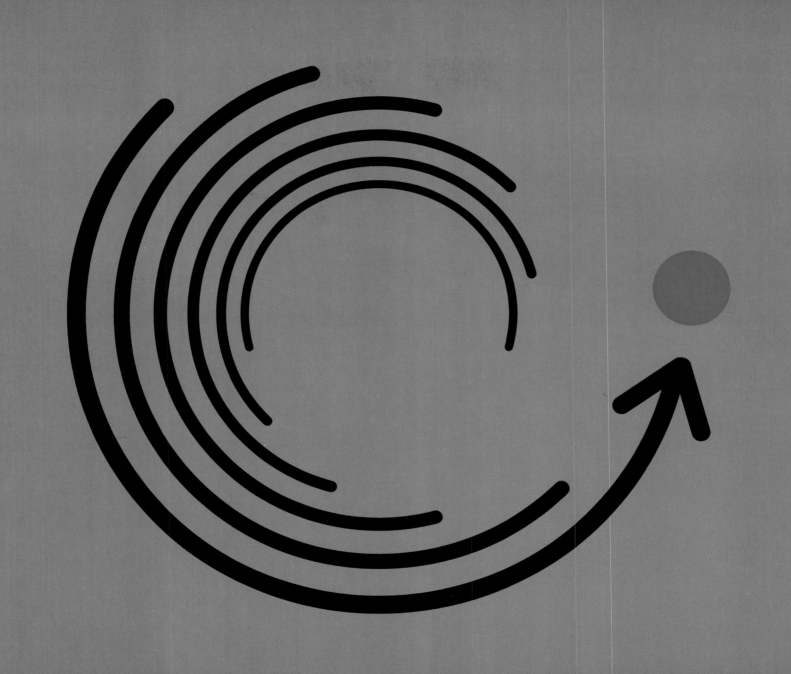

The first step to Venture Building is to make sure you have an idea to incubate in the first place.

At this point, you're probably at one of three stages in the new venture ideation process:

You have one to two specific new venture ideas that you want to move straight to the Incubate phase. If this is the case, you'll conduct a Challenge Framing and Stakeholder Mapping session to structure the jumping-off point and establish the guardrails for the venture.

or

You have a large number of ideas that you need to assess, sort, and prioritize to decide which ones are worthy of incubating and in what order. When we work directly with R&D groups, they almost always have this problem, along with the fact that their ideas are rarely customer driven but rather technology or product driven. If this explains your situation, you'll want to conduct a Portfolio Review to assess, filter, and prioritize the ideas.

or

You don't have a specific venture idea but rather have an opportunity domain, theme, or challenge you want to explore. You may also be hunting to find your internal entrepreneurs and need a mechanism to flush them out. If any of these scenarios sound familiar, you need a few more steps to help you get to venture ideas you can actually incubate. For companies in this third category, we suggest you conduct a Domain Exploration and Ecosystem Mapping exercise or a New Venture Competition.

Regardless of which category you fall into—from "We already have an idea" to "We have too many ideas" to "We don't have incubatable ideas or enough ideas"—there is always work in the Ideate phase

BUT WHAT ABOUT STRATEGY?

You may be thinking, "Wait a minute, before companies can even think about new ventures to launch, don't they first need an idea of what strategic themes or domains they want to explore?" Yes, but many of these large companies work with some of the best strategy consulting firms in the world. We partner with many of them (in fact, some are even our clients). While those firms focus on creating the strategy, we focus on execution. We are there with the catcher's mitt to help turn a company's innovation and growth objectives into thriving startups. This book is not about how you get to the themes in the first place; we leave that to our consulting friends, board members, C-suite execs—the thousands of strategy books published by Harvard Business Review Press and others. We are laser-focused on getting you from those more general themes to revenue-producing new ventures.

that needs to be done; it is just a matter of how much. Feel free to skip to the section that makes the most sense for your current situation, but first let's hit a topic that is relevant to all of you, no matter your starting point—how to quickly assess whether your venture idea makes sense for your company to even consider incubating.

→ New Venture Concept Assessment

Whether a client comes to us with a specific idea or we are sorting through a portfolio of ideas or helping them generate and then prioritize ideas, we do a very simple assessment exercise. To be clear, we do mean simple. Do not spend money or waste time doing extensive analysis, because, as you will discover, the only way to truly assess a venture is to pick up the phone and talk to customers (we cover that in the next chapter). First, let's make sure you have an idea that meets five tests:

Desirability. It starts with customer pain and a belief that there is enough of it to make the venture worth pursuing.

Feasibility. You believe that a product or solution of some sort can be built to solve that pain (you may not know what the product is, but it is not, for example, time travel, which you know you can't make happen right now).

Viability. You believe there is money to be made, and you can imagine one or more business models that could make sense.

Suitability. Even if all of the above are true, does this venture make sense for the Mothership? Do you believe you are the right company to build it? Do you have some unique capabilities or competencies? Can you imagine the venture gaining internal support?

Capability. Can you get the right people to join the venture team—from either the inside or the outside—to make the venture successful?

ASSESS THE NEW VENTURE CONCEPT ACROSS FIVE KEY DIMENSIONS

Desirability	Finding customer need	Does anyone care?
Feasibility	Determining the product or service	What should we build?
Viability	Designing the business	How do we make money?
Suitability	Mothership alignment	Should we build it?
Capability	Venture team	Can we get the right people?

At this point, it is OK for all the discussion to be based on hypotheses, even intuition, because you will test *all* your hypotheses during the Incubate phase, and that testing continues in the Accelerate phase. You just want to make sure that if your company is providing computer technology that the venture idea someone submitted—true story—isn't heated toilet seats. Or even if the venture is cool and you *love* the team, if the idea is just too far afield for the company to reasonably expend resources on—a semiconductor company with a New Venture Team that wanted to do food delivery, for example—versus another more strategically relevant idea, then you need to filter out the idea early in the process. Let's look at the five tests in more detail.

TOOL: DESIRABILITY
THINKING ABOUT THE CUSTOMER

Successful new ventures begin with customer pain. Great ideas come from trying to solve that customer pain.

We wish that truth was obvious and universally recognized, but it's not. Too many companies *do not* start with customer pain. Instead, they jump right into what they think is a great product or service idea, which was likely dreamed up by a senior executive or an engineer. This product-in-search-of-pain problem is the cause of much of the roadkill among Silicon Valley startups as well.

When Paul Holland, Mach49 VC-in-Residence and longtime general partner at Foundation Capital, asks entrepreneurs or Intrapreneurs what customer pain they're trying to solve and they can't come up with the goods, he walks away. No answer, no money. So we go through an exercise in which we make the team start with the customer.

Who is the customer?
- Is there a single customer or an ecosystem? How well-defined?
- If an ecosystem, how are the stakeholders related?
- Is this the right type of customer for the Mothership?

What customer problem are we solving?
- Is there a clear description of the customer pain, fear, or hope?
- If the venture is based on pain, is it acute?
- How easily adopted is the solution by the customer? Are major adjustments required?
- Are there proxy solutions already in the market?
- Are the target customers part of important social or business trends?

Once the team members have asked themselves these questions, we have them rate on a scale of one to five whether they believe there is enough pain to pursue the idea and what their relative confidence is in that rating.

FINDING CUSTOMER NEED: DOES ANYONE WANT IT?

Assessment Scale:

Desirability

WEAK: 1

Customer is not defined.

Pain, hope, or fear is questionable or latent.

Weak underlying market.

MODERATE: 3

Customer definition is specific but may be hard to locate.

Pain, hope, or fear is moderate.

Some evidence of broad market trends supporting the solution.

STRONG: 5

Customer definition is specific with well-defined boundaries.

Pain, hope, or fear is acute with no or few adequate solutions.

Strong underlying market trends.

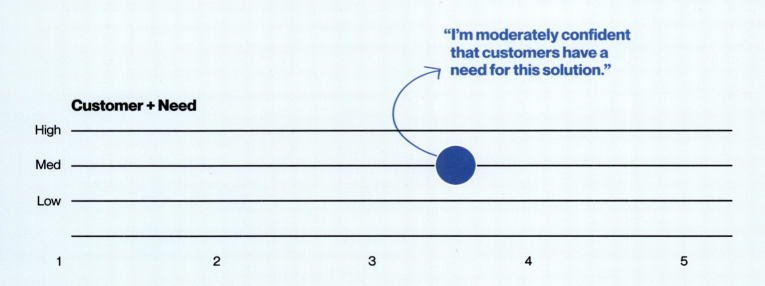

TOOL: FEASIBILITY
THINKING ABOUT THE PRODUCT OR SOLUTION

If they can't imagine the pain, there is no need to go further. But if we believe that, yes, there is potentially tons of pain, then we move to our hypotheses about the product or solution. How obvious is it? Is the user experience clear? Can we build it? In orders of magnitude, how much will it cost to design and build?

Exactly what is the offer?
- Is the domain specific (e.g., expanding middle class in Africa)?
- Is the offer specific (e.g., a mobile app, a tech-enabled service, hardware)?
- How broad is the solution? How many components does the solution comprise?

What are the technology hurdles?
- Do certain risks jump out? For example, for AI/ML, are we confident there is a signal in the data?
- Can each technical risk be mitigated with analysis, prototyping, and iterative testing?
- Is the idea based on unproven science?

Can we build it?
- How broad is the solution? How many components does the solution comprise?
- Is there an extended development road map with components requiring significant development?
- Does it require scarce or expensive resources to design and build?
- Can the solution be built in a series of sprints, and does it lend itself to an MVP?

What other risks stand out?
- Are there external dependencies on development, such as regulator or infrastructure requirements?
- Does the solution require integration with other emerging systems?

DETERMINING THE PRODUCT OR SERVICE: WHAT SHOULD WE BUILD?

Assessment Scale:

Feasibility

WEAK: 1

Offer is poorly defined.

Offer may not be technically feasible.

Development road map is flawed or resources are not available.

Regulatory or infrastructure risks pose fundamental challenges.

MODERATE: 3

Offer is only partially defined, or is in a questionable domain.

Technical risks may be significant.

Development road map or resources are in question.

Regulatory or infrastructure risks may be an issue.

STRONG: 5

Offer is well defined in an important domain.

Technical risks are manageable based on existing solutions.

Development road map and resources are clear.

Regulatory or infrastructure risks are manageable.

THEN WE RATE THE PRODUCT DIMENSION.

"Based on the high-level description . . .
a) I know what the offer looks like, and
b) I believe we can build it."

Product

High

Med

Low

1 2 3 4 5

TOOL: VIABILITY
THINKING ABOUT THE BUSINESS

People often think the order in which we do these tests seems out of order. We can assure you it's not. If there is no pain to solve or the product you are imagining is time travel (I am excited for the day when we have to issue a new release of the book because we do indeed have the technology for time travel, but for now it is my go-to example for a solution that is not currently feasible), then you can save yourself time crunching a bunch of numbers that can't be real because there is no pain or no product. When we turn to the business preassessment, we are asking: Is the revenue model obvious? How big is the market? What might be the unit economics? How could we market and sell it?

How big is the market?
- How big is the total addressable market and how quickly is it growing?
- How big is the initial target segment? Is there entrenched competition?

How do we make money?
- Is the business model specific and does it make sense?
- Are there multiple sources of revenue?
- Are there examples of successful companies with similar revenue models?
- What are the major costs and are they manageable?
- Does the market support high margins?
- Can we grow revenues substantially within a reasonable Accelerate and Scale schedule?

How do we go to market?
- Are the buyers and users both defined? Do both have an incentive to participate?
- For marketplaces, do all stakeholders have an incentive to participate?
- Is there a channel to reach customers? Are sales direct or indirect?
- Are customers expensive to acquire?
- Does our brand de-risk the purchase?
- Are the target geographies familiar?

DESIGNING THE BUSINESS: HOW DO WE MAKE MONEY?

Assessment Scale:

Viability

WEAK: 1

Market is too small or is owned by entrenched competitors.

Business model is inappropriate or undefined.

No defined customers or channel.

Unacceptable timeline to reach Scale.

MODERATE: 3

Market may not be large enough; competition is significant or growth is poor.

Business model is questionable for this offer.

Target customers or channel are in question.

Timeline to Accelerate and Scale is questionable.

STRONG: 5

Market is large with good dynamics, and competition leaves room to enter.

Business model is suitable and established.

Target customers and channel are defined.

Business can scale within reasonable Accelerate timeline.

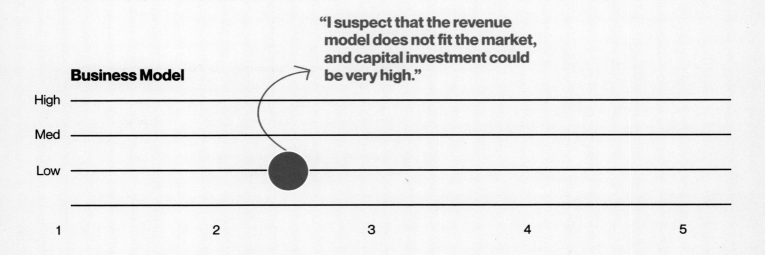

"I suspect that the revenue model does not fit the market, and capital investment could be very high."

TOOL: SUITABILITY
THINKING ABOUT THE MOTHERSHIP

We also address the new venture's fit with the Mothership's reality and strategy. While we want the new ventures to represent a stretch for the Mothership, an opportunity to disrupt itself and create new markets, the idea may just be too many adjacencies away for the Mothership to handle. So we ask: Are we the right people to build this? Do we need to and can we find a home for it? Can the venture gain internal support?

Are we the right people to build this?
- Does this new venture concept align with our strategy?
- How many adjacencies is it from our core business?
- Does it leverage our unique assets and capabilities?
- Are there shared services we will be forced to use?

Can we find a home for it?
- Is there an obvious organizational home for this new venture?
- Are specific executives ready to sponsor it?

Is budget available?
- Which organization will provide the budget for the new venture?
- Are the economies (OPEX, CAPEX, margins) acceptable to the Mothership?

Will it gain internal support?
- How will it interact operationally with the Mothership? Legal, Finance, HR, IT, Procurement?
- Does it have special requirements that are counter to our operating policies?
- Will the new venture have noncash "gives"/benefits for the Mothership?

MOTHERSHIP ALIGNMENT: SHOULD WE BUILD IT?

Assessment Scale:

Suitability

WEAK: 1

Does not fit within current competencies or strategy.

No clear organizational home or budget is unavailable.

No internal support.

MODERATE: 3

Possible fit with strategy or competencies.

Organizational home or budget is in question.

Questionable internal support.

STRONG: 5

Fits well with strategy and competencies.

Defined organizational home with budget available.

Strong internal support.

"I'm confident this new venture aligns well with our strategy and we have a division to own the venture."

Mothership Fit

	1	2	3	4	5
High				●	
Med					
Low					

The Unicorn Within

TOOL: CAPABILITY
THINKING ABOUT THE TEAM

Finally, we imagine the core competencies, skills, and capabilities we might need on a team tasked with leading and delivering a venture in this space, not just at launch, but in the future. Can we build, attract, and retain a team of that caliber? Can we motivate it? Will the Mothership be open to creatively compensating the team? Are internal team members passionate about the idea or do they see the venture as another tour of duty? Can our HR department handle strangely named roles like "growth hackers"?

Can we build a team?
- **Can we staff a mature team with the mix of capabilities across customer, product, and business expertise to drive the new venture to scale?**
- **Is the Mothership willing to hire essential external additions with complementary skills to the core team?**

Can we motivate the team?
- **Do our internally sourced team candidates have the entrepreneurial mindset and motivation?**

Can we compensate the team appropriately?
- **Can we motivate a team to deliver this offer based on available compensation?**

VENTURE TEAM:
CAN WE GET THE RIGHT PEOPLE?

Assessment Scale:

Capability

WEAK: 1
Team does not have the skills to execute.

Serious doubts regarding motivation.

MODERATE: 3
Team capability is in question.

Team motivations and/or compensation are questionable.

STRONG: 5
The team has the right capabilities or external resources can be hired.

Team motivations and compensation are well aligned.

"We have a full entrepreneurial team committed to this new line of business."

Team Capability

High · Med · Low

1 2 3 4 5

The questions we are sharing for each of the five tests offer a starting point. One step you want to take is to determine whether you need to adapt this set of questions to those your company should be asking. When we help build Venture Factories for our clients versus just helping them incubate one venture, one of the many activities we do with them during the Venture Factory design phase (see chapter 9) is finalize the questions they might want to add or edit to assess their new venture ideas on an ongoing basis.

You can also use this concept assessment framework as you move into the storyboard and prototype phase of Incubate to filter the product or service solutions you are brainstorming to test with customers.

For the final ranking, pull all the ideas together and compare them against each other.

You may have lots of great ideas at this point. Now you need to pick one or two to start incubating. If your company is doing its first incubation, our recommendation is start with the one that is easiest for the Mothership to imagine, not the one that is the most disruptive. Do that one second.

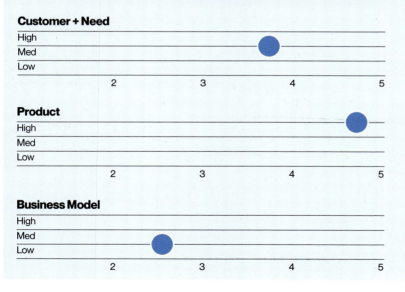

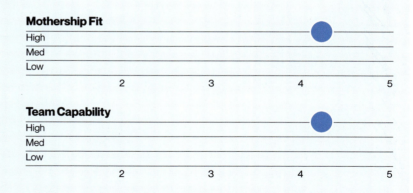

**GO/NO-GO DECISIONS:
HOW DOES THIS CONCEPT COMPARE TO OTHERS?**

Now let's get you an idea that is ready to incubate. Remember the three scenarios:

- You have a venture idea, ready to incubate.
- You have too many ideas, so you need to sort and prioritize.
- There are not enough ideas.

Feel free to read through each scenario or skip to the section that is most closely aligned with your current starting point.

→ Scenario 1: Have an Idea Ready to Incubate

If you already have a venture idea that you want to incubate, that's great. However, before you launch into Week 1 of the twelve weeks of incubation, you need to have two things:

- A *Challenge Statement* that provides some focus and some boundaries
- A *Stakeholder Map,* so you know whose pain you are trying to solve

There's no set rule for which one you tackle first. Sometimes the stakeholders will lead to the Challenge Statement; in other situations, the Challenge Statement helps define the stakeholders.

Let's go through both of these activities.

> **New Venture Board members should take part in the challenge framing and stakeholder mapping exercise. Either they can be part of the session or the team can present them options for the Challenge Statement and a map of the stakeholders in a shorter session to finalize.**

What Is Your Challenge?

A great Challenge Statement accomplishes three things:

- Establishes the aspiration or moon shot the venture is attempting
- Points to some early hypotheses that give the venture a starting point to test through customer pain point interviews
- Provides some guardrails so the venture isn't trying to be all things to all people

Here are the steps for developing your Challenge Statement:

Step 1: Assemble the team. Assemble a core group of team members, ideally the whole New Venture Team plus members of the New Venture Board. Feel free to add other key influencers or subject-matter experts as desired or needed.

Step 2: Establish the idea. Articulate the venture idea you believe you want to build.

Step 3: Identify who matters most. Identify the highest-potential constituents who you believe have the most pain or are most vital to the success of the venture you are imagining. Stakeholders will certainly include customers, but there will be other members of the ecosystem who you need to engage as well, for example, regulators, members of the supply chain, potential channel partners, and so on. This step is so critical, it gets its own section in a few pages.

Step 4: Identify what matters most. Determine the most important trends that could impact your success (social, economic, technical, political, etc.).

Step 5: Asset Jam. Create an inventory of Mothership resources your venture can leverage to help propel your program.

Step 6: Customer pain hypotheses. Take a problem a stakeholder faces and then describe a general solution you can imagine can solve that problem and identify its benefit to the stakeholder.

Step 7: Challenge question. Create a stakeholder-based question that provides a guide for the incubation. We use a very simple template to help clients determine their Challenge Statements.

EXERCISE:
WHAT MATTERS MOST?

Instructions

1. List Trends
In the box below, list some trends to watch—social, economic, technical, political—that might matter to your success and place them on the poster.

2. Cluster
Cluster similar trends.

3. Prioritize
Vote for the trends that matter most above the others. For a successful incubation, which trends must the team investigate?

Domain

Domain Topic Here

Trends

Voting Results

**EXERCISE:
ASSET JAM**

Instructions

Create an inventory of resources your venture can leverage to help propel your business. Examples might include:

Unique Capabilities

Particular skills that help drive your company's growth and profitability

Distribution Channels

The web of businesses and intermediaries currently bringing your product or service to market

Marketing Channels

The shared values, goals, attitudes, and practices that characterize your organization

Brand Equity

The value created by positive stakeholder perception of your brand

Cost Structure

Fixed or variable costs that enhance your competitive position

Partnerships and External Relationships

Successful, long-term, strategic connections with outside entities—business, government, academic, other

Intellectual Property and Know-How

Patents, copyrights, trademarks, and trade secrets that are critical assets for your company

Supply Chain

The network of suppliers who help produce your product or service—activities, people, entities, information, resources

Customer Segments

Groups of customers that are central to your company's success

**EXERCISE:
CUSTOMER PAIN HYPOTHESIS**

Instructions

Based on your insights, state a problem faced by one of your stakeholders while performing a particular activity.

To highlight a pain point, try this format.

**We believe that [this type of person]
needs to solve [problem]
while performing [process or task]**

Hypotheses

Voting Results

EXERCISE:
CHALLENGE QUESTION

Instructions

Create a stakeholder-based question that provides a guide for incubation. We use a very simple template to help clients determine their Challenge Statements.

How might we [goal or result]
for [stakeholders]
in a way that [approach]
so that [benefit or impact]

Elements of a Challenge Statement

How might we...
Describe what you want to accomplish

For...
Describe the people for whom your impact will matter most

In a way that...
Describe the approach, mindset, or values that you want your ventures to embody

So that...
Describe the big impact you want to make

Questions

Consolidation Exercise

Here are some Challenge Statement examples:

CHALLENGE STATEMENT.
B2C Example.

HOW MIGHT WE ...
empower people to take action toward healthy habits and understand their body

FOR ...
adults

IN A WAY THAT ...
is empathetic and personalized, actionable and dynamic, and integrated into their lives

SO THAT ...
they are informed and in control of achieving and maintaining a healthy lifestyle?

CHALLENGE STATEMENT.
B2B Example.

HOW MIGHT WE ...
create the Resource Virtual Marketplace

FOR ...
airlines

IN A WAY THAT ...
compels members to exchange resources rather than using mutual agreements or not using their existing assets

SO THAT ...
it quickly becomes the principal means airlines use to obtain maximum value from their collected resources?

Who Are Your Stakeholders? Who Matters Most?

New ventures do not operate in a vacuum, nor do they exist in a bubble that includes just the venture and the customer. Rather, they are part of an ecosystem that includes end customers *and* other stakeholders.

This reality is obviously true for B2C businesses, but it is even more important for B2B companies. Airbus may sell planes to the airlines, but they must build for the airlines' customers. A food processing company like Archer-Daniels-Midland may make the ingredients used by the big food companies, but it can't forget that those food companies sell their cereal to end consumers, who then feed that cereal to their kids.

Identifying stakeholders is the absolute key to launching a new venture, because without people to interview, you can't validate the pain you are trying to solve. Without clear customer pain, you have no venture.

Let us walk through the steps we use and then we will illustrate the results with real examples.

To create a Stakeholder Map, first get a group of people invested in your idea or venture in a physical or virtual room, hand them a pen and a pack of sticky notes or set them up on a digital Miro whiteboard and go through the following steps.

> **When you create a sticky note for who matters most, it must be a person or a role; it can't be an entity. For example, if a government agency matters most to you, don't write "agency" on the sticky; you can't interview a government agency or a bank or a furniture company. But you can interview the finance minister or the director of retail banking or the head designer. So don't cheat. The people are the ones who actually have pain. People are also the ones with the budget. Marketing departments can't buy; chief marketing officers buy.**

Step 1: Who matters most? Brainstorm a broad list of stakeholders, not just customers but all those who might be part of the ecosystem. Try to include one emotion and one lifestyle or situation (B2B, B2C, or B2B2C).

Step 2: Group similar or related stakeholders.

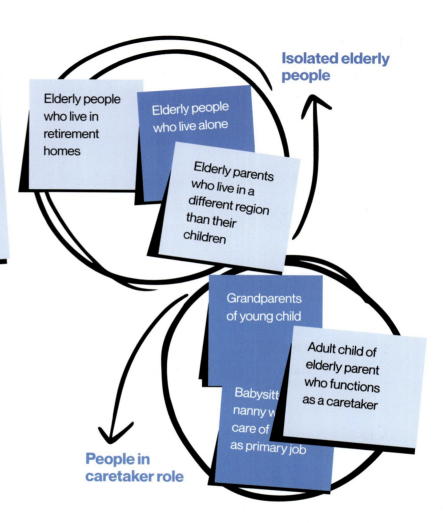

Parents of a 3-year-old girl who both work, feel guilty for not spending enough time with their child, and worry when their daughter is not in their charge.

A Generation X early adopter who worries about her retired father after seeing early signs of questionable decision-making. Living apart, she wants to track his whereabouts to make sure he's safe.

Step 3: Label the groups. These will become the early groupings that will later represent personas you will be designing or solving for.

Isolated elderly people

Elderly people who live in retirement homes

Elderly people who live alone

Elderly parents who live in a different region than their children

Grandparents of young child

Adult child of elderly parent who functions as a caretaker

Babysitter nanny who takes care of child as primary job

People in caretaker role

Step 4: Vote. Have the group vote on which groups represent the best starting hypothesis for who matters most. Soon you will have a map of your stakeholders, and you can begin to identify who you want to interview once you start the Incubate phase.

Your Stakeholder Map does not have to be perfect from the start. It grows and evolves as you begin to interview customers, so don't try to boil the ocean or argue over whether the CFO or chief marketing officer is more important. Instead, interview them both and discard one or the other once you have more information. Identify the people you think have pain and get ready to start interviewing them the first day you start to incubate your venture.

EXERCISE:
IDENTIFY WHO MATTERS MOST

Have the group vote on which groups represent the best starting hypothesis for "Who Matters Most." Soon you will have a map of your stakeholders and you can begin to identify who you want to interview once you start to incubate.

List Stakeholders

≔ List Trends: List all the stakeholders who might matter to your success. Make sure to include both internal and external stakeholders.

Cluster

∴ Cluster: Cluster similar stakeholders by sliding sticky notes into groups. Label each group with the main feature.

Prioritize

↑↓ Prioritize: Vote for the three stakeholders who are the most important for your initial research during the first few weeks of your incubation.

Putting It All Together

When you marry the Challenge Statement with a set of stakeholders, you will have built the foundation for your venture and can begin incubating. For example, a large energy and automation client wanted to build a venture focused on the emerging market around electric fleets. We first developed its Challenge Statement.

Then we married it with all the different segments that mattered most when thinking about that challenge.

But by remembering they couldn't interview a bus company, the team members took it down to actual potential stakeholders, users, buyers, and other key influencers.

Armed with a Challenge Statement that establishes a hypothesis of what the pain is that you are trying to solve and a Stakeholder Map of who matters most so you know who to interview, you and your team are now ready to incubate.

CHALLENGE STATEMENT.

How might we enable and accelerate the transformation to zero-emission mobility?

CUSTOMER SEGMENTS.

Utilities PG&E	Charge Station Operator EVGo	Incumbent OEM GM	Service and Tech Fleet Sunrun
Fleet Management Companies LeasePlan	Yellow Steel Fleet Ranger Construction	Government and Municipality County of LA	Hardware and Technology Tritium
Food and Beverage PepsiCo	Public Fleet Operation TransDev	EV OEM Workhorse	Contractor Black & Veatch
Software Technology Bestmile	Last Mile FedEx	Bus Companies Proterra	Ride Share Uber

CUSTOMER PERSONAS.

Fleet Management Operation Executives	Fleet Manager	Facility Manager
Policy Manager	CFO / Finance Manager	Consultant
CEO / COO	Global VP Real Estate	Sustainability Execs

→ Scenario 2: Too Many Ideas, Do a Portfolio Review

Do you have too many ideas and aren't sure where to start? Here are three steps to sort the ideas, build the pipeline, and determine which ventures to incubate first, second, or third.

Step 1: Conduct Executive Interviews

The New Venture Team and the New Venture Board Sponsor need to conduct executive interviews with the New Venture Board members and any other key influencers or sponsors involved in the development of new venture ideas. Through these interviews, they can build a complete list of all the ideas, collect any research or work that has already been completed exploring the ideas, and understand if there are Mothership issues relative to each of the ideas. The team and the NVB Sponsor may eliminate some of the ideas, thus reducing the list, or they may choose to advance the whole set of ideas to Portfolio Review Day. For more on these NVB executive interviews, see chapter 10.

Step 2: Host a Portfolio Review Day

Run a New Venture Portfolio Review session. The New Venture Team first shares results of the executive interviews and sets the stage for a series of activity sessions. Then for each venture on the list, you will run through six exercises. Usually, we break up the group into teams that each take a set of ventures to work on throughout the day. You don't need more than ten minutes per exercise (with huge thanks to our good friends Greg Galle and Mike Burn at Solve Next, who have been members of the Mach49 family since our founding and have helped us develop these activities and materials).

- **Challenge Framing.** What is the pain this venture is trying to solve? (See earlier instructions and tools for Challenge Framing.)

- **Stakeholder Mapping.** For whom are we solving the problem? (See earlier instructions and tool for Stakeholder Mapping.)

- **Asset Jam.** What core assets, capabilities, experience, talent, channels, and capital does the company have that would provide your venture competitive advantage? (See earlier instructions and tool for Asset Jam.)

- **Anchors and rockets.** What Mothership assets or behavior might become anchors that would hold this new venture idea back? What Mothership assets or behavior might serve as booster rockets for the venture?

- **Mothership readiness.** We use the Mothership test from the New Venture Concept Assessment tool earlier in the chapter for this activity. We also plot the ventures in terms of time horizon on one axis and adjacencies from the core business on the other axis. These hypotheses help us then fill out the New Venture Concept Assessment tool.

- **Venture Concept Assessment and prioritization.** With the earlier hypotheses in hand for each venture, the team assembled for the Portfolio Review now sorts and ranks them using the New Venture Concept Assessment tool we shared earlier.

The People

Almost more important than the agenda are the people who are attending the meeting and helping you review your portfolio of ideas. Attending the meeting should be:

- New Venture Board members
- New Venture Team members
- Venture Factory Team members (if you have an internal incubator and accelerator, or are going to set one up, then have the prospective members of the Venture Factory Team join)
- Experienced Venture Builders from either inside or outside the company

When you have a Portfolio Review Day, include experienced Venture Builders from either inside the company or outside to help you assess the venture ideas. Mach49 is made up of a unique cadre of successful serial entrepreneurs, top-tier VCs, and C-suite executives—an extremely experienced team that has collectively helped generate over $50 billion in market value during our operating careers with companies we have invested in, managed, created, or built. So, when we are involved in these Portfolio Reviews, several of us look at the ideas through the lens of our operating careers. The names are not important (and yes, these are real people), but here are the types of individuals and profiles you want to invite to your Portfolio Review. If you believe your market has global opportunities, be sure to include individuals with global startup experience and success.

By the way, these are the same types of people you want as judges if you hold a New Venture Competition, which we discuss later.

Examples of Types of People to Include

The founder, CEO, board member. A two-time successful entrepreneur and expert in Mothership management, she has spent her whole life deeply immersed in Silicon Valley while living in the C-suites and boardrooms of the Global 500, actively bridging these two worlds for over twenty-five years.

The VC, strategic sales executive. A VC-in-Residence, he spent eighteen years as a general partner at a top-tier venture fund in Silicon Valley. He has many IPOs to his name, including two as a member of the senior executive team with global sales and business development responsibility before his venture career.

The CFO. The CFO is an accomplished finance and operations executive who acts as the virtual CFO for all newly launched client ventures. He has been the CFO and CEO for multiple venture-backed startups and turnarounds over the past thirty years. Before joining Mach49, he provided financial and management consulting services to early-stage high-tech companies in Silicon Valley while also managing private equity-funded mining and real estate investments in the western United States.

The serial entrepreneur. This person has extensive leadership experience in Global 1000 firms and intrapreneurial startups. A CEO and turnaround CEO for seven unique ventures, this person helped run SAP's global business incubator and has spent the last two decades creating disruptive businesses and entrepreneurial cultures inside large companies.

The product guru. The chief product officer has spent over twenty years working with software startups in strategy and product development capacities. In addition to creating several multibillion-dollar digital platforms and products, this person ran the main product line at WebEx (accounting for 80 percent of total revenue) and built the original product and product team at Zuora.

The strategic storyteller. The chief creative officer has over three decades of experience helping technology companies craft compelling narratives. Using powerful visual elements to clearly communicate brand value and value propositions to customers, partners, and employees, he has helped many startups and Global 1000 clients bring innovative products and services to market.

The experienced Venture Board member. A VC and Board Member-in-Residence, he has over twenty-five years as a successful corporate venture capital investor in early- and growth-stage technology-related companies. An accomplished board member, entrepreneur, and business confidant across several industries, his experience spans diverse business models and stages of investment. As an internal entrepreneur at Comcast, he helped build, incubate, and accelerate what is now Sprint (wireless), ultimately generating a $3.5 billion return over five years.

The technology strategist. This person brings thirty years of experience creating new ventures at the intersection of emerging technologies, business opportunities, and human needs. Throughout his twenty-five years in leadership at IDEO (most recently as director of technology strategy), he led teams around the world to create new ventures for organizations like Cisco and Johns Hopkins. With roots in electromechanical engineering and six patents from his engineering work, he takes great pride in creating and sharing his expertise through university programs and Mach49's education programs.

The serial head of product. The product VP and Entrepreneur-in-Residence is a technology product management executive with over twenty years of experience. In addition to leading teams to build web-based products and iOS or Android apps used by millions of people around the world, she led Taulia's product management, user experience, and data science for an enterprise SaaS platform and established a repeatable process to create and launch new products and services at A3Ventures.

Silicon Valley's go-to CEO. A CEO-in-Residence who focuses on the Accelerate phase and getting ventures up and running in the market, he is a Silicon Valley–based technology entrepreneur and executive with startup, growth-stage, and public company experience. He has a track record of building and leading high-performance teams, driving product innovation, efficiently scaling business operations, and delivering revenue growth, profitability, and value to shareholders.

The big-company entrepreneur. This person has over twenty-five years of experience building new high-tech products and businesses inside large companies spanning mobile devices, products, services, IoT, and developer platforms. A serial Intrapreneur, he has successfully led multiple startups within *Fortune* 500 companies from conception through launch.

The strategic customer development guru. The VP of customer research and development has spearheaded user research capabilities for startups and *Fortune* 100 companies across industries for over twenty years. Combining her background in psychology, entrepreneurship, behavioral economics, game design, marketing, and traditional user research, she created innovative customer development processes that quickly and effectively helped companies of all sizes to determine and shape the right products to build.

The entrepreneurial polymath. This Board Member-in-Residence has more than twenty-five years of experience at the intersection of entrepreneurship, technology, innovation, and business. A seasoned C-suite and board-level executive in both private and public companies, he is a serial entrepreneur who has founded or been in executive management at four successful startups. In addition to running a $325 million corporate venture fund, working on dozens of successful M&A deals, and closing more than $2 billion in partnerships, he yielded $100 million or more in returns on under $7.5 million in capital as an investor.

The CTO technologist or entrepreneur. The technology Expert-in-Residence is a chief technology officer with over thirty-five years of expertise in technology product development. In addition to his portfolio of patents and intellectual property, his extensive entrepreneurial background spans multiple industries and has driven many successful ventures, including the incubation, acceleration, and launch of several startups with Mach49.

The corporate investing expert. This person is a partner with years of experience helping global enterprises optimize their external venturing activities. As lead venture adviser for a diverse set of Global 2000 corporations, he augmented deal sourcing, strategic connectivity, and partnership or investment activities across a number of enterprises including the Arizona Commerce Authority, Barrick Gold, DeNA, Southwest Airlines, and UPS Ventures.

The brand builder. A chief marketing officer and strategic thinker, she thrives on execution and data-driven insights. With over twenty years of experience, she specializes in startup and venture capital communications and brand development. She has worked in Silicon Valley, Hong Kong, and the UK helping B2C and B2B companies shape their brand stories for maximum impact.

Step 3: Prepare to Incubate

The last step is to pick the first three ventures you want to incubate and run them through the Preparing to Incubate steps we outlined in chapter 3 to make sure there aren't any logistical issues that might impact the order of incubation.

→ Scenario 3: Don't Have a Specific New Venture Idea But Know the Domains You Want to Explore OR Don't Have Enough Incubatable Ideas

If you need to spend more time on ideation, there are two different techniques:

- Domain Exploration and Ecosystem Mapping
- New Venture Plan Competition

Domain Exploration and Ecosystem Mapping

Often based on their strategy, clients have an idea of the domain they want to explore but don't have a specific venture idea they can incubate within that domain. For those companies, we recommend spending the time up front doing some Domain Exploration and Ecosystem Mapping. The goal of this exercise is to break down the domain into subsegments and then look for opportunities that might be interesting to pursue. Here are some steps to help you frame the work:

- Define the end-to-end value chain and then divide that value chain into segments and subsegments.
- Identify any megatrends that might impact the domains and segments.
- Develop a draft set of criteria and a framework for filtering venture ideas that are relevant for your company. If your company doesn't have a strategic set of criteria to help you filter ideas in place, this is a great opportunity to use the New Venture Concept Assessment tool explained earlier.
- Map the ecosystem of players already active and involved in selected sectors including VCs, startups, private equity firms, corporations, corporate venture capital, and others.
- Capture high-level signals that will shed light on where ecosystem activity is focused and imagine how that activity might impact your company—competition, saturation, business models, potential partners, white space opportunities.
- Identify and propose possible venture ideas and filter or prioritize them through the New Venture Concept Assessment tool.
- Build Stakeholder Maps of who matters most for the prioritized ideas within the most promising segments. As we have discussed, the Stakeholder Maps provide the basis for the first set of interviews during an incubation.
- Conclude the effort by conducting a Challenge Framing session for each domain to develop Challenge Statements for each venture idea of interest. Then rank the ideas and decide whether to take any of the venture ideas straight to the Incubate phase or feed the Challenge Statements into a New Venture Competition.

We have already explained in detail how to run a Challenge Framing session. The key difference between running a Challenge Framing session when you already have an idea versus when you are exploring a domain is that you need to bring the New Venture Board members into the process earlier. Their role is to identify the strategic imperatives and growth objectives they have been working to develop as senior leaders of the company, which will give them a

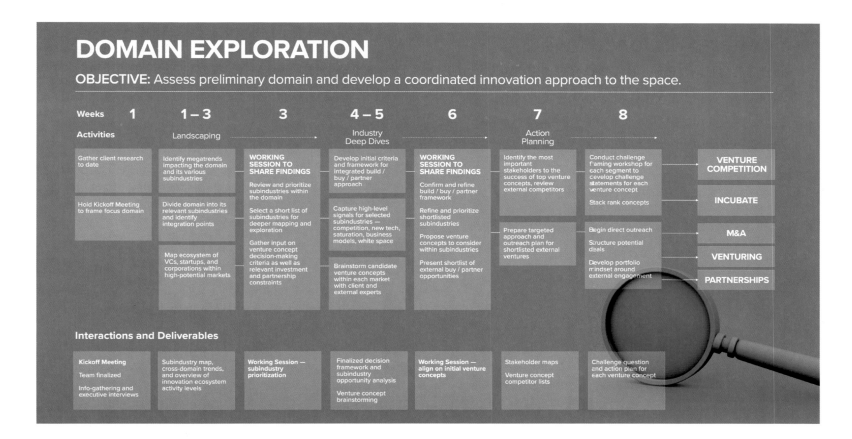

starting point for ventures they might consider. You may even want to conduct one-on-one executive interviews with each of your NVB members as preparation for that Challenge Framing session. (See chapter 10 for sample interview guides you might use with the NVB.)

The other difference is that you are likely to develop multiple challenges. Sometimes the Challenge Statements you write combined with the Stakeholder Map you develop for each challenge are enough to form teams and start incubating. Sometimes those Challenge Statements are the first step to launching a New Venture Competition. For example, a large semiconductor client brought the whole NVB together for a one-day session and identified six themes that the company cared about; the client then wrote Challenge Statements for each one. Those Challenge Statements provided the framework for the New Venture Competition, which yielded five hundred new venture submissions.

New Venture Plan Competition

One great way to identify specific new ventures to incubate is to challenge your internal entrepreneurs with a companywide Venture Plan Competition. Many companies face a garbage-in–garbage-out problem with business plan or New Venture Plan Competitions because they do not spend the time they need to set up a robust challenge (yes, that Challenge Statement is going to come up over and over) or develop a framework for participants to follow. Steps to ensure a successful competition include:

Frame a challenge. Different competitions typically address different challenges. One competition can offer multiple challenges.

Define guidelines for submitting a plan with a template and a set of expectations. By creating a more rigorous submission process, a company ensures that it gets higher-quality proposals from teams committed to doing the work. That's because only those with real passion for their idea will fulfill the requirements of the competition.

Launch the competition with all systems and processes in place before launch. That way there isn't a loss of momentum or delay moving teams to incubation. Answer the following questions:

- Who will review the submissions?
- What criteria will you use to judge the venture ideas?
- Who will be your judges? What criteria are you using to select them?
- How many rounds of feedback and additional presentations will you support?
- Will you be hosting a Pitch Day when only the judges are present or will you allow others to participate?
- How will you communicate results?

Host a Pitch Day including curating judges and sponsors both for the value they might offer in assessing the ventures and also for an opportunity to manage the Mothership and get key influencers to become advocates for the new ventures.

Select winners to incubate using predetermined metrics that need to be identified for filtering.

Provide feedback to those who are not selected to build engagement and capability of all participants.

Enjoy the energy; repeat!

Preconditions for Running Great Venture Plan Competitions

Below is a schematic of how New Venture Plan Competitions work.

New Venture Plan Competitions make the most sense when a company decides it wants to engage a broader group of employees in new venture creation or when a company wants to identify its internal entrepreneurs. One very critical component is to ensure the company has a feedback mechanism in place so those who are not selected feel their effort is valued. Feedback also enables them to learn how to improve their ideas or proposals, should they want to submit a new venture in the next competition. For every venture you select, there will be ten you don't, and most companies overlook how important it is for all those other people to feel good about spending time on their new venture idea and engaging in the process.

One global industrial client came to us with a "great plan" for generating ideas to incubate. The client was going to put out a request to all employees in the organization to submit a two-minute video on "How they might transform our company." We said, "Whoa, that could be a problem." When the client asked why, we replied, "First, that is too broad and too vague a question. Second, it has nothing to

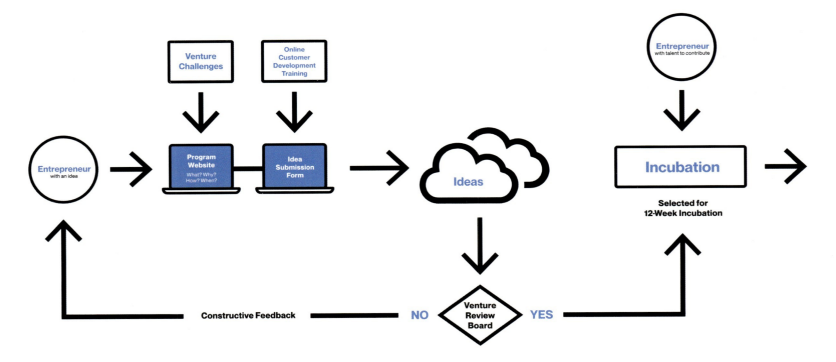

do with solving the pain of your customers, it's all about *you*. And third, just how many employees do you have?" With 160,000 employees, even if 1 percent of employees submitted a two-minute video, who would watch one hundred hours of video and then provide feedback to the submitters so that they would feel their submissions and time were valued?

While New Venture Plan Competitions are a great way to shake out your internal entrepreneurs and have them bubble to the top, you do have to be careful. Once you get those entrepreneurs excited, there is *no* turning back.

For example, another large financial services client said they were very enthusiastic because they were launching their competition as a way to excite next-generation leaders. It was to be an opportunity to recruit and retain the best and the brightest, because they would see their big, mature employer as a place where they could manifest their entrepreneurial aspirations. That is an extremely valid and worthy reason for running a New Venture Plan Competition, but only as long as you work from the future backward and have thought through how you are going to make everyone feel good about the process.

So, we asked the client, "In your first go-round, how many ideas got submitted?" They said, "1,500." Knowing it is impossible to do justice to 1,500 plans, we said, "Great! How many did you take forward from Round 1 to Round 2?" The answer was seventy. We said, "Great, so you now have disappointed 1,430 teams. How many did you take to the final round?" They answered, "Ten."

"Perfect," we told them. "You now have disappointed 1,490 teams with who knows how many team members per team."

Obviously, in life, not everyone wins, but everyone should feel that their participation was valued. And they should have an opportunity to learn from the effort so they can do better the next time.

Too many companies focus on those who win the competition and forget those who don't, then wonder why criticism and grumbling increases every year. Worse, the Venture Factory Team members wonder why they are out of business in three years as the unhappy, talented employees who see themselves as budding, but now disappointed and no more enlightened entrepreneurs, tell their managers that "those Venture Factory people don't know what they are doing." Often disenfranchised participants complain to their executives, who bubble up those complaints to the C-suite, which leads to the inevitable, but avoidable, end of the Venture Factory because it results in the opposite effect of what it set out to accomplish.

Instead, rather than going for the most ideas you can—which often feels like the logical play—go for fewer, higher-quality ideas submitted by teams passionate enough to do the work required to submit a proposal in the first place. In other words, consider these two counterintuitive concepts when designing New Venture Plan Competitions:

- Raise the bar on what it will take for ideas to be submitted in the first place. That way, you actually get a lower ratio of ideas to incubate, while getting higher-quality ideas.

- Get more people to self-select out of the process before you have to turn them away. Ideally, the cumulative number of people you disappoint stays low enough that there's no backlash over time. Once you have a series of successes this problem will go away, but if your ratio of disappointed teams or individuals to people who get the opportunity to move forward is too high too early, your Venture Building process will see a rising tide of complaints that may shut it down.

There are five ways to achieve all the above and keep your internal entrepreneurs happy:

1. Make the Challenge Statement(s) you use to request proposals more targeted. It is OK for the Challenge Statement to be broad (see the earlier examples); it just can't be all things to all people.

2. Make the opportunity to submit a proposal more robust, so that only teams with passion and conviction submit because those are the ones willing to do the up-front work. Requirements can include such items as identifying forty to sixty customers they can interview (don't ask them to conduct those interviews yet but have them identify the target subjects to prove they understand their Stakeholder Map).

3. Give everyone who participates the chance to improve their skills and learn something as they go through the venture challenge process. Even if they don't win, if they learn how to do customer development or get to download a venture plan template in the process, they will benefit and become more valuable resources in their everyday work.

4. Shorten the cycle time from idea to decision. Most venture competitions drag out far longer than they need to, which means teams must invest more time before finding out their idea isn't moving forward. You should not be looking for a full plan, just a customer-pain-validated idea as a starting point.

5. Offer people the option to take an alternative path to entrepreneurship. Often people want to be entrepreneurs, but they don't have a strong idea. If the only option they have to participate in the process is to submit an idea, then they will submit any idea—even if it is crappy—just to be noticed. When we run venture challenges, we always put these two buttons on the web page:

- I want to submit an idea.

- I don't have an idea to submit, but I would like to be considered for a New Venture Team. (For one client, when we launched a New Venture Competition, in just twenty minutes two hundred people submitted their résumés to be considered for a team. The client was thrilled to know it had that many entrepreneurial-minded team members, and now it knew where to find them.)

The New Venture Competition Journey and Timing

The eight key steps to executing a world-class New Venture Competition are laid out in the graphic below.

The steps include:

- **Secure executive and operating leadership.** The leadership owns the competition.

- **Develop the strategy and operating model for the competition.** Work from the future backward to determine the goals, logistics, judging criteria and process, communications plan, and most importantly, the website you need to build to process submissions.

- **Launch the competition.** How are you going to let the company know about the competition? How are you going to create excitement and buzz so your best and brightest engage?

New Venture Competition Journey

Secure Leadership →

Executive Champion
Operating Executive
New Venture Board

Develop Strategy and Operating Model →

Program goals and calendar
Budget (including venture compensation)
Challenge Framing
Submission criteria and tool
Decision scorecard
Employee communications

Launch the Competition →

Leadership call to action (email, web, and video)
Town hall forums
Executive sponsorship

Create Submissions

New Venture Idea teams form, get trained, and build submissions

Individuals apply to be team members

Initial Screening →

New Venture Board screens and filters to the top ~5–20

Finalists selected for Pitch Day

Specific feedback provided to all submitting teams

Finalists Prepare →

Teams get additional training and build their pitch deck

Pitch Day →

Teams present

New Venture Board decides which ventures to incubate

Specific feedback provided to all Pitch Day teams

Projects Chosen

Team members finalized

Travel/job details arranged

Incubation preparation begins

- **Create submissions.** Guided by the template you build for them, teams submit ideas, and individuals who want to be part of a team submit their résumés.

- **Do initial screening.** You do not want to waste people's time going through the whole process when you can't possibly incubate most of the ventures. To avoid that, institute a preliminary gate. Every team that submits a plan receives feedback at this stage either to help it prepare to go on to the Pitch Day or to help coach the members about what they could do better the next time.

- **Help finalists prepare their final pitches.** All teams participate in a training session to address the following topics on which their venture will be judged:
  - Market sizing
  - Team recruiting or formation
  - Customer development
  - Structure of an effective pitch
  - Storytelling and presentation coaching

- **Host Pitch Day.** Invite the following people:
  - All the individuals who submitted ideas, whether they were finalists or not, so they can view the pitches (in person or remotely)
  - Judges
  - The Intrapreneurs who submitted their résumés and demonstrated their interest in joining a team, even though they didn't have an idea—they may see a venture that fits their skills perfectly, and Pitch Day is a great opportunity for networking
  - Company executives who have been supporters and those who you may want to convert
  - R&D lab leaders and other subject-matter experts who may have relevant experience that could benefit one or more of the teams over time

- **Choose projects.** At this point, the Preparing to Incubate activities ensue, including:
  - Working the logistics and freeing up team members for the twelve weeks of incubation and potentially much longer if the venture gets officially launched
  - Finalizing team members, filling any gaps the team may have, ideally with individuals who submitted their résumés to what should now be a very robust internal entrepreneur talent pool

End to end, the first New Venture Competition you execute will take about six to eight months before you launch your first cohort of new ventures to incubate, but after the first one, they go much faster because you have completed all the prework, your systems are running, your website is built, and you are off to the races.

The New Venture Competition Judging

One of the most important elements in a New Venture Competition is the judging. The number one thing is that judging must be fair.

- Eliminate bias
- Create a fair, accessible process
- Run a high-quality program
- Drive for continuous success
- Encourage future submissions

At this point, you create a review panel or panel of judges from both inside and outside the company. The panel members should not merely have seniority, but, if possible, be a mix of company veterans, internal people who have started new companies in the past, or other highly qualified insiders (such as board members), combined with outsiders (venture capitalists, professors, successful entrepreneurs, industry or domain experts, etc.). For reference, check out the types of people listed earlier that we use to help with a Portfolio Review; they are the same people who we use to judge venture competitions.

There are two rounds of judging:
- The initial screening
- The Final Pitch Day

For the initial screening, there are again two rounds:

Round 1. A small group of screeners reviews all submissions, noting level of interest, completeness of the submission, and perspective on fit based on the judging criteria. They will put a number of submissions aside at this point because they just don't fit the criteria or the team has not invested the time needed to produce a top-tier proposal.

Round 2. A larger executive group reviews a smaller batch of submissions, but now, because we have already weeded out the incomplete or lackluster submissions, this round is primarily focused on the judging criteria (see the scoring sheet on page 108 for an example).

For the final Pitch Day, there is just one final round.

The finalists present their pitches to the judges and the audience through a series of fifteen-minute presentations. When we run competitions, that judging takes place in the morning, and then during the afternoon, the teams host booths where they can answer questions and get the community to help them enhance their ideas.

Even if a team does not win, meaning it does not get to move on to incubate its venture inside the company's Venture Factory, often team members continue to work on their idea in the hopes of resubmitting it in a future competition or developing the venture on their own, so this community feedback along with the judges' feedback is invaluable.

PITCH DAY.
Sample Agenda

8am – Noon **Pitches from Teams**
(15 minutes each plus breaks)

Noon – 1pm **Lunch Break**
Judges confer about pitches

1pm – 5:30pm **Engage Community to Help Enhance Ideas**

- Each team has a separate station
- Community participates in facilitated exercises
- Bigger Yes! — solicits ideas to make idea bigger, better, more specific
- Asset Jam — what internal resources can teams leverage to help their ideas?
- Act Now — community commits to support ventures
- Reframe Challenge — based upon input, frame challenge more broadly

6pm **Celebration for all participants in the Venture Competition**

Best in Class

Sample Scoring Sheet

Product/Solution: MVP	20%	How well is the technology/solution understood? Is it based on solid fundamental principles? Has it been validated?	Groundbreaking technology with great technical promise. Clear plan for developing the technology until it is fully validated and ready for scaling steps. Initial IP position considered.
Market Opportunity, Go to Market, etc.	20%	Has the team begun to understand the market size, trends, and competition? Do the identified market segments represent an attractive and achievable opportunity? Is the value to targeted customers and partners well-defined? Has the team identified and/or engaged with customers and strategic partners?	Clear understanding of market dynamics and trend is apparent. The targeted market segment is either highly profitable or achievable. High potential for market penetration. Clearly better than competition. Value to customers and partners is apparent. Partners and customers have been identified and/or engaged.
Problem Statement: Customer Pain	20%	Have costs and potential pricing been considered? Does the team understand the value offered to customers? Is a realistic and scalable deployment conceived at this stage?	The team understands how to build a sound and credible strategy around developing the business and learning customer development/acquisition skills.
Team	20%	Does the team have the technical and business skills, ability, and attitude to adapt and grow as a company?	Outstanding initial management team qualifications identified. Any existing gaps have been clearly identified. The team seems to understand what it will take to attract additional quality team members and advisers.
Why Our Company	20%	How does the proposed business opportunity take advantage of our company's strengths?	The team identified a strong set of Mothership advantages.

On Pitch Day, the judges should evaluate the ventures based on the same criteria they used in the first round but they should also look to see if the New Venture Team members have answered the questions and addressed any issues the panel suggested during the first round.

Once Pitch Day is completed, the judges confer and choose the winners. In some cases, the winners are announced that day, but usually, given how much work all the teams have put in, the company hosts a celebration for all participants that same day and then spends the next week talking to each team one on one, letting the members know if they were selected and what comes next. If they were not selected, they receive thoughtful feedback.

Congratulations, your first New Venture Competition is now complete, and you have a pipeline of terrific new ventures to incubate and excited entrepreneurs ready to dive in.

→ A Starting Point Is All That Matters

As Voltaire warns us, perfection is the enemy of the good. All these ways to ideate have the same objectives—develop a starting set of hypotheses about the pain you are trying to cure and who matters most, those individuals who will make up your Stakeholder Map. In the case of a Portfolio Review or a New Venture Competition, you may also have an early theory regarding potential solutions (but don't get too wed to those solutions). Customer interviews tell you the rest—ensuring you create, build, and launch a venture that can ultimately achieve product-market fit and real revenue.

Large companies too often suffer from analysis paralysis. I promise you the twenty-five-year-olds starting companies in Silicon Valley, Berlin, Tel Aviv, Mumbai, Singapore, London, Brisbane, Amsterdam, and beyond are not spending a lot of time doing strategic studies. Rather, they are developing a hypothesis of what their new company could be and then they go talk to a ton of people.

You need to be similarly aggressive. So, let's take the next step. You have an idea, you have a team, you are prepped and ready to go.

It's time to incubate your new venture.

It's time to pick up the phone and interview your first customer.

Chapter 05

Incubate Phase I: Customer

Does Anybody Want It?

Resolving customer pain is at the core of every successful startup.

Too many startups fail because they are built around products *looking* for pain, as opposed to products or services imagined in the service of *solving* real, identifiable, and validated pain.

Mach49's Expert-in-Residence, Drew Harman, has a memorable mantra that we make all our client team members memorize and repeat:

Customer insights *are* the currency of credibility; everything else is uninformed opinion.

Nobody knew to ask for drone copters, cashless payments, or mobile everything, but everyone feels the pain of commuting in traffic, an empty wallet, and being tethered to a physical object or a physical space (remember landlines and phone booths?). It is up to us to hear their pain and then marry it with the art of the possible in terms of new technology or trends and provide the solution.

A farmer can't tell you that the solution to tractor downtime should be sensors on parts that transmit data to the manufacturer through an industrial internet of things (IIoT) network. Or, that the network should trigger the part manufacturer's sales department to FedEx a replacement part to the farmer *before* the part fails, thus saving weeks and weeks of downtime and money during the imminent harvest.

The bottom line is that customers can't tell you the solution, but they can definitely share their pain. Finding that pain—through a series of relentless and curiosity-driven interviews—kicks off Day 1 of the Incubate phase and continues every day throughout Incubate and Accelerate. We call this customer development.

→ The Art of Customer Development

Why should you care about talking to customers? Because you don't want to build something nobody wants to use or buy. It seems so obvious, but Silicon Valley is littered with roadkill—failed startups that couldn't find a market because the companies didn't bother to talk to enough customers *before* they started to build their "amazing" new product. You want to find a market willing to buy the thing you want to build before you spend millions of dollars, euros, or yen building it. And it is not just whether people buy it; once they buy it, can they use it? And more than loving to use it, as our Board Member-in-Residence, longtime venture capitalist Bill Kingsley likes to say, you want customers to tell you they cannot live without it.

Interviews—not surveys—represent the core of customer development. Surveys are statistically significant but strategically irrelevant, because all you have done is outsource your visceral understanding and empathy for the customer to someone else, who inevitably is going to repackage the results and share them with your competitor. It is not that you will never do any surveying at scale, but we don't want you to start there.

Interviews with customers will help you:

- Understand customer pain, how customers behave, and how they make decisions
- Differentiate between "must solve" and "nice to solve" customer pains
- Validate or invalidate initial hypotheses (and create new ones) about what your new venture is and what it can become
- Tweak your solution designs with feedback from real end users
- Make sure that your solution works as predicted
- Begin to build a base of potential customers who are willing to pilot or buy your product or service after you launch

That last point is very important. These interviews aren't user research; we call the process customer development by design because you should view everyone you speak with as a possible future customer. Every time you interview a customer, you are beginning to develop a relationship, and when you log your interviews into Airtable or Google Drive or whatever database you have chosen for keeping track of those interviews (discussed in chapter 3), you are adding to your CRM system.

Over the course of the ninety-day incubation, you will talk to between 150 and 400 people (B2B numbers tend to be slightly lower than B2C numbers). You should do five interviews per day across twelve weeks. Assuming a 5 percent to 10 percent conversion rate, that's fifty to a hundred reach-outs per day. That sounds like a lot, right? But it can and absolutely needs to be done. No exceptions. We just had a client ask us to remediate a broken venture that someone else had incubated for them. The client was in the Accelerate phase and was wondering why they weren't getting any traction. When we asked how many customers the team had interviewed, they answered, "About ten." Most of them had been Mothership or internal customers (those don't count by the way), so we had uncovered the source of the problem. A bigger problem now emerged; the client had already built the product so wasn't so keen to go back to do the work that should have been done before spending all that money, because what if they found out that no one wanted the product they had built? That's what we call the walking dead. Please learn one lesson. If you have ventures that sound like this one, take your lumps and go back and do the work or just kill the project. Stop throwing good money after bad.

While there are lots of variations, at a basic level those 150 to 400 interviews will span across three different types. These are done progressively, meaning you start with the first and then, once you've hit certain milestones, do the second and third.

1. Open-ended discovery/pain point interviews
2. Value proposition testing/storyboard interviews
3. Solution testing/prototype interviews

→ **The Ins and Outs of Interviewing**

Before we jump into each interview type, let's go over the general process—from recruiting customers through writing scripts to speaking to customers. We'll also provide general interviewing tips, tricks, and best practices. Our advice will prove crucial during pain point interviews but will also serve you well during the storyboard and prototype interviews.

Recruiting Customers

One of the areas of greatest concern for team members is whether customers will talk to them. We can absolutely allay your fears: the answer is yes.

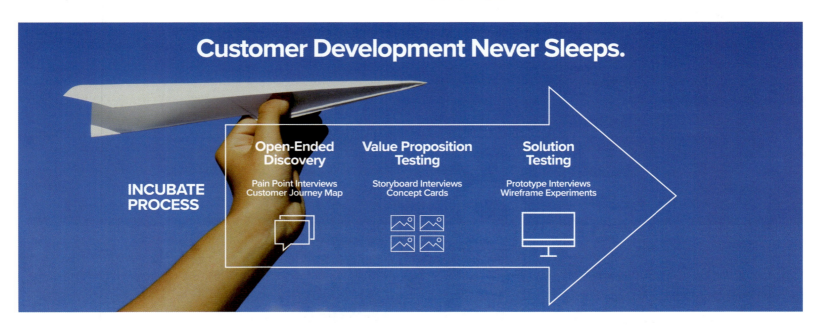

Customers typically are eager to talk, especially if they believe you are actually listening to them and not trying to sell them your preconceived notion of a solution to what you think is their pain. Interviewing (versus surveying) allows you to hear where their passions really lie, where their feelings are the strongest. You need to listen for nuance and emotion. You need to imagine translating the words they use (not your words) into early messaging to frame your value proposition. No survey can do that.

One advantage to launching a new venture from inside a large company is that you should have access to *plenty* of customers. However, that doesn't always work, usually due to company politics or procedures. Also, while it is easier to interview customers you have, you also want to interview customers you don't have, as that may be even more important.

The good news is that you have already determined who matters most and built your Stakeholder Map, so while you may not have your first set of customers to interview lined up quite yet, you know who you are targeting.

With that list in hand, there are three approaches to recruiting customers for New Venture Teams.

Option 1: Leverage the Customer Base You Already Have

You can pull this off by working with your NVB and Sponsor to determine:

- Who in the Mothership can help identify customers in the target segment(s)?
- How can you get access to contact data?
- What is the approval process to approach customers and how can you simplify or streamline this process?
- How quickly can you get access to them? (A venture works in days, not months.)
- What kind of post-interview Mothership notification is required?

> **NVB members, please note that part of your reason for being is to help your teams get access to existing customers, as that is what gives you clear competitive advantage over even the most well-funded startups.**

Option 2: Recruit Customers Outside the Mothership

The following steps are for recruiting potential customers that are new to your organization:

Reach out to your own contacts to interview or ask to be introduced. The list should include friends, colleagues, partners, senior executives, and so on.

Be mindful of the etiquette that is important when using personal introductions.

- Do *not* send an email blast (messages should be personalized).
- Make sure connections understand why you chose them for introductions.

- Include critical content elements about what you are up to.
- State the problem you are hoping to solve with your venture.
- Identify why the connection can help the venture.
- Explicitly ask your connection to forward the email you include (make it easy for them).
- Let them know what you are looking for—the type of person you want to interview, the fact that you only need a small amount of time.
- Offer assurance of privacy that you won't use quotes directly, and that everything will be aggregated and anonymized.
- Express appreciation.

Here is a sample email:

> Subject: Can you help? Share your insights with NewCo
>
> Hello [Name],
>
> Hope you and [name] team are doing well. [Friendly sentence].
>
> I'm reaching out to request your help with a new venture our team is building. We are in an early stage and looking to speak with experts like you to better understand the challenges and experiences of working in the industrial supply chain and construction industry.
>
> We would like to start by setting up time to ask you a few questions. It won't take more than 30 minutes and there's no need to prepare. As a seasoned professional in this space, we would love to learn more from your experiences.
>
> As part of our research, we will aggregate our interviews into an anonymized report. The results will only be used by the new venture team, but we'd be more than happy to share a copy with you once they are complete.
>
> Would you be available for a 30-minute conversation? If so, I'll share a calendar link where you can sign up for a time slot that works best for you.
>
> Thank you so much,

Find contacts on LinkedIn. The social network is a great source; you can see people's bios, job titles, and industry. Here's a primer:

- Contact first-degree connections via personal email address.
- Leverage first-degree connections to introduce you to second-degree connections.
- For all others, upgrade to premium subscription.
- Use filters to identify the best targets.
- Contact directly via LinkedIn InMail.
- Be specific about how they can help.
- Identify the problem you are solving.
- State the amount of time requested.
- Only send ten to fifteen messages at a time so you can test message effectiveness and iterate.
- Don't burn through your leads.

Here's a sample message:

> To: Jane Doe
>
> Subject: LinkedIn Connection Request
>
> Hi [Name],
>
> I'm with NewCo, a new venture from Mothership. We're having informal talks with experts like you who have experience in the construction, building, and design industry. We think you'd be a great fit for our research.
>
> If you're interested, please click on the link below to schedule a time to connect.
>
> [link]
>
> Hope to hear from you!
>
> Best Regards,
>
> John Doe

Encounter off-line. This is the old-fashioned way, but it can be very effective.

- Go where your prospective customers physically go: a grocery store, a conference, a shopping mall, a construction site—the opportunities are nearly endless.
- Don't approach them if they are busy or engaged.
- Keep it short.
- Pitch the problem.
- Ask one question.
- Get contact data.
- Set up a follow-up meeting.

Use a web landing page. Sometimes it is good to attract prospects to a page that explains and legitimizes the project you're working on, especially if you're utilizing social media advertising or Google AdWords or other services.

- Build a page or use a hosted service (remember we said at the beginning that every client team gets a name, a logo, and a very simple, inexpensive website) to establish that you are a real company.
- Use Google AdWords to direct traffic to the page.
- Include a short survey with the ability to follow up (you don't want surveys; you want live people, so this survey is merely to hook them and get them to want to talk to you).

Be scrappy. Keep your eyes open, as you never know when the opportunity will arise to find a potential customer. One of our clients was working from home on a fleet optimization project; he noticed that big trucks passed by his window all the time. So he started writing down the trucking company names and phone numbers on the sides of the trucks and started calling them. Another client was working on a zero-water home venture and started calling local governments of towns where there was a moratorium on building because they didn't have enough water. Everyone was incentivized to talk to them—landowners, contractors, government officials, and local businesses, as all of them wanted a solution to help them lift the moratorium.

Option 3: Engage a Professional Recruiting Agency

This option is always the last resort because with a startup, you need to be cautious of burning cash without trying every other effort, but in some cases, you may need help.

Interviewing Customers

Many startups fail because people just don't like interviewing customers. But while it is sometimes hard to get that first pain point interview, if you do the interviews well and *really listen* and don't talk, then the interviewees will realize that you aren't there to sell them something but to solve their pain. Once they realize that, they will want to be part of the later storyboard and prototype interviews because they will want to make sure they have a hand in how you solve their pain. We have customers during every Incubate phase who offer to be pilot customers, and many times they even ask if they can invest in the venture. That's when you know you are really onto something.

The team should follow a rigorous, disciplined process when interviewing customers. A prepared script is important to ensure you get quality insights across interviews conducted by different interviewers. The script needs to be somewhat adaptive to allow you to react in real time with shrewd follow-ups, should an interesting line of questioning emerge, but you need to make sure you document everything.

The scripts will evolve as you begin to interview, but even in their earliest form, they add a layer of discipline that is very important. Each type of interview should have its own script (examples are in later sections).

WATCH FOR BIAS

There are five types of bias that teams should watch out for:

Confirmation bias. People hear only things that confirm their original beliefs.

Choice-supportive bias. After they make a choice, people seek out information to confirm that all other options were terrible choices.

Social desirability bias. Interviewees overreport good behavior and underreport bad behavior. They want to answer questions in a way that makes them look good, so the interviewer doesn't judge them and so they feel better about themselves.

Projection bias. Human beings are notoriously bad at understanding and predicting their own behavior. People believe that next week they won't face as many obstacles as this week, that life will be smooth sailing, and all of their future choices will be logical and rational. ("My diet starts on Monday.")

Consistency bias. People want to answer questions in ways that seem consistent. If someone asks you if you are the kind of person who donates to charity and you say yes, if they then ask you to donate to their charity, you will likely say yes.

Once you've nailed the script, you're ready to talk to customers. Here are some tips for asking great questions and getting meaningful responses.

Question Tip 1: Ask Open-Ended, Storytelling Questions

Ask open-ended questions to prompt stories. Don't ask questions that can be answered yes or no.

- "Tell me about the last time you . . ."
- "Tell me about an experience you've had with . . ."
- "Can you tell me a story about . . . ?"

Question Tip 2: Get Recent or Extreme Info

People remember the extremes of experiences, the best, or the last part of an experience. So, ask for recent stories and extremes.

Don't ask:

"Tell me about your vacation."

"Tell me about your job responsibilities."

Do ask:

"Can you tell me about a moment in your most recent vacation that was extremely positive for you?"

"Can you tell me what, if anything, is frustrating about your current job?"

Question Tip 3: Past Instead of Future

Don't ask "Would you do this?" or "Would you download this?" It is more effective to dig for previous stories.

Don't ask:

"Would you use a caretaking service for your plants?"

Do ask:

"Tell me about services that keep your house running smoothly."

More Question Tips

- Start simple
- Ask one question at a time
- Avoid leading questions
- Favor more-specific questions over general
- Ask what advice they might give to others

AVOID THESE INTERVIEW TRAPS

Lots of people will tell you "Of course, we conducted interviews," but often those interviews exhibit several consistent flaws:

They lead the witness. You assume you are brilliant and already have a great idea, so you bring confirmation bias into the interviewing process to make sure the customer agrees with your insights. You do more talking than your customer does. And, in the end, you convince yourself you got the answer you wanted. (By the way, most senior executives suffer from this problem. It's why they want to insert their opinions into the Incubate process. The venture team has to slyly ask the executive where their customer quotes are so it can add those to the customer interview database. That usually exposes the fact that the executive's comments are merely personal opinion with no empirical basis.) Instead, you must park your agenda—don't suggest answers, and don't try to persuade the interview subject about anything, period.

Apples to oranges. If everyone on the team is using a different script and asking questions in their own way, your data is useless. You need to find patterns, but you can't find those patterns in a sample set of one. Thus, you must be very disciplined about writing a script, following it, and then being in lockstep with your other team members as you execute that script. You will make dozens of changes to those scripts, especially in the early days as you are triangulating on the topics and the personas, but whatever version you are on, make sure everyone interviewing is using the same script.

One-stop shop. Especially in the early phases, if you only have one person at a time interviewing, you will never get full value out of those interviews. It is just too hard to ask questions, listen for insights and quotes, and document simultaneously. At a minimum, you need an interviewer *and* a scribe. You also need each other to keep yourselves honest.

Hear no evil. You were super-disciplined, kept quiet, and didn't lead the witness. You let them talk, but their answers didn't fit your hypothesis, so rather than realize you probably need to kill or pivot your new venture idea, you doubt yourself and the way you are conducting interviews. One of our poster-child clients (poster child because they have been doing an amazing job ideating and incubating all on their own) came to us while they were incubating a new venture and said, "We need you to come in and do some quality control on our interviewing because nobody wants what we are imagining and we think we are doing the interviews wrong." So, we sat in on a few interviews and noted that the interviewers were doing an awesome job. However, the harsh reality was that no one wanted what they were hoping to sell. They were trying to build a digital platform to build the "book" for an IPO. The problem was that the people they were targeting to use the platform had no interest in buying digitally. They liked the personal relationship and being wined, dined, and wooed into making an institutional purchase of an IPO. The lesson? The interview process is not the answer in itself—it is the *path* to the answer.

Mind like a steel trap . . . not. Do not believe you will remember what the customer said, especially after hundreds of interviews. You and your fellow interviewers should pause after every interview to synthesize the insights you gained from that interview and load the customer information and insights into whatever database you are using. If you have asked the interviewee for permission to use audio, then capture quotes and get those in the database as well. Interviews inevitably blend together if you don't get your notes down quickly. And those specific customer quotes will be invaluable on Pitch Day. Documentation is especially important for large enterprises that want to incubate dozens of future new ventures; documentation is what provides the institutional memory on new venture creation so that the venture you create two years from now can learn from the work completed by the venture you are building now. Moreover, if the parent company is good at AI and ML, the data you collect can become an invaluable predictive success resource over time.

Remember, the ultimate goal of the interview process is to capture useful data from an accurate spectrum of stakeholders, determine the nature and magnitude of key pain points, obtain honest and uninfluenced results, and record those results in a manner that is directly comparable with the results of the many other interviews and interviewers.

We've talked about who to interview, how to find them, and how (or how not) to conduct the interview, and the importance of rigorous documentation. Now let's jump into our first interview type—pain point interviews.

→ Pain Point Interviews

The most powerful tool for early testing is informal and qualitative dialogue with carefully chosen people from your Stakeholder Map about their pain, challenges, or opportunities.

In the interests of not reinventing the wheel, we present the work of two of our compatriots: Julie Price, the brilliant partner in charge of our customer development practice, and our Mach49 good friend and MachNet member, Cindy Alvarez—a longtime practitioner of the art of customer development and author of *Lean Customer Development: Building Products Your Customers Will Buy*. Together, they perfected the Open-Ended Pain Point Interview. As Cindy likes to say, "Customers can't tell you what they want, but they can't hide what they need." Here's what we have developed together.

Whether you represent a startup or a product development team, the first step is to develop a hypothesis of the pain that exists and then test whether that hypothesis is true by interviewing real customers, iterating and pivoting your interviews until you hear a pattern. Solving pain always trumps pretty or price when it comes to customers actually buying what you want to sell. Pain points always take priority in their purchasing plans.

Here's an overview and answers to questions you may have.

What Are Pain Point Interviews?
- Thirty- to forty-five-minute interviews, usually remote by phone or Zoom
- Led by one person using the script or guide
- Supported by at least one other note taker
- Focused on hearing stories from the interviewer

What Is the Goal?
- Listen for pains, their severity, context, and any processes surrounding them. If one person is conducting the interview, the others listening need to take notes on stickies throughout the interview. Try to capture pains, insights, quotes, and magic-wand wishes on different stickies so you can post them on a big whiteboard (or on your Miro board, if virtual) and move them around as you see patterns.
- Scripts evolve between sessions, patterns emerge, and eventually your interviews start to focus on the prioritization of pains versus the digging for pain.

Who Are You Talking To?
- At least ten people per stakeholder group
- Multiple stakeholder groups
- Of the 150 to 400 interviews you do over the course of the whole Incubate phase, 40 to 80 will be pain point interviews

When Do You Stop?
- When you reach diminishing returns from doing another interview
- When you can almost predict what they will say
- Usually about two to three weeks into your twelve-week incubation process
- It is typical to see several major shifts in the interview script before starting to find consistency in common pains; when you can start to finish people's sentences, then you know you have found common pain and common pain is where you find big markets

What Do You Learn?
- Explicit pains, per stakeholders
- Severity of pains
- Context and processes surrounding each pain

Developing a Hypothesis
The Open-Ended Pain Point Interview process always starts with a hypothesis crafted as follows:

- I believe (insert type of person)
- Needs to solve (insert problem)
- While performing or doing (insert task)
- Which will give them (insert new ability or benefit)

For example, we believe that CEOs at *Fortune* 1000 companies need to shorten the time it takes to expand into new countries, which typically happens while working with foreign government bureaucracies. This prevents them from selling products and services in new markets and making more money.

It's helpful, at this stage, to craft multiple hypothesis statements and to talk about them as a team.

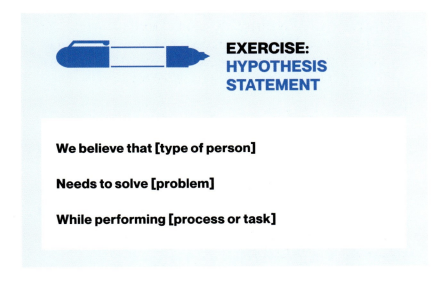

**EXERCISE:
HYPOTHESIS
STATEMENT**

We believe that [type of person]

Needs to solve [problem]

While performing [process or task]

Develop several hypothesis statements

I believe pet owners feel uneasy about their pet's safety and happiness when they aren't physically with them because they don't know how they are doing

I believe pet owners feel anxious when taking their pet off-leash

I believe pet owners don't know as much about the health of their pet as they would like to

Write down the topics on sticky notes

Diet + Health

Vacations + Work

Technology + Monitoring

Open a shared doc and list the topics

Topics: *Extract the related topics from the hypothesis above*

- Vacations and work—Dan
- Diet and health—Gary
- Technology and monitoring—Ann

Add bullets with questions relating to your topic

- Vacations and work—Dan
  - Can you tell me about the last time you went on vacation and weren't able to take your pet?
    - Where did your pet stay while you were away?
    - Can you tell me about a time when leaving your pet while on vacation didn't go so well?
  - Can you walk me through a typical work day and what you do before you say goodbye to your pets when you leave?
  - Can you tell me about a time when you were away from the home and an incident happened involving your pet?

- Diet and health—Gary
  - What's your biggest worry with regard to your pet's health?
  - How do you monitor your pet's health?
  - How do you know when your pet is unhealthy or needs to be taken to the vet?

- Technology and monitoring—Ann
  - How do you monitor your pet when you're not with them?
  - What extra security measures do you currently use when you're not home with your pet?
  - What forms of technology (if any) do you use for your pet?
    - What caused you to start using ____?
    - Why did you choose to use ____?

Developing Topics
Next, write down the topics—what you want to learn about—that relate to your hypothesis statements.

Write the Script
Once you've developed multiple hypotheses and related topics, and memorialized them in writing, open up a shared document.

Everyone should write their topic name and place their own name next to it.

Then add lists of questions relating to your topics, using these prompts to guide you.

- Tell me a story
- Tell me about your frustrations
- Tell me a process

As a team, vote on what topics to include, and choose one point person (editor) to incorporate the questions into the script and one to two background questions as well. Then test the script on a friend or colleague who's not on the team. Iterate and edit as needed.

Here's a sample script:

PAIN POINT INTERVIEW SCRIPT
WEEK 0

INTERVIEW SCRIPT

INTRODUCE YOURSELF

- Is this still a good time to talk?
- Thank you again for your time!
- I am talking to experts like you to ask informal questions about your experience at _____. This is an early step in our process to design solutions that might support you, and I can follow up with you at a later time to share where these conversations have led us.
- I'm interested in learning about your experiences and understanding the frustrations you've encountered as it relates to _____.
- I have a note taker with me, although you and I will be the only two speaking. Everything we discuss today will be completely confidential.
- Are you comfortable if I record our session? This is just so I can go back if I forget anything. The recordings are confidential and it's perfectly fine if you say no.

GENERAL QUESTIONS

Goals: Get your stakeholder warmed up for storytelling. Keep it light and informal.

- Can you tell me a little about your role?
- Where do you spend most of your time?

MAIN QUESTIONS

If you're not following a path toward specific pain points that come up naturally, use this list. You will refine it regularly as you learn more about where to dig. List only 5 to 7 here.

Examples:

- Tell me about how you do _____ today. Tell me about the last time you _____.
- Do you use any tools to help you get _____ done? What tools do you use for _____?
- How often do you do _____? Let's say, how many times in the past month?
- When this problem occurs, how much additional time or money does it cost you or your company?
- Who else experiences this problem?
- When you do (or use) _____, is there anything you do immediately beforehand to prepare? Last time you did _____, what were you doing right before you got started? Once you finished, what did you do afterward?
- If you could change one thing about how you do _____ today, what would it be?

SECONDARY QUESTIONS

If the list of 5 to 7 questions above are not enough, the moderator might choose a question from this list.

Examples:

- If you had [target feature] today, how would that make your life better?
- Is there anything else about _____ that I should have asked?
- How do you use _____ in your job today? How has it changed over the years?
- What makes _____ particularly difficult? Can you list your biggest challenges and tell us about each one? (Look for stories.)
- What parts of your work require particular care? Can you tell me what sort of practitioners are the most effective? What makes them effective?
- Could you delve a little into the nature of work you did with _____? Do you have any stories about _____?
- If you were going to give advice to another company trying to do what you've done, what would it be?
- Let's say tomorrow you get a new job. What's the one thing you'd be happy you don't have to do anymore?

FINAL QUESTIONS (5 MINUTES)

Save time to ask these questions:

- If you had a **magic wand** to make your work experience better with one change, whether it is **technically feasible or not**, what would you change?
- I'm looking to understand the various frustrations in your daily work life. Are there any other questions I should have asked you?
- *Check Slack #questionsduringtest to see other questions from the team.*

- *[Depending on team philosophy]* Also, I'm happy to send you anonymized aggregated observations from these interviews, if that would be interesting to you. Would you like me to send them?
- Thank you for your time and thoughts today. Would you mind if I reached out in the future to hear what you think as we move forward and have some ideas to show you for your feedback?
- I'm continually looking for feedback from people like you. Is there someone else who you think would be comfortable giving us their thoughts?

INTERVIEW QUESTION TIPS

- **Start simple.** A great first question is "Can you tell me about your role?" or "Can you tell me a story about _____?"
- **Ask open-ended storytelling questions** to prompt stories (don't ask questions that can be answered with "yes" or "no").
- **Get recent or extreme info.** People remember the extremes of experiences, the best or the last part of an experience. So ask for recent stories and extremes.
- **Past instead of future.** Don't ask "Would you do this?" or "Would you download this?" It's more effective to dig for previous stories.
- **Ask one question at a time.** Be careful of double questions (e.g., "Which do you prefer and why?")
- **Don't ask leading questions.** Stay as neutral as possible; repeat their words back to them instead of introducing new words and concepts. When in doubt, pause for them to fill the silence.
- **Specific over general.** Ask questions about specific moments in time or specific processes rather than asking general questions, which they may misremember or misinterpret.
- **Advice to others.** Often people do not like admitting their weaknesses or do not see their challenges clearly. It can be helpful to ask them what advice they would give others to find their biggest challenges rather than asking them directly.
- **Solicit impossible questions.** Ask the magic wand question in every interview. "If you had a magic wand to make your [work] experience better with one change, whether it's technically feasible or not, what would you change?" The answers to this question are sometimes the most interesting of the whole interview.

INTERVIEWING BEST PRACTICES

- Listen for emotions. Changes in pacing, pitch, laughter, breathing—these are all signs of emotional moments, and you can dig deeper at these points to ask directly about these moments.
- The goal of the interview is to listen for pains, judge their severity, and learn more about the context and processes surrounding them and where they occur.
- Don't suggest answers to your questions. Even if they pause before answering, don't help them by suggesting an answer. Ask questions neutrally and be open when you hear surprises. Allow a three-second pause before asking the next question.
- Don't be afraid of silence. Often if you allow there to be silence, a person will reflect on what they've just said and say something deeper. Attempt to be as invisible as possible.
- Stay on the same path of a question. Respond to what your interviewee offers and follow up to go deeper. Use simple questions (like "Why is that?") to get the person to say more. For example: "Oh, why do you do it that way?" and "What were you feeling at that point?"
- Be aware of nonverbal cues if you are in person or on video. Consider body language and facial expressions, and try to appear neutral as much as possible.
- Let one person moderate the conversation while others take notes. Only the moderator speaks and owns the interview.

FOCUS ON THEM, NOT US

- Park your own views before the interview—your goal is not to persuade anyone on the merits of your opinion, and the interviewee is always right.
- Don't overdiscuss your plans and background. Stay focused on them instead of you, and if they force the conversation, save it for the end of the interview and invite them back to see your progress later.
- Be careful not to share new ideas. Questions like "Would something like this solve your problem?" or "Do you think you'd use a solution like this?" are unreliable and can hurt our ability to learn the truth.

Effective Note Taking

Earlier we said that interviews should always be done, at a minimum, in pairs. One person is the interviewer and the other person is the note taker. When you are note taking, listen in particular for comments that:

- Invalidate what you believed
- Validate what you believed
- Are the customer expressing emotion (note the emotion)
- Surprise you by being unique and different
- Indicate preferences and the rationale behind them
- Offer any other interesting surprises and insights

The other role of the note taker or someone other than the interviewer is to send the interviewer a real-time message (our teams use Slack for this) if you think there is something worth pursuing or that the interviewer may have missed a question you think needs to be answered. Every interview is precious, so don't miss the opportunity to dig.

Improving Interview Techniques

At the end of every interview, teams should debrief with the person who was doing the interviewing. The goal isn't to judge the person but to improve the quality of the information they are getting. Everyone rotates through the interviewer role, so everyone gets this type of feedback. Some good questions to ask an interviewer, especially in the early phases of interviewing, include:

- How did the interview start off?
- Which leading questions did you (accidentally) ask?
- Which questions need adjusting or rewording?
- Which questions were missing that you should ask next time?
- Where should you have asked more follow-up questions?
- Is there anything else you should do differently next time?

The first interviews are hard. They may even be uncomfortable. Some people on the other end of the phone may ask why you are asking them these questions. That does not mean you are doing the interview wrong. It reflects the fact that the team is in the early phases, and you are triangulating on who matters most, who really are your target personas. Just as you tweak the scripts, you will also start to refine who the real potential customers are. Do not give up because your first few interviews are uncomfortable or embarrass you. Refine the script and reflect on the target personas. Give the script a chance with multiple personas. And welcome to the world of entrepreneurship. It sometimes takes a while to find the right mix of interview questions and target customers. Resilience and perseverance are key.

> **MORE TIPS FOR INTERVIEWING**
>
> **Be quiet.** After you've asked the first question, force yourself to be silent for as long as possible.
>
> **Ask why.** Even when you think you know the answer, ask people why they do or say things. The answers will sometimes surprise you.
>
> **Encourage stories.** Ask questions that get people to tell stories. A story should go on as long as it needs to.
>
> **Look for inconsistency.** Sometimes what people say and what they do are different. These inconsistencies often reveal interesting conflicts.
>
> **Notice nonliteral cues.** Be aware of voice inflection. For face-to-face interviews, watch for body language and facial expression.

Validating That the Pain Is Global

In some cases, you may have specific markets you want to go after first or you may think that the market you are targeting is big enough so if you find enough pain in that one market, it will be worth launching the venture.

Often, however, for the opportunity to scale to the point where the growth is sufficiently meaningful to the Mothership, that venture needs to scale at least regionally and, in many cases, globally. You may also find that there are different segments of the market, and you may want to test to see if the solution or at least parts of it are relevant to a wider variety of segments.

Typically, if we have a venture we know needs to scale globally, or is looking at multiple segments, rather than start the pain point interviews from scratch with each region or segment, we pick the one geographic market or segment we believe could be large enough to validate the venture, conduct all our pain point interviews there, and then travel (physically or virtually) to other markets to validate that result. In the first market, you ask completely open-ended questions. Then, when you are validating those results, you use the pain points you identified with the first segment or geographic market to see if they are the same, similar, or completely different in other global markets.

The reason this knowledge is important is that if a new venture only has to mildly tweak its offering to localize, adapt, or augment for a different segment or geographic market, then that is both expected and fine. But, if it turns out you have to build something completely new for every segment or geographic region, that is not scalable, and either the team would have to believe that the one market is huge enough to drive growth on its own or you need to pivot the solution or kill the venture.

For example, the largest bank in Africa was searching for a way to bring order out of the chaos that was the current consumer packaged goods (CPG) ecosystem across Africa. The bank was looking at two different scenarios:

Regional. It could choose to start in South Africa and then validate the pain it found there in Kenya and Nigeria, both of which had very different demographics and settings.

Segment. It could understand the pain that existed in the modern CPG space (commercial retail establishments that look like first-world retail stores) versus the pain felt in the traditional CPG space, such as Spaza shop owners in South Africa and vendors in a marketplace in Nigeria.

Below is an example of what the bank found and could communicate to its New Venture Board:

Similarly, a large insurance provider client was not interested in just producing another insurance product; it had much bigger aspirations—dealing with the issue of aging. Given the rapidly changing culture and demographics, where children are no longer around to care for aging parents, the client chose Asia as its first market and picked two countries in that region to study, South Korea and Taiwan.

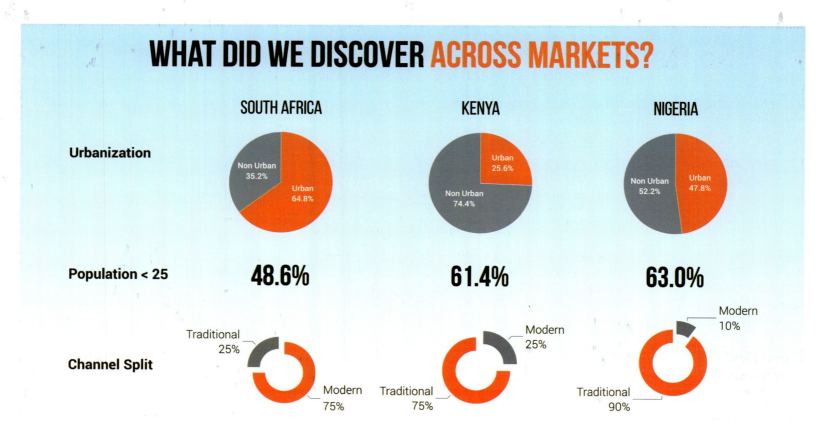

In the end, the insurance company realized that not only was there huge pain in Asia regarding the issue of how to help post-retirees and the elderly feel useful, connected, socially active, safe, happy, healthy, empowered, and engaged, but this market also represented a massive global opportunity. The company had found a fantastic solution to the problem as rated by the customers interviewed. While the South Korean market might become its MVP test market, the company knows it can quickly scale globally because the trends and themes are consistently heard everywhere.

Below is how it shared what was common and different among the markets.

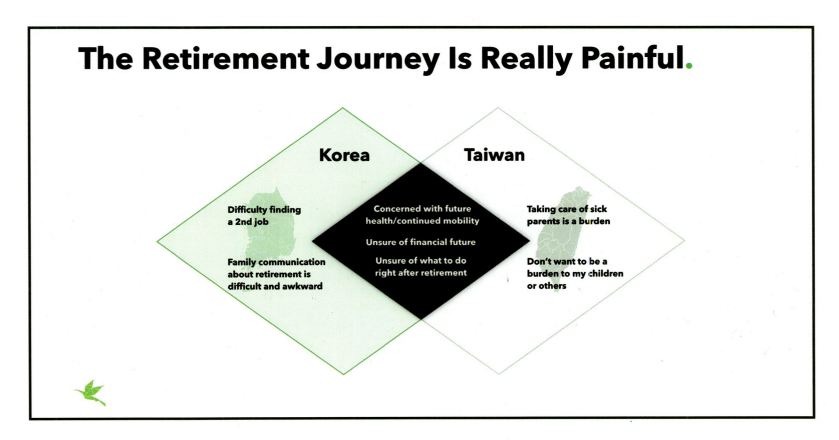

Putting It All Together

The pain point phase ends with a summary and synthesis of the pains the team heard. Here are a few examples:

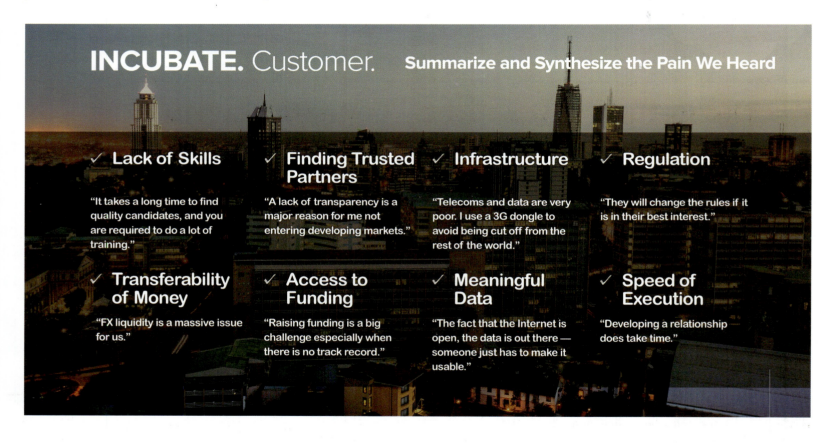

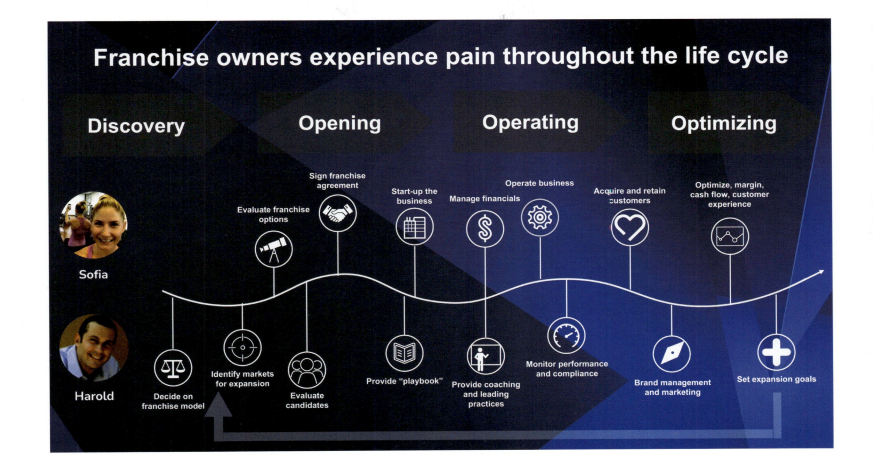

Synthesis is the art of making meaning and finding direction from disparate and contradictory inputs. Synthesis is a way for teams to aggregate, edit, and condense what they have learned to establish a new perspective and to identify opportunities for inspiration. The process takes teams from inspiration to ideas and from stories to solutions. The feedback you derive from the synthesis exercises will also help you edit and integrate your interview scripts.

Here's how you do it:

Step 1: Tell stories from the field. Put the data and thoughts from your interviews into a manageable form by summarizing key points from each interview.

Step 2: Look for patterns. Identify key themes and then assemble a preliminary hierarchy and priority based on feedback from stakeholders.

Step 3: Extract the key insights. What lies beneath the surface of what people told you? Go beyond just what was said.

Step 4: Craft the message. Find the strongest way to convey the message and meaning. Craft "How Might We?" statements:

Example 1:
How might we . . . reduce the barrier to entry for hardware development

In a way that . . . enables quick iterations across the entire system and offers a simple way to develop and scale products,

So that . . . hardware developers have flexibility, time to market, reduced development costs, and productivity improvements like those in agile software development?

Example 2:
For . . . developers and managers of buildings and properties, who are both consumers and producers,

How might we . . . provide turnkey solutions for on-site energy optimization

In a way that . . . reduces cost and increases resiliency,

So that . . . we can deepen customer loyalty while also enhancing systemwide visibility and control and driving our portfolio to net-zero carbon as rapidly as possible?

With the synthesis of your pain point interviews in hand, you now have a complete overview of the situation—in particular, where your potential customers and their stakeholders see dangerous weaknesses in their businesses or personal lives.

The team needs to study these results and then ask itself:

Is there real pain?

What is the pain?

Is there a lot of it?

If the answers to the first and third questions are no, or if the answer to the second question is indeterminate, then—and this is hugely important—THE TEAM NEEDS TO *KILL* THE VENTURE *NOW*.

Needless to say, such a decision will be difficult for the team to make. After all, team members have spent many hours racking their brains to come up with what seems like the best idea for a new company, then followed that with even more hours in interviews to confirm the brilliance of their choice. Now, after their collective heart is behind the idea, they must abandon it and move on to something else.

But that's how it works. Consider how many independent startups die because they pursue headlong a new business idea—burning up both time and money—only to discover that the perceived demand for its product or service just isn't there. Indeed, many Unicorns started out with one strategy, abandoned it and then luckily had enough capital left to pivot to a new business.

Obviously, this process is incredibly wasteful, and that's why the histories of places such as Silicon Valley are littered with the remains of thousands of failed startups. The world only remembers those that survive.

This process is cold-blooded, made especially difficult because the team has likely already fallen in love with their new business idea. However, the goal is not to realize the team's dream, it is to create a successful business. And if the target customers are experiencing no pain, there is no business. So, it's time for the team to cut its losses and move on to the next new venture idea.

However, even if you have to kill off your first idea, if the team has been true to the process and really listened to its interviewees, it will likely find real pain it can still solve. For example, one large industrial client thought it could build a venture related to road safety. As logical as that sounds, the client couldn't find any particular pain directly related to road safety. However, two other new venture ideas emerged that were much bigger opportunities that had corollary safety impacts. One dealt with commercial surface management (think of a grocery store parking lot in the winter). The other came from interviews about trucking and safety where the real issues proved much bigger, centering around what we called agro-logistics and optimization (think bulk products that need to be trucked when no one knows in advance where those loads are and if they can get where they are needed on time).

Once you know you have found real pain—and a lot of it—the team can move on to the really fun and creative part of the incubation process: imagining opportunities to solve that pain. It's time to move to storyboard interviews.

→ Storyboard Interviews

Now, let's look at the more likely, happy scenario: the interviews uncover significant pain and thus an opportunity that the new venture idea (with or without modifications) might solve brilliantly.

Now the question is: How do you dial in that idea so that it makes the best possible fit with that intense market need?

The answer is found through humanity's oldest and most powerful diagnostic tool: *storytelling*. Its power lies in the fact that a story can do what impersonal appeals to logic or statistics cannot: it can touch human imagination and manifest empathy.

In our case, the vehicle for storytelling is the *storyboard*. Similar to that seen in movie and television productions, it resembles a comic strip, with simple figures acting out a finite number of actions that show the need for the proposed product or service, its use, and the happy result.

Storyboards can come in many forms, but we primarily use hand-drawn storyboards.

The creation of storyboards arises directly from the pain point interviews. The team dissects, synthesizes, and analyzes the results of the interviews, once written up. The team members then chart them, along with any useful interviewee feedback. They usually do this with a whiteboard and sticky notes (virtual or physical), which allows them to group and regroup patterns of pain they think they can solve.

The storyboard enables the testing of lots of different product or service ideas that might become the core of the new venture. The process of developing storyboards occurs through rounds of brainstorming to develop multiple stories about possible products or services you could offer to solve the pain. Once you have brainstormed these ideas and clustered them thematically, you are ready to create storyboards to test.

The storyboard format should always be the same. Clockwise from the upper left, the drawings in each panel work as follows:

Panel 1. Set the context.

Molly loves her dog and wants to know how he is feeling when she is away.

Panel 2. Introduce a tension.

Her neighbor informs Molly that her dog barked for hours while she was away at work, but she has no idea why.

Panel 3. Resolve the tension.

Molly uses a new app that monitors her dog's emotions and stress levels and alerts her when he is anxious or unhappy.

Panel 4. Show a positive result.

With the app Molly discovers that the automatic vacuum has been scaring her dog, and instead takes him for a walk during cleaning time!

Not all of these stories are equally valid, but, just as in the Ideation phase, the goal is not to try and pick winners, but to get down *all* ideas that answer the customer desires expressed in the pain point interviews. With storyboards, quantity is key, and there are no bad ideas. Even feasibility is not considered at this point. In the case of this client, literally the pain that dog owners felt was that they wished their dogs could talk to them and tell them how they were feeling. There is a lot of science looking at humans and heart rate variability that can indicate happiness, boredom, pain, and depression. It turns out that the same science applies to dogs as well.

Yes, everyone can draw a storyboard; once you realize that it has nothing to do with talent, you can really be prolific. (In fact, the less polished the better; if something looks too polished, people think you are farther along than you are and won't be honest in their feedback because they feel sorry for you and don't want to hurt your feelings.) There are some tips for storyboard creation included in the sidebar.

STORYBOARD CREATION

Mach49's customer development aficionado, Chelsea Hare, put together these tips for creating storyboards.

TIPS FOR STORYBOARD CREATION.

Refine drawings so they show enough context, **but not so much that the details distract** from the purpose of the storyboard.

Use text to supplement visuals in a storyboard.

ANYONE can sketch a storyboard!

CONTEXT — TENSION

SOLUTION — BENEFIT

HOW TO SKETCH.
People

KEEP IT SIMPLE.
Find a style and stick to it.

HOW TO SKETCH.
People

SWITCH THINGS UP.
Differentiate characters with hairstyles.

HOW TO SKETCH.
Emotion

MAKE IT OBVIOUS.
Use icons or speech bubbles.

WORRIED CONFUSED FRUSTRATED — SURPRISED EXCITED HAPPY

HOW TO SKETCH.
Tech

OVERSIMPLIFY.
Less is more.

SMART PHONE

DESKTOP — LAPTOP

As with the pain point interviews, when you run the storyboard interviews, you should document and codify the feedback and data from those interviews (into Airtable, Google Drive, or whatever database tool you choose to use for reference) so you can use it in current and future product development. You should log every storyboard, capture every interview, and record all insights throughout the process. The short-term and long-term value of rigorous documentation cannot be overstated. You will not remember everything that happened after hundreds of interviews, and you may not be around several years from now when a similar venture idea resurfaces.

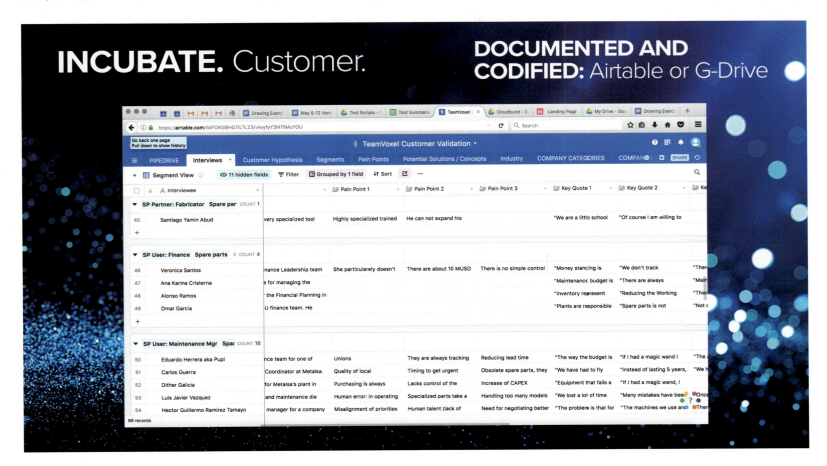

→ Storyboard Interviewing

Now you understand how to build your storyboards. But what are you actually doing in the storyboard interviews and what are you learning? Here are the salient characteristics of good storyboard interviews:

- Every storyboard interview compares three stories that introduce three new products or services to solve a problem.

- Each story contains a setting, conflict, resolution, and benefit.

- Each story is presented from the mindset most relevant to that stakeholder. For example, you may have three ideas that are presented differently to two stakeholders, resulting in six storyboards shown.

- You learn how people respond to each story, how they would improve each story, how they would rank each story in their own lives, and if they would want to combine the stories in any way.

- The interviews should teach you which pains are most painful and which solutions resonate with respondents.

- You iterate each storyboard and rotate which ones you present, until you arrive at three to five that are most attractive to each stakeholder.

- Each storyboard usually needs to be shown to five to eight stakeholders (segments) to achieve consistency. That said, you can throw away specific storyboards earlier if they are failing for good reasons.

- You can mix and match approaches to aid comparison. For example, you can present one storyboard, one video, and one landing page as a test.

- You cannot use this type of testing to arrive at your final solution. You *can* rule out wrong solutions. And you can get closer to options you want to develop further, because the ultimate goal is to use the storyboards to determine what you want to present during prototype testing (see chapter 6).

What You Should Learn from Your Storyboards

- How stakeholders respond to different solutions that may help them.

- How desirable each of these solutions is.

- How close you are to detecting real pains and the situations where they typically are encountered.

- How easily potential customers will believe the solutions you are proposing can be executed. Sometimes people cannot get past their disbelief; this is something you need to account for in prototype testing.

You should conduct a storyboard interview in a manner similar to a pain point interview. We use this script:

STORYBOARD INTERVIEW SCRIPT

PHILOSOPHY

The intent of this script is to let the customer share their stream of consciousness while interacting with multiple storyboards. Listen to their answers, interrupt only when necessary, and save most follow-up questions for the very end of the interview to avoid influencing their thought process.

Since the interview should only be scheduled for 45 minutes, you should watch the clock and move them to the next storyboard when needed to get through each storyboard and to ask a few final follow-up questions before running out of time. **Try not to ask questions while participants are going through the scenarios so you don't alter their line of thinking.** *Questions like, "Can you elaborate on that?" or "Why did you just laugh?" are good guides, while most other questions should be saved until the very end of the "Final questions" section.*

BEFORE INTERVIEW

- Assign a moderator.
- Assign a note taker and open notes in Airtable.
- Email the tester with final call-in.
- Create a site order for the day for each test participant (e.g., ABC, BCA, CAB).

FOR ZOOM

- Set up Zoom with the "Start without video" option.
- Email the tester with final Zoom info a few minutes before and/or at the start of the call.
- Have the storyboards open in the browser and close all other tabs.

STORYBOARD INTERVIEW SCRIPT

INTRO

Is this still a good time to talk?

Thank you again for your time!

I am talking to experts like you to understand how you feel about various solutions that might support you. I'll show you these in the form of hand-drawn stories and ask you to share your honest feedback about them so that we can improve upon our ideas.

I'll start by asking you some general questions, but before I do, I want to let you know that I have someone with me taking notes, but you and I will be the only ones talking. Is that OK?

Thank you.

BACKGROUND QUESTIONS (cut them off after five minutes and move on to scenarios):

- Can you tell me about your role?
- Or
- *A different question for those we've already interviewed.*

Thank you. I'm now going to show you my screen—I'll get us set up.

ZOOM

- Click "Share Screen."
- Choose the window to share (your browser window with the storyboard link open).
- *If they'll be controlling the screen:* Choose "Remote Control" and select interviewee.

You should be able to see my screen. **If they'll be controlling the screen**: You'll also have the ability to move the mouse and click on what you'd like.

STORYBOARD INTERVIEW SCRIPT

INSTRUCTIONS
- I'm going to show you three storyboards describing three different scenarios.
- Please read through them, thinking out loud as you go.
- Thinking out loud is like talking to yourself.
- If you're reading, please read out loud—otherwise, share your stream of consciousness as you go.
- Just know that I didn't design anything personally, and nothing you say will offend me or hurt my feelings.
- The best thing you can do is be honest as you go along and keep thinking out loud.
- *If you're controlling the slides vs. them controlling the screen:*
  Also, when you get to the end of a slide, just let me know when you want me to move to the next slide.

Use predetermined site order (e.g., ABC, BCA, CAB).

[Hit "Present" in Google Slides]
Please start by clicking on Storyboard ____ and read and think out loud as you go.

STORYBOARD 1: (LIMIT: 5–10 MINUTES) DIRECT THEM TO LINK

Ask a subset of these questions (only what they haven't answered already). Positively reinforce the second they think or read out loud correctly. "You're doing a great job thinking out loud, thank you, just keep doing that."

- If you were talking to a friend and telling them what this system is, what would you say?

  [If they're describing it incorrectly]: "For today, let's assume that the system actually [*describe system*]. Does that change how you feel about it?"

STORYBOARD INTERVIEW SCRIPT

- On a scale of 0–10, how likely is it that you would recommend something like this to a friend or colleague (with 0 being not at all likely and 10 being extremely likely)?
- Why is that?
- What sort of person would this be for?
- Is there anything you would change or add?
- You did a great job thinking out loud and sharing your feedback as you went. Please click on "Home" and do exactly what you did before and click on Storyboard ____ .

STORYBOARD 2: (LIMIT: 5–10 MINUTES) DIRECT THEM TO LINK

Ask a subset of these questions (only what they haven't answered already).

- I'm going to ask you similar questions.
- If you were talking to a friend and telling them what this system is, what would you say?

  [If they're describing it incorrectly]: "For today, let's assume that the system actually [*describe system*]. Does that change how you feel about it?"

- On a scale of 0–10, how likely is it that you would recommend something like this to a friend or colleague (with 0 being not at all likely and 10 being extremely likely)?
- Why is that?
- What sort of person would this be for?
- Is there anything you would change or add?
- Can you click on the last Storyboard ____?

STORYBOARD 3: (LIMIT: 5–10 MINUTES) DIRECT THEM TO LINK

Ask a subset of these questions (only what they haven't answered already).

- I'm going to ask you similar questions.

STORYBOARD INTERVIEW SCRIPT

- If you were talking to a friend and telling them what this system is, what would you say?

  [If they're describing it incorrectly]: "For today, let's assume that the system actually [*describe system*]. Does that change how you feel about it?"

- On a scale of 0–10, how likely is it that you would recommend something like this to a friend or colleague (with 0 being not at all likely and 10 being extremely likely)?
- Why is that?
- What sort of person would this be for?
- Is there anything you would change or add?

FOLLOW-UP QUESTIONS

It's important not to ask specific follow-up questions until the prioritization question.

- Which of these three solutions would you want in **your own life**? Feel free to go back and look at them again.
  - Why?
  - Which would be your next favorite, in your own life?
- Would you want to combine them in any way?
- *Quickly take them back to slide 2 for each system and ask them the following question:*
  On a scale of 0–10, how big a problem is this for you personally (with 0 being not at all a problem and 10 being a serious problem)?
  - Why?
- *Elaboration questions here!*
- *Ask any questions you'd like to probe on here. (Earlier probing should have included only things like, "Can you elaborate on that?" or "What do you mean?" or "Why do you say that?" or "What's going on?" or maybe even "How was that experience?")*

STORYBOARD INTERVIEW SCRIPT

- *Check Slack #questionsduringtest to see other questions from the team.*
- **Do you have any other questions for me?**
- This was really valuable feedback. As we move into the next phase of our process, we'll be testing drawings of specific solutions based on your feedback today. We would love to talk with you further to improve on these newer ideas. Can I reach out to set up another session like this to get your thoughts?
- I'm continually looking for feedback from people like you. Is there someone else who you think would be comfortable giving us their thoughts?

JUST IN CASE THEY DON'T UNDERSTAND THE STORYBOARD

Sometimes teams find that their storyboards are not quite right for a few possible reasons, in a very extreme way. If that's the case, there is an extra question that can be inserted as the first in each grouping before the *describe the system to a friend* question. This question should be used only if:

- People are getting hung up on specific details that are wrong about the storyboard/what doesn't apply to them
- You're not articulating the context, conflict, or benefit in the right way
- You want them to stop criticizing and instead help with rewriting
- By using this tactic, you can't use any of the ratings/rankings from that interview
- This should be used fairly rarely

The question to insert:

- You mentioned [*language they used to indicate you got something wrong*].
- Because we're at such an early stage, I'd love to get your help to refine what's missing. *[Bring them back to the area of the page where they had the challenge.]*
- Can you help me rewrite this? Feel free to think of yourself as a movie director and let me know how you prefer it to read.

In the end, as the image below suggests, you will have created hundreds of storyboards that you have rigorously documented, rated, and ranked.

Let's pause and discuss ratings and rankings, as this is an extremely important continuous exercise the team needs to perform. You will notice that for every storyboard or scenario you share with a customer, you are asking that customer, "How likely is it that you would recommend this solution to a friend or colleague?"

That question gets you to a net promoter score. NPS is a metric Fred Reichheld pioneered in his seminal 2003 *Harvard Business Review* article, "One Number You Need to Grow." NPS is critical to the interviewing process.

Using Reichheld's technique, depending upon the answer to that question, respondents are grouped as follows:

- Promoters (score 9–10) are excited enthusiasts likely to buy your product or service and refer others, fueling growth.

- Passives (score 7–8) are satisfied with what you are proposing to them but are potentially unenthusiastic customers who are vulnerable to competitive offerings.

- Detractors (score 0–6) are those who have zero interest in your product or solution as it is currently imagined. They could impede growth through negative word of mouth.

However, for a new venture, as important as that 0–10 NPS rating is, it is only half the equation. The other critical component is the ranking. For example, customers may rate what you share with them as a 10. But that may be a 10 on a feature that is solving a pain that only ranks tenth on their list of pains. That will not be enough to help your venture reach escape velocity and succeed.

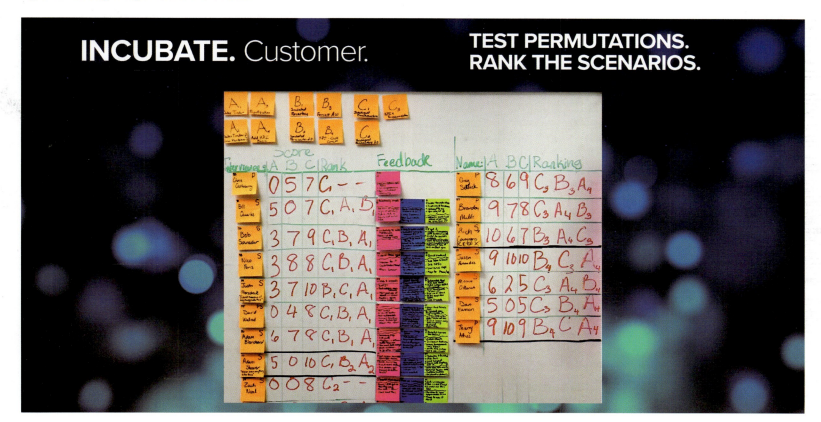

With B2C new ventures in particular, once a storyboard scenario begins to show a strong sense of customer ratification, the team now has the opportunity to quickly take that idea to another level of validation through in-market testing. For example, you can quickly run lots of different types of tests leveraging social media and other tools at low cost. For the pet-owner product, with just $14,000 of investment in in-market testing on Facebook, we ended up with 10,000 people signed up for a product that didn't yet exist. So, if you have a consumer product, doing A/B in-market testing while still incubating can be very efficient and effective.

From Pain to Product

The ultimate outcome of the storyboard interviews is that magic moment when the team has made the leap from pain to actual product, solution, or service idea. In addition, the storyboard interview phase will have yielded three more very practical and tactical outcomes:

Market segmentation. The combination of the pain point interviews and the storyboard interviews provides an effective means not just to identify a market need, but also to segment that market into submarkets by variations in that need and by differences in application. This segmentation at the beginning of the process is a huge advantage over what independent new startups often face, which is typically a large monolithic market. Trying to go after a market that is too big and undefined can waste both time and money (sometimes fatally) as the startup may try to be all things to all people. To build an MVP, you need a persona or segment to target that ultimately helps you get the flywheel going and you can expand and pivot from there. Throwing spaghetti against the wall and hoping it sticks is really not a viable startup strategy.

Customer persona. The interviews also enable the team to begin the process of understanding the nature of its customers, not just their pain points, but their personalities, work, life, career goals, and so on. Personas are typically one-page descriptions of composite people based on the team's stakeholder interviews and their new knowledge of the space. (See the Customer Persona exercise you can do with your team and an example from a real venture.) Building personas is very important for several reasons:

- It helps to humanize the users.
- It allows you to test scenarios to see if they serve particular user needs.
- Teams can gain and maintain empathy for the end user when making decisions.
- Personas connect what you build to actual user needs and pain.

Early messaging. Startups, even new initiatives by established companies, tend to commit themselves to new products because they are appealing to decision-makers, because they represent a proprietary technological breakthrough, or simply because of an intuition that the market will love it. And too often the result is an impressive new product for which there is *no* real market, or if there is an identifiable market, the company has no idea how to reach it. The advantage of the storyboard testing and, if relevant for the particular venture you are working on, A/B testing right at the start is that the new venture can hit the market with a message that has already been proven congruent with the market's desires or identified pains.

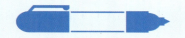

EXERCISE:
DEVELOPING PERSONAS

Ideally a team identifies one to five personas per project. Any more than that and you are starting to design for outliers and not core customers or users.

CREATING A PERSONA.

Name

Sketch a person with
an emotion and a quote of need

Behaviors

(Identify 5)

Demographic

(Identify 5)

Needs and Goals

(Identify 5)

Sample final persona:

CREATING A PERSONA.

Jane

Behaviors

- Checks Zendesk phone app twice an hour while on call three nights a week
- Follows subreddit called DDoS attacks
- Organizes security tickets by risk to infrastructure
- Attends security conferences twice a year
- Keeps a tab with "traffic" up at all times in the browser

Demographic

- Security Engineer Manager at Etsy
- CS degree
- Lives in Brooklyn
- 42 years old
- Been with Etsy for 3 years

Needs and Goals

- Worries that she will miss an alert about a security problem that is her responsibility
- Wants to stay up-to-date on all news of hacks across the industry to make sure she is aware of any new threats
- Values keeping infrastructure safe from immediate threats over scheduled maintenance
- Fears DDoS attacks over all others because the risk that the system would be down for days is high
- Wants to be promoted to director

Let's move to the product phase and the last type of customer interview you need to learn and apply: the prototype interview.

On to the next chapter.

→ A Final Note

Customer development is a continuous process of widening the aperture and developing relevant and actionable insights that drive you to the next stage—a process repeated until you get to the big opportunity and the MVP.

With a huge pain to solve and equipped with a set of product, solution, or service ideas that can solve that pain, the team is now ready to move to the *product phase*. The task now is to flesh out what that product is going to be through prototype interviews and to determine how feasible it is to build that solution.

Chapter 06

Incubate Phase II: Product, Service, Solution

**What Should We Build?
Can We Build It?**

The magic moment in any Incubate phase is not Pitch Day.

It is that moment when your team figures out how to move from pain to an exciting product, service, or solution.

That magic moment—when we graduate from storyboards and a singular focus on interviewing customers and move to the Product phase to begin testing real products or services—usually starts around Week 6 of the twelve-week Incubate process.

As we shared in an earlier chapter, while everyone is doing customer development work during the first phase, during the Product phase, the team splits into two parts.

Some of the team continues to work on customer development, conducting prototype interviews. Meanwhile, the members of the team selected for product vision and skills now focus on the design and early iterations of the product or service itself.

→ Product Phase 101

The fundamental questions to answer during the Product phase of the Incubate process are:

1. What should we build?
2. Can we build it?
3. Can we deliver it?

Here in the digital age, in the empire of Moore's law, a natural human tendency is to assume that anything we can imagine can be constructed. After all, so many great ideas that have been plucked from the imagination have—in short order—been realized: personal computing, craft beer at scale (oxymoronic as that may sound), global mobile telephony, smartphones, a worldwide repository of all knowledge, legitimized couch surfing, veggie meat, VTOL drone taxis, and so on. Each seems like a miracle, and each underscores the belief that the only limitation on invention is our imagination.

The reality is that we only focus on these inventions or solutions as inevitable in retrospect. But if you read the histories of those products, they were anything but inevitable at the time. Moreover, a lot of great ideas never become real products or services. It's not that they can't be created; especially with software, they almost always can. And in this age of advanced materials science, CAD/CAM, and robotics, most hardware inventions can be realized as well.

No, the problem is not the ever-closing gap between idea and creation. Rather, most new inventions founder on the shoals of cost, time, and demand for the following reasons:

Cost to manufacture. Many products prove impractical because the cost to build them exceeds what the market is willing to pay.

Scalability. This challenge almost sunk semiconductors in their early years: prototypes could not be practically built in volume because the yield rates of finished devices were just too high.

Reliability. The products can be built without failure, but quickly break down in use or are too expensive to repair.

Novelty. Some new inventions, solutions, or services are *too* new; that is, customers don't really understand the advantages of these new products and don't want to take the time and training to learn.

Commoditization. A superior new offering isn't valuable enough to attract customers away from existing lower-cost or reduced-performance versions.

Marketability. The product can be built—or the service can be designed—but there are no existing distribution and sales channels in place to deliver them without the expense of building those channels.

Complexity. The product can be built, but it has so many features that the average user only uses one or two of them and therefore doesn't see the value.

While all these reasons are important—and we address them all—the biggest obstacle to a new product's success and the issue we must address first in the Product phase is this:

Need. The product does not address any of the prospective customers' pain points that you have by now meticulously explored. Therefore, it remains nonessential, or a novelty buy, and it will never scale to the point that the idea will be a major growth business.

There are two different parts of the Product phase—continuing customer development and very early product development.

→ Activity One: Continued Customer Development

Enter the next round of customer development and the third type of interview we use during the Incubate phase: the *prototype interview*. As Steve Jobs famously said, "It's not the customer's job to know what they want."

The beauty of the prototype interview is that it helps customers imagine solutions and, as a result, helps you refine those solutions. The type of pain or opportunity your venture is addressing determines the type of prototypes you build; for example:

- If your solution is digital, you can use wireframes, sample websites, or digital simulations as your prototype.

- If your solution is hardware or a physical product (hard goods, food, airplane seats), you can build mockups or samples.

- If your solution is a service or an experience, you can create simulations, shoot a video, use actors, or immerse a potential customer in virtual or augmented reality.

The bottom line is that the number of options you have for prototypes is limited only by your team's imagination and creativity. Whatever option you choose, the goal of your prototype should be users having an authentic experience of what using, eating, riding, engaging with, and so on your product or service will feel like. It must mimic the actual experience.

Usually, at this stage in the process, clients pepper us with questions about this next phase. Here are answers to the ones they ask most often.

Why Prototype?
You prototype for lots of reasons:

- Get more reliable and specific feedback on the concept
- Refine your solution(s)
- Determine functionality and feature set
- Further narrow who the solution might be best for
- Help define your go-to market strategy—especially potential evangelists and early adopters

There's a reason that all the interviewing we do falls under what we call customer development (not just user research). Every interview you do while incubating your venture should be building your brand, raising awareness, and developing interest among potential customers to be early users, become a beta site, or run a pilot.

Plenty of people are impatient and want to start building before testing. They think prototyping is too expensive and gets in the way of getting to market faster. But as Ralf Speth, the CEO of Jaguar Land Rover, has said, "If you think good design is expensive, you should look at the cost of bad design."

When to Move to Prototype Interviews?
How do you know when you are ready to prototype? Is it always Week 6? No, honestly, it could be Week 4 if you are hearing tons of consistent pain early, guessed right, and your early storyboards tested incredibly well. On the other hand, it could be Week 8 if you have had to pivot multiple times to really find pain or develop storyboards that consistently get nines and tens on your NPS.

You know you are ready to move from storyboard to prototype interviews when:

- Users are getting hung up on details of functionality and how it works in your storyboard interviews.
- User responses are fairly predictable, and you are getting diminishing returns on each subsequent interview.
- Rankings are consistent among particular customer segments.
- Potential customers are repeatedly giving high rating scores on some specific storyboard concepts (value props).

How Do Prototype Interviews Work?
As we move the team into the Product phase and begin designing prototypes, we have some housekeeping items and tactics for sequencing and managing the prototype interview process.

You first need to create and agree to the prototype testing scope, goals, and weekly cadence—alternating between testing and iterating or designing. A typical model would look like this:

Testing scope or goals:
- Each test = three wireframes tested by five to seven interviewees
- Tests 1–4: Find fit against target audience
- Tests 5–7: Find product vision (features and functions)
- Tests 8 and 9: Find MVP hypothesis

Testing and iterating cadence:
- Monday a.m.: Design; p.m.: Test 1
- Tuesday a.m.: Test 1; p.m.: Design
- Wednesday a.m.: Test 2; p.m.: Test 2
- Thursday a.m.: Design and synthesis; p.m.: Test 3
- Friday a.m.: Test 3; p.m.: Design

If you are working in multiple languages, be sure to leave time for translation. If you are working in multiple time zones, be sure you have factored that timing into your week. You also need to:

- Build a shared calendar for scheduling interviews aligned with the testing cadence so the team is aligned and clear on what is happening when. As if the pace isn't already crazy, it really picks up at this point, and unless you have added people to your team, you have fewer people specifically focused on interviewing.

- Finalize the logistics:
  - Determine whether the team will use Zoom or another technology it is approved to use to share prototypes with customers.
  - Develop templates for outreach emails with Zoom, Microsoft Teams, or WebEx information to ensure your interviewees can access, view, or interact with your prototypes.
  - Schedule a prototype workshop, script review, and a test of the test with a friendly participant. On the first day of real interviews, the team should run consecutive, not concurrent, interviews so everyone can observe the first round together.
  - Before each test, assign a moderator, note taker, recorder, and which prototypes you will show the interviewee and in what order.

- At the end of the day, when necessary, before you forget:
  - Update the prototypes.
  - Update the personas you think the prototypes are most relevant for.
  - Update Airtable or Google Docs or whatever database you are still using to rigorously document your interviews and insights.

→ Prototype Tools

With the tactics out of the way, let's talk about building the prototypes themselves.

The Starting Point

At this point, you're probably still trying to determine what direction in which to take the product. To really get to the next level on those details and vet them, you have to switch to low-fidelity interactive wireframes or prototypes. Also, at this transition point, you usually have specific questions you want to solve, including the biggest question of all: *Which ideas really do resonate with the different segments or stakeholders?*

Prototyping, wireframing, or even test landing pages help the team determine which of the now limited subset of ideas—narrowed through the storyboard process—are really the ones to pursue. Typically, teams are down to three big ideas at this point, sometimes more, sometimes less. A good goal is three. At this point, with a turnaround public company client, we were down to just one big idea with a few variants, which is also fairly common.

When we work with New Venture Teams at Mach49, we control our testing very differently from how typical usability researchers control their tests. We don't jump right to building something—a cardinal sin of many failed startups. We're still looking to choose an idea, refine the concept once we have one, and then isolate the features to build gradually into a product road map.

What to Build

Start with something that looks simple. Why? Because people should focus on the essence of the idea and not the design of it. The higher the resolution, the more people talk about the details and *not* what they should care about in the early phase, which is, are we heading in the right direction?

The two main differences between our wireframes and traditional wireframes or prototypes are:

- We make the screens or prototypes interactive (using InVision, real mockups, or simulations).

- We don't use filler text like *lorem ipsum* or squiggly lines.

We do this because we want our prototypes to allow viewers to pretend they are actually using a system, working with a product,

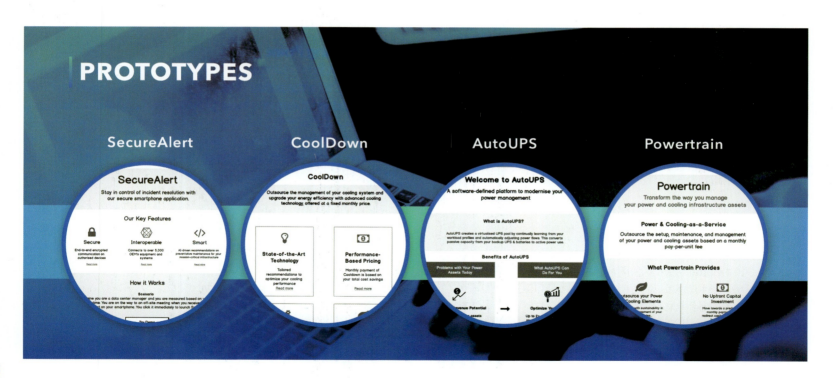

KEY PROTOTYPE

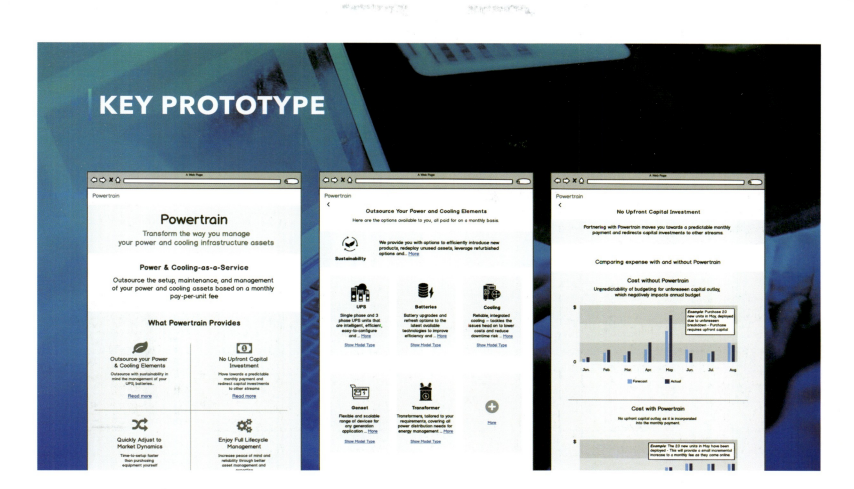

or engaging in an experience. We want them to get immersed in the details that matter—the story that unfolds relating to them using a product in a certain situation. We do that so they can precisely respond to that experience.

The rationale is that people have difficulty looking at something and telling you if they like it or not, or just generally how they feel about something in a reliable way. They'll give you confident answers, *but they'll be wrong 50 percent of the time*. Don't have them imagine it—let them use it.

> **PROTOTYPE INTERVIEWING TIPS**
>
> 1. Have a person think out loud and capture that aha moment when they understand what something is doing. At that moment, you see their pure, unfiltered reaction, before they've had a chance to overthink.
>
> 2. Make sure what they're seeing is as real as it can be, with real information and real data, that follows a real and believable story.
>
> 3. Compare different situations, stories, or clickable prototypes against each other. If you show someone one thing, they'll say, "Yes, I like that. I'd use it." They forget they have options. They forget they've tried and failed at other solutions. They forget they have crowded and busy lives. Showing multiple solutions, especially those that differ greatly, helps get past this issue and helps the customer really prioritize the quality of the experiences.

Writing Your Prototype Script

We will provide you with a sample script; however, it is important to understand the main components of a prototype script in case you want to write your own. These include:

- Greeting
- Ask the interviewee to introduce themselves, their role, and their company, whatever relevant information you want to help you define personas later
- Explain the test and the process you are going to use
- Run through each of the tests or prototypes you are sharing (typically three)
- After each experience be sure to ask:
  - How was that experience?
  - How likely is it that you would recommend this system to a friend or colleague on a scale of 0–10?
  - Why is that?
  - If you were talking to a friend, what would you tell them the system is and does?
- After sharing all your prototypes, ask follow-up questions relevant to your new venture. For example:
  - How might you prioritize the three in your own life and in what order?
  - Would you want to combine them in any way?
  - Was there anything you expected to see in any of the systems, but didn't?
  - Was there anything that surprised you about any of them?
  - What might you do to improve on any of the systems?
  - Ask anything specific that came up during the test that you'd like to drill into more deeply
- Have them ask you questions

PROTOTYPE INTERVIEW SCRIPT

PHILOSOPHY

The intent of this script is to let the customer share their stream of consciousness while interacting with multiple prototypes. Listen to their answers, interrupt only when necessary, and save most follow-up questions for the very end of the interview to avoid influencing their thought process.

Since the interview should only be scheduled for 45 minutes, you should watch the clock and move them to the next prototype when needed and ask a few final follow-up questions before running out of time. **Try not to ask questions while participants are exploring the prototypes so you don't alter their line of thinking.** Questions like "Can you elaborate on that?" and "Can you give an example?" are good guides, while most other questions should be saved until the very end of the "Final questions" section.

BEFORE INTERVIEW

- Assign a moderator.
- Assign a note taker and open notes in Airtable.
- Email the tester with final call-in.
- Create a site order for the day for each test participant (e.g., ABC, BCA, CAB).

FOR ZOOM

- Set up Zoom with the "Start without video" option.
- Email the tester with final Zoom info a few minutes before and/or at the start of the call.
- Have the prototype open in the browser and close all other tabs.

PROTOTYPE INTERVIEW SCRIPT

INTRO

Is this still a good time to talk?

Thank you again for your time!

I am talking to people like you to understand how you feel about various solutions that might support you. I'll show you these in the form of stories and ask you to share your honest feedback about them so we can improve our ideas.

I'll start by asking you some general questions; however before I do, I want to let you know that I have someone with me taking notes, but you and I will be the only ones talking. Is that OK with you?

Also, are you comfortable if I record our session? The recordings are confidential and mainly so I can go back if I miss anything. It's perfectly fine if you say no. Are you comfortable if I record our talk?

Lastly, I want to confirm, are you at a computer?

Great, thank you.

BACKGROUND QUESTIONS (cut them off after 5 minutes and move on to scenarios):

- Can you tell me about your role?
   Or
- *[A different question for those we've already interviewed.]*

Thank you. I'm now going to show you my screen—I'll get us set up.

ZOOM

- Click "Share Screen."
- Choose the window to share (your browser window with the InVision [software] link open).
- Choose "Remote Control" and select interviewee.

PROTOTYPE INTERVIEW SCRIPT

You should be able to see my screen, and you'll also have the ability to move the mouse and click on what you'd like. Please click on the "Begin" button.

[KEEP THEM ON THE "BEGIN" PAGE WHILE YOU GIVE INSTRUCTIONS].

[If it doesn't work, email them how to go to the prototype on their own and get them to screen share if possible. Otherwise, they can use the prototype and think out loud].

INSTRUCTIONS

- I'm going to ask you to read a scenario and then click through some drawings.
- As you look at the drawings, only some of the links and buttons will work, but I'll ask you to keep trying to click on anything as you would if you were really using the system on your own.
- As you go, I'll ask you to think out loud. Thinking out loud is like sharing what you're thinking as you go along. If you're reading, please read out loud—otherwise, share your stream of consciousness as you go.
- Just know that I didn't design anything, and nothing you say will offend me or hurt my feelings. The best thing you can do is be honest as you go along and keep thinking out loud.
- Keep in mind these are early concepts, so I'd love feedback on the overall concept rather than the screen design itself.
- Please click on the "Begin" button to get started.

Use predetermined site order (e.g., ABC, BCA, CAB).

FIRST SYSTEM

Please read System _____ out loud and think out loud as you go.

[When they first think or read out loud correctly, positively reinforce them]:

PROTOTYPE INTERVIEW SCRIPT

"You're doing a great job thinking out loud; thank you, keep doing that."

[If they're not thinking out loud, try the following questions in order]:

- Do you mind thinking out loud as you go?
- What's going on?
  After they answer, "Thank you, that's really helpful. If you can keep sharing thoughts like that as you go, that would be wonderful."
- After two tries, just stop reminding them and you'll get your answers at the end of each prototype and at the end of the test.

[If they're commenting on the design or grammar issues]: "For today, I'd love your feedback on the product rather than the design, so if you could focus there, that would be very helpful."

AFTER THEY'RE DONE

- How was that experience?
- If you were talking to a friend and telling them what this system is, what would you say?

  [If they're describing it incorrectly]: "For today, let's assume that the system actually [*describe system*]. Does that change how you feel about it?"

- On a scale of 0–10, how likely is it that you would recommend this system to a friend or colleague (with 0 being not at all likely, and 10 being extremely likely)? Why is that?
- *[If there is time]* Who is this for?

SECOND SYSTEM

Now we're going to do the same thing with a different system.

Please do the same thing you did before with System _____.

PROTOTYPE INTERVIEW SCRIPT

AFTER THEY'RE DONE

- How was that experience?
- If you were talking to a friend and telling them what this system is, what would you say?

    [If they're describing it incorrectly]: "For today, let's assume that the system actually [*describe system*]. Does that change how you feel about it?"

- On a scale of 0–10, how likely is it that you would recommend this system to a friend or colleague (with 0 being not at all likely, and 10 being extremely likely)?

    Why is that?

- [*If there is time*] Who is this for?

THIRD SYSTEM

Now we're going to do the same thing with the last system.

Please go to System _____.

AFTER THEY'RE DONE

- How was that experience?
- If you were talking to a friend and telling them what this system is, what would you say?

    [If they're describing it incorrectly]: "For today, let's assume that the system actually [*describe system*]. Does that change how you feel about it?"

- On a scale of 0–10, how likely is it that you would recommend this system to a friend or colleague (with 0 being not at all likely, and 10 being extremely likely)?

    Why is that?

- [*If there is time*] Who is this for?

That was great feedback, and you did a wonderful job sharing your thoughts! I have a few questions about all three systems, so I'll bring us back to the home screen.

PROTOTYPE INTERVIEW SCRIPT

FOLLOW-UP QUESTIONS

- Which of these three solutions would you want in **your own life**? Feel free to go back and look at them again.
    - Why?
    - Which would be your next favorite, in your own life?
- Would you **want** to combine them in any way?
- *[Ask anything specific that came up during the test that you'd like to drill into more deeply. You should have saved most of your questions until this point.]*
- Was there anything you expected to see in any of the systems, but didn't?
- Was there anything that surprised you about any of them?
- What might you do to improve any of these systems?
- **Do you have any questions for me?**
- Would you mind if I reached out to you in the future to hear your thoughts as things evolve?
- *[Depending on team philosophy]* Also, I'm happy to send you anonymized aggregated observations from these interviews if that would be interesting to you. Would you like me to send them?
- ***[Only if this is a first-time interviewee]:***

    I'm continually looking for feedback from people like you. Is there someone else who you think would be comfortable giving us their thoughts?

Sample Prototypes

As noted earlier, prototypes typically go through three stages of ever-increasing fidelity—getting ever closer to what you might actually launch as an MVP. In the early phases, keep the prototypes simple so the customers you are interviewing don't feel sorry for you because you have "worked so hard and made it so pretty."

In those situations, they won't want to tell you the truth, which is what you desperately need at this phase. However, as you keep refining the bigger picture of what the opportunity is, you begin to refine the actual product, service, or solution, going deeper and deeper into questions of usability, features, functions, and the other finer points of the product development process. Here is the progression we might use for a digital solution and examples of companies we took through the process.

Low-resolution
- Majority of testing takes place at this stage because you are testing lots of solutions

- Tools used: Balsamiq, InVision

- Three steps for each wireframe to help the user see how the idea will help achieve objectives (you add more detail over time)

- Test three different wireframes against one another

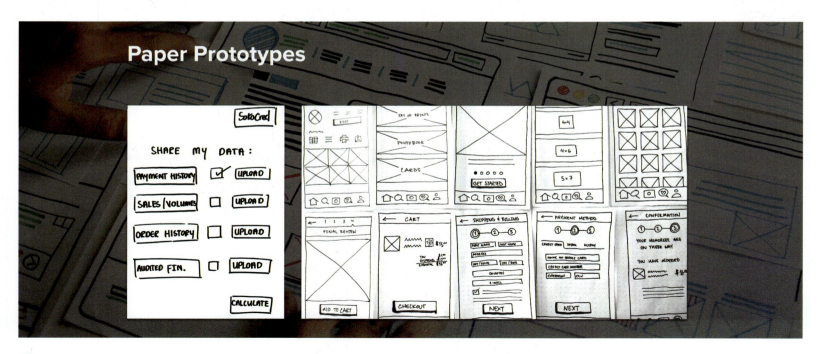

Paper Prototypes

Mid-resolution

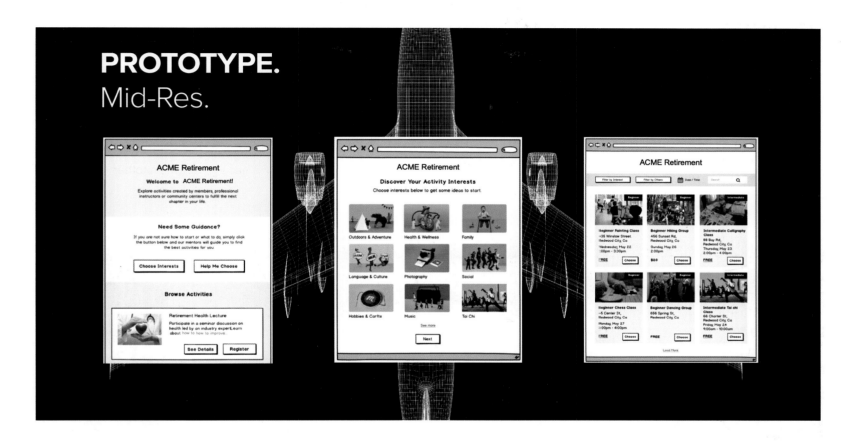

High-resolution

- Gives your New Venture Board a sense of a real product that is achievable and exciting
- Tools used: Sketch, InVision
- Use of full visual design: color, typography, and imagery
- Test at the end (otherwise people get caught up in visual details and forget they should be thinking about the experience)

Scoring Prototype Tests

Just as with storyboards (as you can see in the sample script), you are still scoring your prototypes using NPS scores and rankings of the options you are sharing with each interviewee. You also are still capturing all the data in your Airtable, Google Drive, or whatever database you have chosen to rigorously capture your interview results and insights.

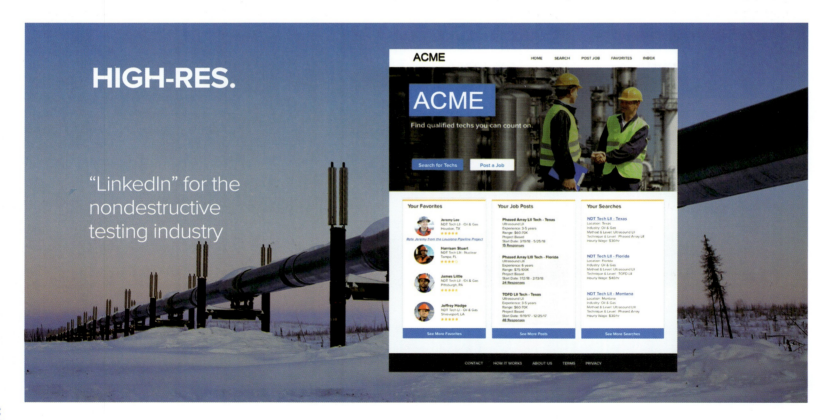

HIGH-RES.

"LinkedIn" for the nondestructive testing industry

Hardware or Hard Goods versus Software or Digital

Some say, "Well, wireframes work as prototypes for software or digital products, but what about hardware or hard goods? How do you prototype for those?"

In fact, at Mach49 we have worked on a bunch of projects that involved hardware or hard goods. Our approach is to design the test based on what we want to learn. We break down prototype development into two possible questions that determine how we will test the product or service:

Do we want to learn about the design of the physical object?

or

Do we want to learn if the decision-maker is interested in buying that physical object if it works the way it was meant to?

How you answer that question determines how to test it. One large industrial client was pursuing a drone for a mine operator. We brainstormed possible test approaches. Julie Price asked, "What do you want to learn?"

Did the team want to learn about the drone design and the use of the drone?

or

Did it want to learn if there was a drone that operated a certain way or achieved a certain goal, would the mine operator be interested in one?

Ultimately, teams *do* have to answer option 1, but making sure they are building a product anyone cares about should almost always be the first step.

If determining interest and excitement are the goals, you need to build a marketing or landing page that describes the product, the benefits, and the usage. For that task, we use Balsamiq, a prototyping tool, but your team may choose to use another tool. Your teams also must determine who would go to this landing page and what they would be curious about (e.g., a video, testimonials, features, benefits, etc.).

Another valuable aspect of this type of test is that you can compare different types of products against each other—say, one hardware solution against a software solution against another service solution. In our experience, people have little trouble responding authentically in tests where you compare options and present them in different ways.

One of our favorite tests is to compare an idea against a product or solution that already exists. It's cost effective and easy to learn from someone else's work, and again, people don't mind testing in different resolutions in one test. Recently, for a turnaround public company, we started testing its biggest competitor's product against the company's new idea. Specifically, we took the competitor's live site and put it head-to-head against our hand-drawn alternative in Balsamiq. It went amazingly well.

That's not to say that the actual design of the hardware doesn't matter or that we won't have to creatively test physical objects. It's just important not to let the tail wag the dog and test what's obvious without taking a hard look at what we want to learn from that test.

Once you know you are building the right product, you can move on to determine what you want to learn next.

Some of the numerous topics a team may determine it wants to explore may include:

Uses. What applications should the proposed product or service be able to perform?

Specs. At what level of performance should the product or service be able to operate?

Interface. How should the customer use the product, service, or web page? How complex should the user interface be?

Packaging. In what form should the product appear? Physical? Mobile? Footprint? Size and weight? If a service, should it be offered at a physical location? If an experience, how should a customer engage with it? If food, does it have a shelf life or an expiration date to consider?

Input or output. How should data be entered into the product? What form should output take? Display? Print? Upload to the cloud?

Compatibility. What platforms, programming languages, networking protocols, and operating systems are commonly used—even standardized—in the customer's industry? With what other devices and networks will the product most commonly connect?

Price. Given the above, what is a competitive price for the product or service?

Support. What standard level of service and support does the customer consider superior in its industry?

Special features. Are there any other features—rechargeability, waterproofing, hardened packaging, recyclability, multiple languages, and so on—that the interviewee considers standard for the industry? Or better yet, what features would confer on the product or service an immediate perceived advantage over competitive offerings?

Be aware of when you need to learn something about the customer or market, never assume you already know. There are certain topics about which it makes sense to go deep during the Incubate phase. Other topics, you may want to wait and test during the Accelerate phase as part of launching your MVP. For example, you certainly want to know during the prototype interviews if people would be willing to pay for your product or service, but you may want to wait until you have launched your MVP to test *how* they want to pay for it by testing different payment models during your pilots. Remember, customer development never sleeps. Whenever you have a question, ask the customer.

How Should You Structure the Prototype Phase?

Looking at it from a high level, the prototype activity during the Product phase operates roughly at the following pace.

Week 6: Prototype or wireframe training. Wireframes start with three, three-page wireframes and a scenario screen for accessing those wireframes (not counting log-in or registration screens).

Week 7: Elaboration. Either continue with the short three-page wireframes, adding new concepts to the triads tested, or start building out a few wireframes so there are more pages. The goal is to find one or more wireframes that resonate with the target segment.

Week 8: Interviews. Continue wireframe interviews to get to the MVP and vision: What is the *big* opportunity for the venture? Most of Mach49's clients are multinational, multibillion-dollar companies, so merely building an app is not a venture. Rather, big companies need opportunities that start with an MVP but have a product or solution road map that demonstrates that the team is building a substantive venture or business. Also, sometimes the MVP is more obvious; then you test for vision. At other times, it's the opposite. The big opportunity is clear, but the right MVP to launch with may need additional testing.

Week 9: Check-in. As we mentioned in chapter 2, Week 9 is when we typically host the New Venture Team's first formal Check-in with the NVB. As a reminder, during this meeting, team members presented summaries of their customer pain findings from open-ended interviews and the early solutions they are considering, based on customer storyboard interviews and the first set of prototype interviews. The Check-in agenda covers the work of the New Venture Team to date, including:

- Segmentation and stakeholders
- Target personas
- Stakeholder processes
- Customer pain findings
- Storyboard research findings
- Opportunity framework (the big picture for the new venture at scale)
- Early product vision and MVP focus
- Risks
- Next steps
- Executive session

During the Check-in, the team should listen to the feedback from the NVB and note the most important questions or risks it raises that are relevant to customer development. From that session, you should be able to identify the biggest unknowns that can translate to testing goals for the remainder of your time incubating. You should design tests going forward that can map back to those unknowns and provide you with answers you can share in your final pitch deck, Week 12. There are lots of additional testing strategies; we are only highlighting a few. For example, kitchen sink testing (if you want to dig into vision), splitting apart features and comparing MVP options (A/B testing), or blowing up or disaggregating the MVP to answer specific questions. The questions could be UX or UI related or could be specific questions the NVB has asked regarding important unknowns.

Week 10+: Advance. Continually update your biggest unknowns or test goals and map the number of test cycles against the calendar, designing the appropriate tests accordingly. Engage closely as a team to make sure you work on the most important goals through to the end of the Incubate phase, which at this point is rapidly approaching.

→ Activity Two: Early Product Design

At this point during the Incubate phase, you are looking for two outcomes:

1. What is the big opportunity?
2. What is the MVP?

Remember that you are not in the business of building apps, because those rarely move the needle in terms of driving growth for large companies. Rather, you are here to build a *new venture*, a substantial new business.

One big energy equipment client had a new venture, code-named GreenFleet. The team realized that there was huge opportunity in electrifying fleets for large companies globally. The ultimate opportunity was to offer electric fleets as a service—zero emissions mobility with zero risk for large companies.

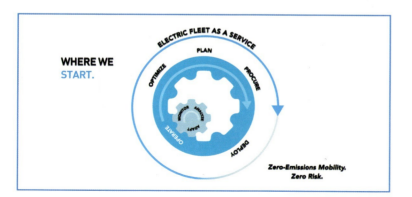

However, every great startup begins with an MVP. For GreenFleet, the MVP started with helping large companies *plan* to electrify their fleets using data and analytics to figure out how and where to start, based on lots of different data inputs.

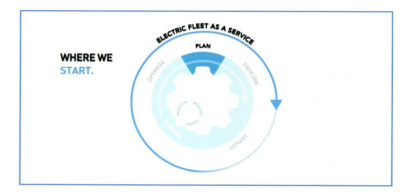

Thus, GreenFleet's MVP became "GreenFleet Evaluate," a program providing the analysis and planning required to optimize the conversion of fleets to electric vehicles.

We explore more examples of the big opportunity, MVP, and product road map in the next chapter as we move to the third phase of Incubate: the business. There, we pull it all together and show how to build a truly robust business and execution plan. For now, let's focus on what else is happening in phase II: *Product*.

While part of the team continues to conduct customer interviews, the other part of the team—charged with ultimately designing and building the product, service, or solution—begins to ask four big questions:

Can we actually build what we are imagining (or is it a fantasy)?

Can our company build it?

How should we build it?

If we can't build it, can we buy, partner, or invest in other companies to get it built?

Let's look at each of these more closely.

Can We Actually Build What We Are Imagining (or Is It a Fantasy)?

Earlier we said that successful ventures start with customer pain. They then marry that customer pain with the art of the possible—the trends and technology that currently exist that the venture can bring together to solve that pain.

Uber and Lyft could not have been built before the advent of mobile phones, GPS, and real-time payment capability. The challenge for many large companies is that they do not stay current on the art of the possible. One of the reasons that most large companies should have a corporate venture capital (CVC) fund is because, if designed and managed correctly (the topic of our next book; stay tuned), the CVC fund team can keep the Mothership current on the art of the possible. If you don't have a CVC scanning the globe for you, then your New Venture Team members need to assess what technology, tools, and trends exist that convince them the solution the customers you are interviewing imagine and hope for can actually be built.

We actively encourage New Venture Team members to be their own sensor network. You *must* stay current; the world may change, even during those twelve weeks. Whatever industry you are in, there are conferences, blogs, newsletters, meetups, demo days, and starving graduate students who would love to share what they are working on in exchange for a stipend or a meal. They can help keep you up-to-date and informed. The world is moving too fast to think that what you knew five years ago is relevant today. Product teams, in particular, whether building a digital platform, developing a new food sensation, or imagining a theme park, have to seek timely inspiration for what they are trying to achieve.

If what you are imagining is still outside the bounds of reality, physics, human tolerance, or capability, this is a second reason why you

CUSTOMER PAIN
↓

Big Data . Predictive Analytics . AI . IoT . Fintech . Blockchain . AR VR . Wearables . 3D Printing . Material Science . Synthetic Biology

↑
ART OF THE POSSIBLE

might kill the venture. Even if there is customer pain, if there is no way to alleviate that pain, there is no way to build a successful business.

However, if the tools and technology *do* exist to make it happen, then you get to ask additional questions.

Can Our Company Build It?

One of the activities New Venture Teams perform early on is what we call an *Asset Jam* (refer to page 84). Created by our partners Greg Galle and Mike Burn of Solve Next, the Asset Jam is a quick way to identify and categorize the core competencies, assets, and capabilities the Mothership's organization has that it can leverage to build the solution that solves customer pain and creates competitive advantage (especially against those pesky startups).

How Should We Build It?

At this point, the team begins to prepare the prototypes, while at the same time beginning to contemplate how the product might come to life.

Here are some of the key topics to address during this part of the Product phase.

Who Builds It?

Can we build the product or service ourselves? In hardware, this means tooling, manufacturing line equipment, robots, hired assemblers, testers, inventory storage, and so on. In software, this means code writers, quality control, secure distribution, and so on. If a service, can we find the people we need to provide the service and can or will what we imagine scale globally in all countries and across all cultures? And, given that no service these days comes without some digital interface, do we have the means to reach our customers effectively?

This is a time to be realistic: if you cannot afford to do the manufacturing, development, or design—or don't believe you can get the parent company to invest at this level—it doesn't mean you necessarily must abandon the project. There are other viable scenarios. For example, the Mothership can:

Buy

Partner

Invest

You may be able to find a strategic partner willing to work with you in exchange for equity. Or, you can off-load the job to a contract manufacturer or service provider. You may be able to replace some planned proprietary component and instead buy it from an existing retailer. Or find a fellow corporate partner that wants to coinvest to fund the build.

Needless to say, the answer to this question is not something you can pull out of a hat. You need to research potential alternatives and, eventually, contact the most likely vendors or partners to obtain terms and an estimate of costs.

What's the First Step?

The first step is determining the MVP that the venture can bring to market to ultimately determine and validate product-market fit. Mach49 friend Steve Blank is the chief guru of the lean startup methodology, much of which we have adapted for the Global 1000. He explains what an MVP actually is:

> *It is critical to understand that an MVP is not the product with fewer features. Rather it is the simplest thing that you can show to customers to get the most learning at that point in time. Early on in a startup, an MVP could simply be a PowerPoint slide, wireframe, clay model or sample data set, etc. Each time you build an MVP you also define what you are trying to test/measure. Later, as more is learned, the MVP's go from low-fidelity to higher fidelity, but the goal continues to be to maximize learning, not to build a beta/fully featured prototype of the product.*[1]

Sound familiar? Every subsequent revision of your offering should be defined by what you want to learn. The Product phase is a constant back-and-forth between what the team believes is the big opportunity and the steps it needs to take to get there, starting with the MVP and then iterating and even pivoting to the ultimate solution that the new venture can scale to the market.

Mach49 partner Dave Blakely, SVP Client Capability Development, sits at the intersection of design thinking and hard-core engineering. This block diagram is one Dave worked on for an early version of Pear.ai, the very successful venture launched by a big German utility whose NVB sponsor, Patrick Lammers, and venture CEO, Sukhjinder Singh, represent extraordinary role models for how to build ventures right. The diagram shows how the team imagined the entire architecture, earmarking the MVP features with yellow Post-its.

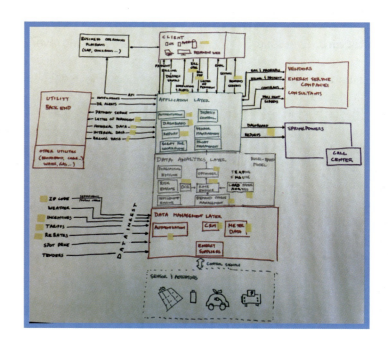

Democratizing System Architecture

Dave believes that even system architecture can be shared by all members of a New Venture Team, whether they are technical or not. In Dave's words, here's how.

Everyone on our venture teams, technical or not, can contribute to a diagram like the one on the facing page for Pear.ai. Here are the basic concepts all team members should understand:

Stack. Any software-based system is configured as a stack. The basic concept is that the deeper the layer, the more complicated and riskier a change will be. For example, on the Pear stack, it's easier to change the online dashboard than to modify the signals from an installed energy meter.

Architecture. Everyone on the team should understand every block conceptually. As an example, everyone on the Pear team understood the notion of a "settlement engine" for transactions. That said, advanced technical knowledge, such as understanding the analytics behind settlement, was not necessary.

Data flow. How will the various architectural blocks "talk" to each other, and what information will be passed between them? It's important for everyone on the team to understand which blocks are managed internally, and which blocks require more difficult interfacing with external sources, called "APIs." In the architecture diagram, information on tariffs and rebates is gathered from external sources by the "Data Management Layer."

Using this approach, everyone on the Pear team collaborated to create the final architecture for the system and, eventually, came to a consensus on the vision for the MVP. Despite the fact that several members of the venture team had no software experience, they were more than able to develop a complete understanding of the system, even to make valuable contributions. This diagram became the specification tool for external developers to begin development in earnest once the new venture was launched.

The title MVP does not just apply to the product; ultimately it applies to all the features of the new company you are building, from the business model and pricing to go-to-market options, brand messaging, and more. We'll talk more about that in chapter 8.

As the Product phase unfolded, a global industrial client's very successful Australian venture could articulate its product vision:

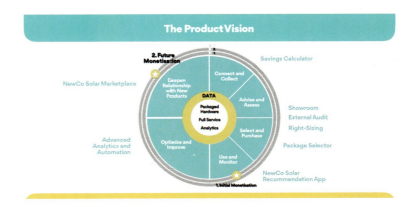

Its starting point—the MVP.

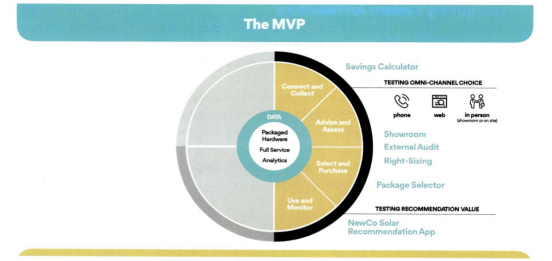

And, ultimately, by the end of the twelve weeks, the preliminary product and technology road map that would ensue during the following twenty-four months post-launch.

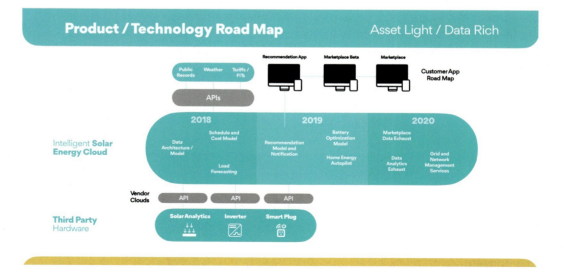

Risk and the MVP

The purpose of the first phase of the Accelerate phase, Building to Validate, is ultimately to mitigate risk. Andy Rachleff, one of the visionary founders of Benchmark Capital, developed this insight:

> *In Silicon Valley we look at funding like an onion and every layer of onion is a layer of risk, it could be market, technical, or financial. [At Mach49, we add "governance" to that list, because the Mothership may love its new ventures to death or starve them of oxygen.] The best entrepreneurs know how to remove the greatest amount of risk on the least amount of capital.*

Earlier we said that what the Silicon Valley does best is understand customer pain, marry it with the art of the possible, and place a series of small bets. In the Product phase, we marry the understanding of customer pain with the art of the possible and then we place a series of small bets in the form of customer pilots, experiments, and tests we run at low cost to continue to learn. In the best companies, we design those small bets to prove that we can mitigate a risk and are held accountable by the metrics and milestones we have identified that tell us we have indeed mitigated that risk. Only then does the team unlock the next round of funding.

When the new venture gets to the point where it is contemplating risks, that is a very good sign because it means the team has found significant pain to solve and believes it has identified a viable solution. Now, on to the final question:

How do we make money—and a lot of it?

It's time to move to the final phase of Incubate and do the work required to build a very robust business and execution plan to launch and grow the venture.

Chapter 07

Incubate Phase III:
Business

**How Do We Make Money?
What's Our Plan?**

We are now in the home stretch of the twelve weeks of incubating your new venture.

You are past your official Check-in session with the NVB and have been given the green light to keep going.

Part of the team is still doing customer development work conducting prototype interviews. The product team continues to feed them prototypes to test while working on the MVP, the product road map, and early engineering and development. As we move into this third phase of Incubate, the group now splits again, and those people recruited to the team to focus on the business side of the venture, typically led by the team lead or CEO, get *really* busy building the business, execution, and operating plan.

The team members defining the business are responsible for the following:

- Sizing the market
- The business model, pricing model, and monetization plan
- The funding ask
- The operating and execution plan including staffing and organizational chart
- Governance
- Gives and Gets
- Risks and competition
- Why us?

Once the business team has completed the business-related research and analysis, it pulls together the results into a final business and execution plan that also includes the work of the customer and product teams. Much more than a traditional startup pitch deck, what you are preparing is a very robust and rigorous business case along with a detailed execution and operating plan that the team presents to the NVB (in about three to four weeks) to get the final fund and launch decision. To make sure you know what the NVB is expecting, as we go through each of the business team's activities listed above, we use real case examples from actual venture plans, so you understand the outcomes you want to achieve.

With regard to the structure of the business and execution plan, while VCs are quite happy seeing many different types of business plans from startup founders, that lack of standardization does not work for large-company new ventures. Because your goal is to build the capability to create not just one new venture but a pipeline and portfolio of new ventures, it is critical that companies adopt a repeatable and scalable model for their business and execution plans that is consistent across ventures and over time.

To avoid the apples-to-oranges problem, you must prepare a business and execution plan to deliver to your NVB on Pitch Day that has exactly the same agenda covering all the same material that the ventures before yours and the ventures after yours will adopt.

While the actual content obviously varies from venture to venture and the order of the presentation may shift around, the framework regarding what the team *must have completed* during the twelve weeks and is expected to cover in its business plan at Pitch Day is the same every time. That way the NVB won't be distracted by the process, wondering if you checked the box on this item or that item; the board will see the table of contents, recognize it as familiar, and know you have completed all the required work to produce a great venture. Check the process box; let's focus on the content.

INCUBATE. On Pitch Day Every Venture Will Have a Full Business, Execution, and Operating Plan.

Where We've Been
The Market
The Pain We Heard
The Opportunity Framework
The Customer Journey
The Product Vision and MVP
Product and Tech Road Map
GTM and Monetization
Operating and Execution Plan
The Ask
Governance
Gives and Gets
Risks and Competition
Why Us?
Do It on Monday

→ **Building the Business Case for the Venture**

As we move to the Business phase, the *storyteller* becomes critical. Cross your heart and promise that you will not produce a bunch of boring PowerPoint slides with too many words crammed on a page and not a single icon or visual. Just as design matters to your product or solution, so too does how you tell the story of your new venture.

We will share lots of examples to help you understand how high you need to set the bar on storytelling, as well as step-by-step guidance for every slide you need in your deck.

The moment has arrived; let's get this venture funded.

The Cover: Tell Them Who You Are

Too often, startups fail to actually tell their audience, from the very first moment, what the venture is all about. I have watched too many startup pitches where, about halfway through, I have to ask, "What is it that you actually *do*?"

Within the first two pages, you must give your audience something to be excited to learn more about. From the very first week of incubation, our New Venture Teams have a name, a logo, and a website. By Pitch Day, they also have a story.

You may ask why an appealing and relevant cover matters—after all, you merely flip to the next page quickly once you start your presentation. Does it really matter? Yes. Your cover slide is up on the screen before the NVB members have fully assembled (whether physically present or virtually by video), so it is the image they are looking at from the time they walk into the room, or log into the video conference, until you begin the presentation.

Why does it matter? Because, according to Malcolm Gladwell, in *Blink: The Power of Thinking Without Thinking*, decisions often occur instantaneously or, at most, within two seconds. According to Gladwell, "people think without thinking, and they thin slice whenever they meet a new person or have to make sense of something quickly or encounter a novel situation." Your cover represents that first impression, so make it intriguing.

The cover should include:

- The name of the venture
  - It can be a code name for now, as you will not have spent time or money on an extensive branding exercise.
  - It can also be presented as a stand-alone venture or indicate the parent company; often "powered by" is a great way to share the glory.
- The logo
- The tag line or pain you are solving
- A strong, simple, and clear typeface
- An enticing image that sets the tone for the story; design matters (an illustration, screenshot, or stock photo)

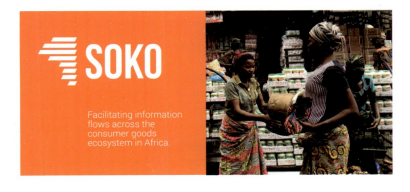

Where You've Been

As part of the founding team, you have been living, eating, and breathing the new venture every day since the first day of the Incubate phase. By comparison, while the NVB members have been engaged (or should have been; more on that in chapter 10), they are not as fully immersed in what you have been doing and may not remember the activities you have completed to date. In addition, you are not presenting to a traditional venture capitalist; for the NVB members, reviewing new ventures is unlikely to be their area of expertise. Most won't intuitively understand all that you have accomplished so far. This fact is especially true if you are one of your company's early ventures. For that reason, your team will be very happy that it has been rigorously documenting the process the entire time, because you have all the data, information, quotes, and other artifacts at hand to build this part of the business plan.

The "where you've been" section should include:

- Your original Challenge Statement and the new one, if you pivoted from the original once you started interviewing customers
- A snapshot of the overall incubation plan and where you are now in terms of your timeline
- A refresher on the process you used to demonstrate how rigorous and robust your work has been or what may have been unique about how you incubated the venture
- A summary of the number and types of customer interviews the team has completed as a reminder of how customer obsessed and customer driven your new venture is

You would not be in the room pitching this new venture to your NVB if you had not found significant customer pain. The numbers also remind the NVB that *customer insights are the currency for credibility—everything else is uninformed opinion*. This means that if the NVB members want to weigh in on whether there is real pain or what the product or opportunity should be, the team has every right to ask them to share the customer interviews and the quotes from customers that validate their point of view. Then, if they do, log those validating quotes in your database of everything you have done to date. Since very few board members have the time to actually *talk* to customers and virtually none of them will have conducted their interviews the way the team has, their perceived customer pain is almost always just opinion that evaporates when

INTERVIEW. DEBRIEF. DOCUMENT.

it encounters real, empirical data. The team members are now the experts. Trust yourselves.

The previous two slides are examples representing the "where we've been" features, including what activities you may want to highlight and share with your NVB and ways to present them.

The Market

The market section provides the team the opportunity to share the big picture and the context within which the new venture will live. Market sizing is one of the activities that the business viability team works on during the last month to make sure that the market the venture is pursuing is big enough for the Mothership to make money. The business plan includes a summary of the New Venture Team's research and findings relative to the size of the expected market. Basically, if the opportunity isn't huge, then the team should not be wasting the NVB's time. The definition of huge, however, can be more than just money; it can also be the opportunity to change the world or make a difference in people's lives.

IF IT'S NOT BIG, STOP!

Until now we have identified two critical moments when the team or the NVB should kill the venture and not spend any more time or money:

- During the customer phase, if the team finds *no customer pain* or not enough of it to make the venture worth pursuing.

- During the product phase, if the team finds that there is a ton of pain but to solve it depends on time travel or some other yet unavailable future technology to emerge. In other words, the *product is unbuildable*.

Now we may encounter a third inflection point that might cause the team or the NVB to kill a venture:

- The *market just isn't big enough* or the Mothership can't make enough money to drive meaningful growth over time. When we run Week 0 for the New Venture Teams, we have a very simple statement they need to absorb for this business phase.

If it's not big, if the venture can't move the needle for the Mothership, stop!

Information in the section on the market may include:

- The current problems relevant to the space in which you will operate.
- Any insights you gained from taking a customer-driven dive into this space versus any assumptions and opinions that represent commonly held beliefs that no one has bothered to test in a while (if ever).
- Trends that were meaningful relative to customers and why they might be ready for what you want to bring to the market now. Also, technology trends that make your product or solution feasible.
- Market statistics including the state or size of the opportunity area today. Also, any growth metrics, including quotes from stakeholders the team interviewed, that you find meaningful.

Explain and frame the market, citing any relevant trends, insights, or statistics you found.

Demonstrate the Size of the Market

Mach49 cofounder and CFO Russ Lampert, who helps every one of our clients' new ventures with market sizing, business model, pricing options, funding requirements, budget, and overall financials, teaches our clients the following process for market sizing.

When looking at market size, there are typically four numbers your NVB may want you to calculate:

Total market opportunity (TMO). Assuming 100 percent market share, the total potential value of the product or service sold over a specified time frame.

Total addressable market (TAM). The overall revenue opportunity that is available to your new venture assuming you achieve 100 percent market share in a particular customer segment. TAM takes into account that the venture cannot go after every product or every segment.

Serviceable available market (SAM). The part of the TAM that is served by the company's product or service.

Serviceable obtainable market (SOM). The total value of SAM divided by the expected percentage market share that the company believes it can capture.

VCs and large companies alike need big market opportunities before they make the commitment to invest in a venture. Typically, the easiest way to size a market is through a top-down approach that allows you to determine the revenue potential of new product markets or customer segments.

According to Russ, a pretty straightforward formula looks like this:

Number of people in a population
×
Percent of target customers
×
Purchase frequency
×
Quantity per purchase period
×
Price per unit
=
Market size

The Customer Pain

If the team does not find customer pain early on, it will not make it to Pitch Day. As noted in earlier chapters, the Week 9 Check-in meeting is the first formal presentation to the NVB and the entire Check-in presentation is focused on customers, early segmentation, personas, the customer journey, and pain. To remind the NVB of the previously shared information, many of those slides get updated and repeated in the customer pain section of the final Pitch Day presentation, including:

• Segmentation and stakeholders

• Target personas

• Customer pain findings

The segmentation and stakeholders section often includes the original Stakeholder Map, which captures the universe of possible customers. It then identifies the target personas who the NVT thinks have the greatest pain and are the most likely buyers based on all their interviews. Earlier we explained how to actually create personas; here we share how to address those personas in your business and operating plan.

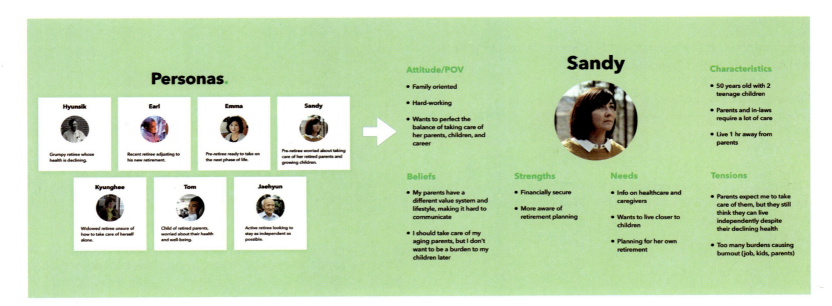

Remember, *people* buy products, services, and solutions; companies do not. So you have to identify real people to sell to and you have to understand them very well.

Summarize the Pain
With segmentation and personas clearly defined, summarize the pain you are solving for them. These summaries have three goals:

Empathy. Make the NVB feel the customer's pain. Often we embed audio clips of customers so the board members can actually hear the emotion in their voices.

Distinctiveness. Show why your insights and plan are unique compared to the status quo. What truths have others missed because they failed to actually conduct customer interviews?

Commonality. As we discussed in the pain point interview tutorial in chapter 5, to the extent that your opportunity is global or multinational in any way, share how the pain is consistent across segments and markets so the team won't have to completely rebuild the product to serve the much larger global opportunity.

The Opportunity
So now the NVB is very excited, you have demonstrated the rigorous and robust work the team has conducted, the size of the market is huge, and the customer pain is palpable. Before you get into the details of how you are going to launch the company, the team needs to now prove to the board that it is planning to build a real business, not just an app. What is the big opportunity that the Mothership should pursue to drive growth? We shared a few of these stories in chapter 6 when we discussed the difference between the MVP and the big opportunity.

The Customer Journey

One of the most effective ways to demonstrate the value of your new venture is to share a Day in the Life of your customer before your venture existed, then, what that day will look like once you are in the market.

The Current Experience

Why Is My Bill So High!?

 I do not understand my bill; I do not understand my electricity costs; I do not know where I use the energy in my home.

Who Can I Trust?

 I do not know who to trust; the information is confusing; I do not know what options are out there to reduce my energy costs.

I will ask my friends and family to see if they know an installer.

Home Visit

 I organize an installer to visit my home and quote for a solar system.

I am not told about monitoring or other features that may be of interest to me. I trust the installer knows what he is doing.

$ Make Deposit

 I pay a deposit and schedule an installation date with the solar installer.

$$ Installation

 The solar installer arrives at site, installs the solar system and leaves; I presume the solar system is operating.

It Works!

 My first energy bill shows that my energy costs have gone down, so I guess the solar system works, but by how much?

An uninformed customer ⟶ **No Deeper Engagement**

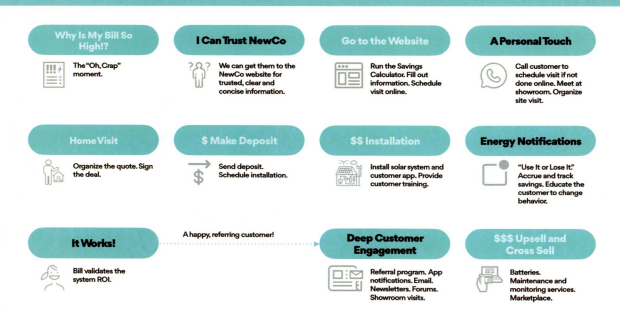

From early on, when you are conducting pain point interviews, you are mapping the customer journey or experience. Once you have finalized the storyboard interviews and have moved on to the prototype interviews, the venture team should have a very good understanding of how its product, service, or solution has solved the customer's pain. Whether you are a B2B, B2C, or B2B2C venture, you should be able to demonstrate your value proposition through the lens and life of your customer.

Great business plans are built on not only financials and storytelling, but also *empathy*. Your Day in the Life stories, as they are rewritten and refined, must manifest that empathy. When you can put yourself in customers' minds and know the customers as well—if not better—than customers know themselves, you are ready to sell your vision of the customers' future to your NVB.

The Product Vision and MVP

We have already dedicated an entire chapter (chapter 6) to product vision and the MVP. However, we want to give some additional examples of how other New Venture Teams have communicated those topics in their final business and execution plan.

Product and Tech Road Map

We also covered the product architecture and road map topics in the prior chapter. So, here we want to give you additional examples of ways you can communicate your product plans to your NVB.

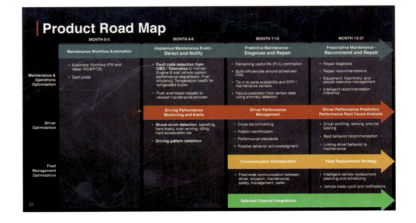

Go to Market and Monetization: Business Model

Just as you place small bets and experiment through rapid prototyping and market testing as you evolve the product, so too do you place small bets by piloting and experimenting with how the new venture will go to market and how it will make money. Identifying the go-to-market options and pricing models to try is another task the business team must do during this last phase of Incubate.

Oliver Gassmann, Karolin Frankenberger, and Michaela Csik of the University of St. Gallen have written an excellent white paper and subsequently a book, *The Business Model Navigator*.[1] They conducted extensive research, first defining and then cataloging all the possible business models a new venture could adopt. In their words:

> *Before discussing how to innovate a business model, it is important to understand what it is that is to be innovated... In general, the business model can be defined as a unit of analysis to describe how the business of a firm works. More specifically, the business model is often depicted as an overarching concept that takes notice of the different components a business is constituted of and puts them together as a whole. In other words, business models describe how the magic of a business works based on its individual bits and pieces.*

> *To describe the business models throughout our study, we employ a conceptualization that consists of four central dimensions: The Who, the What, the How, and the Value. Due to the reduction to four dimensions the concept is easy to use, but, at the same time, exhaustive enough to provide a clear picture of the business model architecture.*

In the end, the authors determined that there are only *fifty-five business models* an enterprise or new venture can choose from.

We won't go into all the details of each of the business models; read the book, as their work is excellent and an easy read. We share some examples of how some of our new ventures have developed their own go-to-market and monetization plans.

Based on the industry you are pursuing and the personas you have identified, you can hypothesize and experiment with the best business model for that industry and those customers. You should experiment with *how* you will go to market and *all the ways* the new venture can make money. Based on the results of all this work, you can then run experiments to determine which model makes the most sense.

55+ BUSINESS MODELS

DEVELOPMENT	PRICING	SALES CHANNEL	MARKETING	PLATFORMS
Add-On	Auction	Cross Selling	Aikido	Affiliation
Crowdsourcing	Barter	Direct Selling	Customer Loyalty	Integrator
Digitization	Cash Machine	E-Commerce	Experience Selling	Long Tail
From Push To Pull	Crowdfunding	Franchising	Fractional Ownership	Open Business
Hidden Revenue	Flat Rate	Licensing	Guaranteed Availability	Orchestration
Layer Player	Freemium	Make More Of It	Ingredient Branding	Peer-to-Peer
Leverage Customer Data	Pay-Per-Use	Self-Service	Mass Customization	Revenue Share
Lock-In	Pay What You Want	Trash-to-Cash	Robin Hood	Shop-in-Shop
Mass Customization	Performance-Based Contracting	User Design	Target The Poor	Solution Provider
Open Source	Rent Instead Of Buy	White Label	Ultimate Luxury	Supermarket
Razor and Blade	Subscription			Two-Sided Market
Reverse Engineer				
Reverse Innovate				

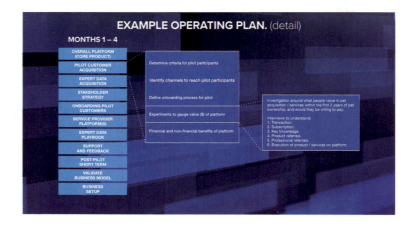

Your operating plan is dependent upon what exactly your venture is going to be. Here are examples from real ventures.

→ Operating and Execution Plan

Now we get into the nuts and bolts of what the new venture looks like as it moves through the Accelerate phase. We examine each topic in this section.

Operating Plan Approach Including Phases and Milestones

The goal is to build an execution plan with a series of pilots, experiments, and small bets that prove you can remove the greatest amount of risk with the least amount of capital. Every phase should have a set of objectives—and metrics and milestones the team and the NVB are able to use—to know when the venture has achieved those objectives and is ready to unlock the next round of funding.

Your operating plan will lay out all the categories of activities you need to pursue once launched. Each category then lays out all the key initiatives you need to pursue in each category. Then, most importantly, it must show what you need to learn as a result of conducting those activities.

The Critical Numbers

The NVB has been very patient to this point. The members likely wanted the numbers from the outset, but your board members have stayed true to the preconditions for success and stayed focused on pain and product first. With those two key phases behind you, now is the time for the venture team member who was recruited to take the lead on the actual business plan to begin crunching the numbers.

Which numbers? The operating plan needs to include:

1. Sales forecasts
2. Organization chart and staffing plan to build out the various parts of the company—typically the biggest driver of cost in an early-stage venture
3. Cash flow, budget, and expected use of funds

The key here is to remember that the new venture is a startup and needs to continue to behave and spend cash like a startup—meaning the team will need to manage its *burn rate* to stay efficient and lean as it starts to grow.

Don't forget to identify follow-on streams of revenue that your venture can pursue, for example, monetizing the data exhaust or estimating the amount of pull-through revenue your venture will drive for the Mothership's other products and services.

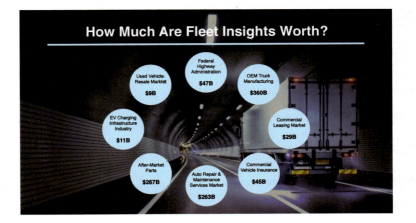

Organization Chart and Hiring Plan

Also included in the operating and execution plan section is an organization chart. It should outline the following:

Duties. What roles the founding team will play (if any; in some cases, team members who were part of the incubation may not have the right skill sets or appetite for risk to help the new venture launch. In those situations, those team members typically return to their former positions, forever changed and hugely valuable).

Recruiting. What roles need to be filled and how they will be filled—hired, outsourced, or contracted? Short term versus long term?

Forecast. Based on the phases laid out in the operating plan, ideally the team can provide an assessment of how the organization and head count will grow over time, which it can then feed back into the numbers.

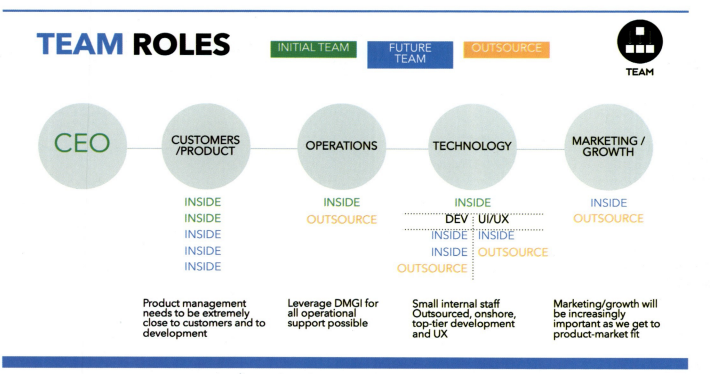

The Ask

Besides the sales forecasts and budgets, the other information the NVB will look for is how much money the new venture requires to achieve the various milestones the team has identified. To provide that information, the team needs to share two primary insights:

- How much seed funding and subsequent rounds of funding will the new venture need?
- How will the team spend that funding?

There are many sources of information to determine these numbers, including:

- Preliminary proposals or contracts from outsiders that the team may want to use
- Reports that share aggregated data on startup costs, such as compensation or product development costs

- Board members or experts—such as the Mothership's accounting firm
- The Mothership's finance organization—if it understands startup economics (otherwise the costs it identifies may be inflated)

When working with any department of the Mothership, beware the dreaded "transfer pricing." Sometimes internal groups cost more than if you went to an outside contractor. Also, when using resources outside the New Venture Team (whether internal or external), be sure to get multiple bids so you can get to a solid use of funds cost.

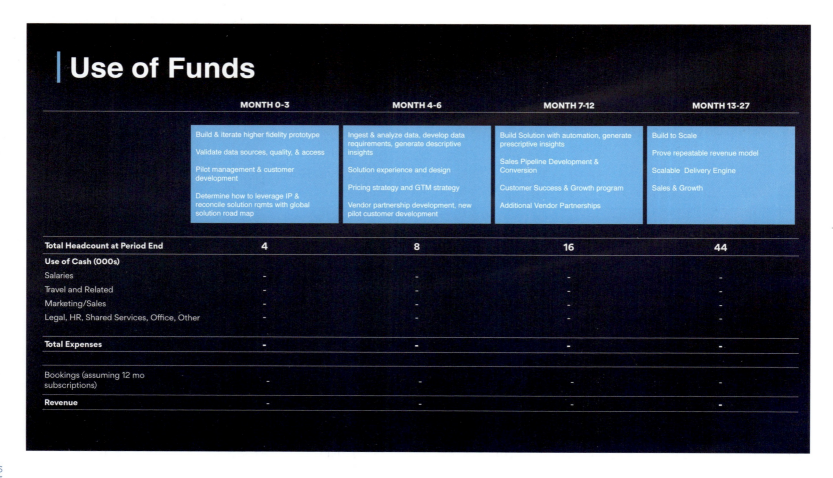

Use of Funds

	MONTH 0-3	MONTH 4-6	MONTH 7-12	MONTH 13-27
	Build & iterate higher fidelity prototype / Validate data sources, quality, & access / Pilot management & customer development / Determine how to leverage IP & reconcile solution rqmts with global solution road map	Ingest & analyze data, develop data requirements, generate descriptive insights / Solution experience and design / Pricing strategy and GTM strategy / Vendor partnership development, new pilot customer development	Build Solution with automation, generate prescriptive insights / Sales Pipeline Development & Conversion / Customer Success & Growth program / Additional Vendor Partnerships	Build to Scale / Prove repeatable revenue model / Scalable Delivery Engine / Sales & Growth
Total Headcount at Period End	4	8	16	44
Use of Cash (000s)				
Salaries	-	-	-	-
Travel and Related	-	-	-	-
Marketing/Sales	-	-	-	-
Legal, HR, Shared Services, Office, Other	-	-	-	-
Total Expenses	-	-	-	-
Bookings (assuming 12 mo subscriptions)	-	-	-	-
Revenue				-

Governance

Until Pitch Day, the NVB is the governing body for the new venture. However, once the business is about to launch, a number of decisions need to be made that relate to governance.

The NVB needs to decide which of the following three options it will pursue for the venture:

- Spin out the new venture, taking outside funding and accepting governance determined by those outside funders.
- Create a wholly owned subsidiary, keeping it inside the Mothership but setting it up as its own line of business, allowing the venture team to go outside for services, such as accounting, legal, HR, marketing, and so on, if it needs to for speed or specialized services.
- Spin in to an existing business unit, which usually means the new venture needs to leverage the shared services of the Mothership to obtain economies of scale.

The calculation of whether to set up a wholly owned subsidiary able to go outside for services or spin in to an existing business unit with shared services comes down to whether duplicating costs by going outside results in faster time to market and revenue. If so, then it is worth paying extra for outside resources and no friction. If not, because the Mothership manages friction well, or there aren't any time savings, then by all means use the shared parent company services; they will likely be cheaper due to Mothership bargaining power and economies of scale.

If the decision is to spin the venture into an existing business unit, then that likely dictates the governance model for the new venture.

The same people governing the business unit now govern the venture. That said, it is normal and useful for at least some members of the existing NVB to stay on for continuity for as long as the venture takes to develop momentum. (We address this again for the benefit of NVB members in chapter 10.)

Gives and Gets

Access to core competencies, assets, capabilities, channels, data, customers, and so on all represent huge advantages for an internally developed new venture, but only if those advantages are managed effectively by the Mothership and channeled efficiently to the new venture. Creating new ventures must be a two-way street, a mutually advantageous, reciprocal relationship between the Mothership and every new venture that gets launched.

GIVES AND GETS

MOTHERSHIP

Assets
- Data and process support with customized APIs
- Energy and market expertise from internal team
- Network-building support using SE expertise
- Cybersecurity expertise

Relationships
- Desired medium business clients
- Supplier relationship acceleration
- Renewable developer relationships

Brand Recognition
- Risk mitigation for recruited brokers
- Accelerate attractive third-party partnerships

STARTUP

Technology
- Updated Supplier Portal

Growth
- Accelerated and streamlined organic and inorganic growth
- Access to new small and medium business markets

Industry Transformation
- Standardization
- Trusted energy ecosystem

Done well, good governance can give an internally developed new venture the ability to beat even the most well-funded startups at their own game. We memorialize this relationship in the Gives and Gets section of the business plan. It builds off the Asset Jam exercise the team completed earlier when it brainstormed Mothership fit and competitive advantage while assessing the new venture ideas during the Ideate phase. To start, the new venture must hold up a mirror and share with the Mothership why the venture matters to the growth of the parent company. Why should the Mothership care about this new venture? What is the new venture going to *give* to the Mothership? Revenue and growth are obviously key, but there are many other ways the new venture can add value to the Mothership.

Once it demonstrates its value to the Mothership, the new venture can articulate what it needs to *get* from the Mothership to be successful. It can also explain how, with the help of the Mothership, the new venture can create moats the competition can't cross.

To identify Gives and Gets, list everything that needs to or will flow between your new venture and the Mothership—for example, new customers, data, use of brand, website, PR, skills, cross-selling, upselling, and others, and capture them in your pitch deck. Should the NVB decide to fund and launch the venture, one of the NVB's primary jobs is to help the venture seize the Mothership advantage by providing access to those items identified by the venture team.

Risks and Competition

While the NVB will likely be most focused on the numbers, it *should* pay more attention to the risks the team has identified and what small bets, experiments, and pilots the team will use to mitigate those risks, including identifying actual or potential competition.

The team needs to be methodical as it thinks about risk, not least because it will make the eventual presentation of those risks to the NVB more persuasive. At Mach49 we walk the team through the following four steps:

1. **Identification.** What are your biggest risks? Or what's the target journey you want and what are the risks along that journey?

2. **Testing.** What experiments are you running or will run to address those risks?

3. **Support.** What do you need to run those experiments (product, people, money, permission, etc.)?

4. **Metrics.** How will you measure success of your experiments? How will you know you can mitigate or eliminate those risks?

WE WILL MEASURE, TRACK, AND EXPERIMENT TO DRIVE THESE METRICS	**Add, Edit, Favorite** or **Share** Listings **Connect** with Tenant/Broker/Owner **Downloads** of Tour Companion App **Tour** a Space (take pictures, reviews) **Connect** to Service Provider (e.g., lawyer, contractor) **% Engaged** in Both Find & Acquire in Life Cycle

Risks can be broadly categorized into market or customer risks, product or technical risks, business or financial risks, and Mothership risks. For example:

Thinking about the customer:
- How well can you define the target customer?

  – Is it vague, as in "enterprise"?

  – Or specific, as in "CFOs in US companies with <$100 million in industries X, Y, and Z"?

- How aware are customers of their pain?

  – Is it a priority or something nice to have?

  – Have they already hacked together proxy solutions?

  – How easy will it be for them to adopt the solution? (That is, do they have to dramatically change the way they currently live or work?)

- How many customers are there?
  - Is there a single customer?
  - Is it a marketplace with a small, identifiable number of constituents?
  - Is it a potential customer base that numbers in the thousands or millions of members?

Thinking about the product:
- How obvious is it?
  - Is the definition very specific (for example, a digital platform, hardware, a tech-enabled service, an entertainment platform, or a new food)?
  - How many components does the solution comprise (for example, web app, or hardware and app, etc.)?
- Is the user experience clear?
  - Can you easily create some user scenarios?
  - Is the user experience easy or difficult to define or articulate?
  - Does the product have clear functional boundaries?
- Can you build it?
  - Do the solution components seem easy or difficult to build?
  - If there is a predictive or learning component, are you confident that there's signal in the data?
  - Does it require integration with other solutions?
  - Does it depend heavily on "gets" from the Mothership?
- How much will it cost to build?
  - Is the solution footprint large or small?
  - Does it need scarce or expensive resources to design and build?
  - Is it a monolithic solution or can it be built incrementally (that is, it's an MVP and agile friendly)?

Thinking about the business:
- Is the revenue model obvious?
  - Is there a single source of revenue (for example, one-off purchase, subscription, etc.)?
  - Are the user and the economic buyer the same person?
  - If it's a marketplace, do both the buyer and seller have an incentive to participate?
  - Are there examples of successful companies with a similar revenue model?
- How big is the market?
  - How large is the TAM? How much of that is the United States and how much the rest of the world?
  - What's the serviceable market?
  - How big is the initial target subsegment?
- What are the unit economics?
  - Are margins high or low?

- Is the cost of goods sold significant?
- What are the cash flow dynamics (for example, does it require large inventories)?

• How do we market and sell it?
  - Will it be expensive to find and acquire customers?
  - Will your brand de-risk the purchase for the buyer or user?
  - Can you sell it through your existing channels, or do you have to build a new channel?

• From which companies do we see existing or future competition?
  - Do you have competitive advantages against those companies, and if so, what are they and how will you deploy them?
  - Can you build a moat around your fledgling venture?

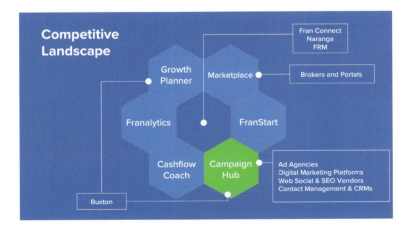

Thinking about the Mothership:
• Are you the right people to build this?
  - Does this new venture concept align with your strategy?
  - How many adjacencies is it from your core business?
  - Does it leverage your unique assets and capabilities as a decisive competitive advantage?
  - Does it conflict with regulatory constraints?

• Can you find a home for it?
  - Is there an obvious and palatable organizational home (inside or outside) for this new venture?
  - Will someone be willing and eager to sponsor it?
  - Is there budget to fund it? Are the economics (operating expense, capital expense, margins) acceptable to the Mothership?

• Will it gain internal support?
  - How will it interact operationally with the Mothership? Legal, finance, HR, IT, procurement?
  - Does it have special requirements that are counter to your operating policies?
  - Will you be able to hire and compensate the right team to build this?

These are just a few of the questions the team must ask as it builds the business and operating plan. Throughout the incubation, great New Venture Teams keep a "parking lot" for risk items they know they will need to address.

Risks and Mitigation

	MONTH 0-3	MONTH 4-6	MONTH 7-12	MONTH 13-27
Risks	• Access to data • Converting prospects to pilots • Mothership governance	• Quality of data • Differentiating from existing services • Leveraging existing IP	• Challenge showing ROI to customers • Vendor Integrations	• Direct sales model is difficult to implement • Customer conversion • Customer retention • Synergy realization
How Will We De-Risk	• Customer provides data on regular basis • Pilot gives and gets • Operationalize mobility steering committee	• Test data received from pilots • Continuous MVP validation testing • Conduct additional customer development interviews • Deploy IP on pilots • Create Mobility Dashboard	• Co-create ROI model with pilots and vendors • Select vendor partners with highest market penetration with an open culture	• Market acceptance of price point and subscription terms • Tracking CSAT and NPS and usage metrics • Leverage phase gate process

Why Us?

Here we make the definitive case for why the combined might of the venture plus the Mothership can and should *win*. We address the key competitive advantages that makes launching this venture a logical and exciting proposition.

Immediate Next Steps Post-NVB Decision to Launch and Fund

Remember, this venture has been a real startup since the first day it started incubating. This effort has not been an abstract or theoretical exercise; you have been sitting for months in that physical or virtual room to create, build, and launch a new venture to drive meaningful growth for the Mothership. Although the official Incubate phase is twelve weeks, Week 13 comes immediately afterward, and your team needs to be ready to work on your newly funded startup.

At this point, you are likely to have pilots lined up and beta customers wanting to be served. While the NVB may not make an immediate decision, until it does, your team needs to maintain its momentum. The Do It on Monday list identifies the immediate next steps for the team once the go/no-go decision is made.

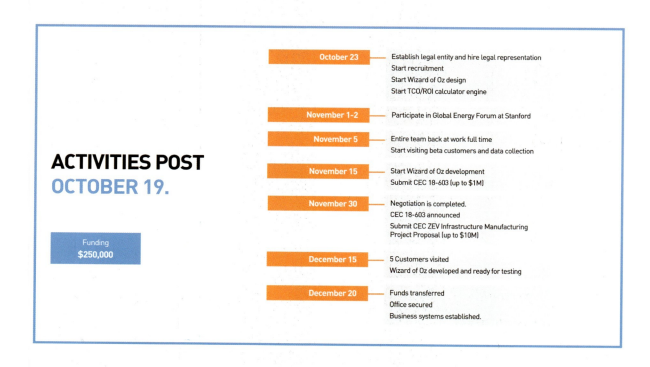

DO IT ON MONDAY

☐ Identify Branches and Client Sites for Experiments

☐ Initiate Experiment Partnerships

☐ Engage with Pilot Branches and Locations

☐ Define Data Needs and Low-Impact Data Capture

☐ Adjust Experiments Calendar with Branch Input

☐ Develop Communications Strategy and Cadence

You rock! For your venture to get to this point, it has successfully demonstrated:

- Lots of customer pain
- A huge market
- A big opportunity to drive growth for the Mothership, and
- A product or service that is eminently buildable

Congratulations! Having rigorously demonstrated all of the above, your venture *should* get funded, or the NVB, not you, has not been doing its job.

While the team members deserve a few days of downtime, they will be excited to maintain the momentum and move to the Accelerate phase. There's no rest for the weary; your excited pilot customers are waiting.

Let's launch this venture.

Chapter 08

Accelerate

Moving Ventures from Funding to Product-Market Fit and First Revenue

Your New Venture Team has now traveled, in just twelve weeks, from the glimmerings of an idea to a business plan and, most importantly, to *funding*.

This achievement is extraordinary. Now is the moment to stop, catch your breath, and put what you've just accomplished into perspective. And please celebrate.

Always celebrate the milestones in a company's story. It builds morale, binds the team together in a sense of shared accomplishment, and marks a point of transition between one critical company era and the next, in the process, motivating the players to take on the next set of tasks. So, go out and have a great dinner. Raise toasts to each other. Tell war stories. Get a good night's sleep. But get ready: in the morning, the *real* company history begins. In the long run, you will look back on these twelve weeks—as vital as they have been—as a mere prelude. Now, the challenge becomes taking that nascent enterprise and building it into a robust and fast-growing company.

→ Accelerate 101

Too many people believe that getting funded at the end of the Incubate phase means the venture has *arrived*. However, it is actually during the Accelerate phase that the proverbial rubber meets the road. If Ideate is getting to a venture idea that can be incubated, and Incubate is getting from the idea to a fundable startup with a robust business and execution plan, Accelerate is where you take that great venture, launch it, and grow it—achieving product-market fit and early revenue. In fact, when we say our success rate is 90 percent, we don't mean the number of funded ventures coming out of the Incubate phase. That's the easy part. We calculate that number based off ventures that are in the market, with customers demonstrating a willingness to pay—giving the venture its first real revenue.

At Mach49, we understand this phase vividly, having gone through it ourselves, often many times. Clement Wang, Mach49 executive vice president and co-head of our Venture Building business, was part of the early leadership team driving product for both WebEx and Zuora, both extremely successful startups. In the early days of incubating Mach49, our MVP was centered around Ideate and Incubate. However, Clement quickly realized that in the end, getting ventures through the Accelerate phase to first revenue was *really* what was going to matter most. He recognized that, especially as we launched new ventures inside large companies, we were going to have to help these startups fight their two-front war (as Steve Blank defines it)—the external front, competitors in the market including other startups, *and* the internal front, the inertia, friction, orthodoxies, and antibodies that might prevent the ventures from reaching escape velocity. Beyond managing the Mothership, we needed to ensure the ventures could seize the Mothership advantage to beat the startups at their own game.

He was right. So, Clement; David Charpie, EVP and co-head of Venture Building and seven-time CEO of both internal and external startups; Bill Kingsley, twenty-five-year veteran venture capitalist, now Mach49 SVP, Growth and Scale, and Board Member-in-Residence; and James Beriker, one of Silicon Valley's super-successful serial entrepreneur CEOs, who is Mach49's SVP, Global Venture Success and Development, and CEO-in-Residence, leveraged their collective wisdom and experience to build an Accelerate framework that our clients' new ventures all live by post–Pitch Day.

We focus significant energy on the Accelerate phase—especially when the Mothership wants to accelerate the new venture on its own—because getting the company up and running; securing passionate, motivated early team members; piloting your business and go-to-market model; launching the MVP; and getting to first revenue are major milestones that are critical to ensuring the venture can help drive growth for the Mothership.

Once the flywheel is turning for the venture, large companies are usually terrific at scaling. But they tend to look at the Accelerate phase merely as the pause between Incubate and Scale. That is a dangerous attitude, because the Accelerate phase is just the opposite.

You need to be as conscious and deliberate during the Accelerate phase as you were during the Ideate and Incubate phases. This is not the time to let your attention lag.

REAL-LIFE INTRAPRENEURSHIP

If you Google "how to start a startup," you will see hundreds of results, such as:

- **The 8 Best Startup Books**
- **31+ Best Startup Books for Entrepreneurs to Read**
- **12 Books You Should Read Before Starting a Business**

And the beat goes on. If you go on Amazon, there are pages and pages of books on the subject. Look more broadly, and there are hundreds of blog posts and podcasts as well.

The reality is that many of these books and articles are fine but too many deal only with theory. They don't give you practical advice on what you need to do on a daily basis to build a company, because they can't; they aren't sitting next to you every day dealing with real-time issues as they emerge. If you are in the midst of starting such a new venture, if you either are on the NVB or are one of the founding Intrapreneurs, you probably won't have time to read one of the books, let alone all of them. So, instead, we are going to lay out how we recommend approaching each stage of the Accelerate phase.

If you do want to explore some startup resources, two sources stand out by providing practical and

tactical advice on growing your company (which is what we care about, since we are 100 percent focused on execution):

- **Steve Blank and Bob Dorf's** *The Startup Owner's Manual*
- **Sam Altman's curated and celebrated** *How to Start a Startup* **class, offered in person at Stanford University but available online.* Sam was the successor CEO to Paul Graham, the legendary founder of Y Combinator, the original startup incubator in Silicon Valley.**

*"How to Start a Startup," https://startupclass.samaltman.com/.

→ Preconditions for Moving to Accelerate

More and more, clients are coming to us with ventures they incubated on their own but are finding the Accelerate phase is not going well. They typically want us to assess those ventures to see where there might be gaps, determine what they need to do to remediate the venture (often they didn't interview nearly enough customers), or help them build an Accelerate plan to take them forward faster. If you are one of those teams that has already incubated a venture and just wants to jump straight into the Accelerate phase, let's review, at a high level, the preconditions for moving out of the Incubate phase and into Accelerate:

- The incubation process has discovered real pain, hopes, or aspirations through rigorous customer development interviews that have led to a product or solution to address that opportunity.
- The target segment and customers have been identified, and there are pilot customers who have expressed an interest in participating once you move to the Accelerate phase.
- The product or solution has potential to result in a material innovation to an existing product, technology, business model, or other type of innovation that opens a new greenfield opportunity.
- A detailed ecosystem or competitive mapping exercise has been completed, resulting in:
  – A belief that the venture can address a significant opening in the market in a differentiated way.
  – Initial validation that the market is large enough to support meaningful revenue and profit at scale for the Mothership.
  – Confirmation that there are no entrenched leaders in the market that have a business model or other significant advantage over the new venture. (Competition is fine, especially if the Mothership is seriously engaged in helping the new venture. However, if you find that, for example, some PE firm has already committed billions of dollars to the exact space you are targeting, the Mothership is unlikely to commit to that level of investment, nor should it, so move on. There are plenty of other sandboxes to play in.)
- The Mothership has a right to play in this market and has assets that can provide the venture with an unfair competitive advantage versus others.
- There is a short-term, in-market experimentation framework or plan focused on de-risking the business killers and validating core assumptions of the venture.

If you have been reading our how-to guide from the beginning and followed the steps we have laid out thus far, your business, execution, and operating plan should have confirmed all that and more. However, if you are a team that didn't follow our method and can't check the box on all the points above, please go back and start the book from the beginning.

→ Accelerate Pro Tips That Really Make a Difference

While you may review blogs, videos, web posts, articles, podcasts, or any number of other sources for inspiration, the number-one best action to take when your venture moves to Accelerate is to surround yourself with *industry veterans*—people who have built a successful startup or started a business from scratch. "A" players bring "A" players, and there is no substitute for experience to teach a venture how to launch and scale.

When we founded Mach49, we did not hire traditional consultants; instead, we banded together an experienced and wise group of successful entrepreneurs who had *actually* built companies with successful outcomes. As serial entrepreneurs, we also had some failures under our collective belt, which gave us unmatched perspective on what works and what does not. In fact, Silicon Valley VCs often back entrepreneurs who have failed before. Why? Because they are savvier and unlikely to make the same mistakes twice. The bottom line? Experience can make or break startups, so as the venture moves to the Accelerate phase, do not ignore the following steps.

Step 1: Curate a Great Support Network for the New Venture

There are a number of ways to surround and support the new venture with talent and wisdom as it launches as a now-funded company into the marketplace. The team can:

- Add to and augment the NVB
- Build an advisory board
- Hire experienced team members (from either inside or outside the Mothership)
- Find experienced subject-matter experts to tap into as needed

Silicon Valley evolved as a result of what could be described (in Californese) as a karmic sense of collaboration and commitment to helping others. Why? Because *what goes around comes around*.

But a team does not have to be in Silicon Valley to find helpful peers. Almost every city has incubators and accelerators that the team can visit or get involved with to find support. Because internal venture teams are part of a large company with core competencies, assets, capabilities, and customers, the team members have a built-in advantage by making use of those resources. Conversely, don't forget that the team itself has singular talents, not to mention a very up-to-date understanding of new technologies and the state of the market. Thus, the team can reciprocate in a meaningful way for the help it has received to date by making its own members' expertise available to the Mothership, say, the venture team's big data expert consulting to the parent company's IT operations.

Networking is an invaluable skill for entrepreneurs, especially during the Accelerate phase. For ad hoc external support and wisdom, teams can often find individuals who are happy to do a one-off review or take a meeting to address a topic. For longer-term engagement, ideally, all of these people can be given a monetary incentive that enables them to share in the upside of the new venture in some way. Since that is true of team members as well, we discuss compensation options for ventures that remain inside the Mothership in chapter 10.

If the venture is lucky enough to have a successful, serial entrepreneur on the founding team, this can be a real advantage. In that scenario, the venture probably doesn't need any more help beyond its board, ideally a small group of engaged, experienced, and useful board members drawn from both inside and outside the Mothership.

In other cases, the founding team is remarkable, with tremendous potential, but the opportunity it has surfaced does not fall neatly into its experiences or networks. For those ventures, the team should look to find experienced operators as advisers.

Some examples of the types of people who can be helpful are:

- Venture capitalists
- Global sales executives
- Former founders or startup CEOs
- Product gurus
- Go-to-market experts
- CFOs or startup finance specialists
- Faculty from local universities
- Subject-matter experts focused on critical aspects of the venture

Step 2: Review, Retain, Remove, or Recruit the Right NVB for the Accelerate Phase

In addition to looking for additional support, internally and externally, the NVB now needs to reflect on its continuing role and, in particular, whether its current membership, which made sense during the Incubate phase, still can make a contribution during the Accelerate phase.

The goals now are to swiftly and effectively:

Make initial pilot customers successful

Build and iterate the product or service to achieve product-market fit

Subsequently drive to full business traction

Most importantly, the NVB must keep managing the venture like a startup, *not* the company's core or legacy businesses.

Thus, the NVB continues to play a significant role during the Accelerate phase, which we cover in chapter 10.

Step 3: Finalize or Find the Venture's CEO

In some cases, we have found that the Mothership or NVB has already attracted a founding CEO candidate with the requisite experience for the upcoming launch and Accelerate phase. In this circumstance, a Mach49 Board Member-in-Residence (BMIR) helps guide the CEO (as "CEO whisperer") and assists the NVB in its role as the startup's venture capitalists. This individual can also help additional team members as they transition to being entrepreneurs. The CEO needs at least *one* person on the board who can play the Mach49 BMIR role—someone the team respects and who has experience starting companies from scratch to provide the CEO support. As you move to the Accelerate phase, you need to find a similar mentor, either someone who currently sits on the NVB, a new person identified from inside the parent company, or an individual recruited from the outside.

In other cases, the new venture may now need an experienced startup CEO whose sole focus and job is to get the venture properly launched and running. While you may have thought you had a CEO or business owner candidate leading the team during the Incubate phase, sometimes the opportunity is just too different from what was originally imagined and the person in the interim CEO role or team lead role just doesn't have the experience required to lead the venture forward.

So, while this team member remains a highly valued member of the founding team, they have to accept what might feel like a demotion but really isn't. They are still a founder, and in any of the startup ecosystems that matter, that is a badge of honor, with or without the CEO title attached. From the outset, that person should already have been prepped that they might need to step aside as CEO to ensure the success of the company. If a venture finds itself in that situation, it has to recruit to fill that role. Often that search can take time, so it may be necessary to bring in *another* interim CEO from either inside or outside the Mothership to take the company forward. The goal is to help launch and lay a great foundation for the venture without losing time and momentum.

With a terrific board, a valued set of advisers identified as part of the new venture's ecosystem, and the right CEO in place, it's time to *move*.

→ Accelerate "Stages" and "Swim Lanes"

The Accelerate phase can be divided into three stages:

1. Build to Validate
2. Build to Automate
3. Build to Grow

3 ACCELERATE PHASES. The Silicon Valley Startup Approach.

"Seed" Funding
6 – 12 Months

Series "A"
12 – 18 Months

Series "B and beyond"
18+ Months

Build to Validate

- Major risks addressed
- Core assumptions validated
- Business model confirmed
- Minimum Viable Product launched
- First revenue recognized
- Strong founding team prepared for next phase
- Series "A" Pitch (Plan and Budget) developed

Build to Automate

- Product-market fit achieved
- MVP advanced through rapid iteration
- Core go-to-market capabilities developed
- Operating processes automated
- Reference customers attained
- At least $1M in revenue / ARR run-rate achieved
- Customer engagement metrics positive
- Core team expanded

Build to Grow

- Product-market-channel fit achieved
- Repeatable sales and revenue model developed
- Attractive unit economics achieved
- Operating playbooks developed for scaling
- 3x revenue / ARR run-rate achieved
- Leadership team built out
- Administrative functions developed

- Business Ready for Scale **Financing or Spin-in**
- Compelling **Transformative Purpose**
- Fully Formed **Functional Team and Board**
- Proven **Product, Business Model, and Pricing**
- **Reference Customers** Advocating for the Product
- Monthly **Revenue Growth**
- High **Customer Retention**
- **Repeatable and Measurable** Processes for:
    - Customer Acquisition
    - Customer Success and Retention
    - Product Development
    - Growth Marketing and Sales
    - Partnerships and Channels
    - Operations
- Scalable **Product Infrastructure**
- **Mothership Assets** Being Leveraged
- Operating Plan to **Scale Revenue at Optimized Unit Economics**

Swim Lanes

In addition to thinking about Accelerate in three stages, we further segment the work the venture team does during each stage of Accelerate into five "swim lanes." While most people obsess about the product, when you launch a venture, you can't forget all the other strands of work that need to happen to build a company. To keep it simple for clients, we describe five categories of activities that need to take place from here on out. Those swim lanes include:

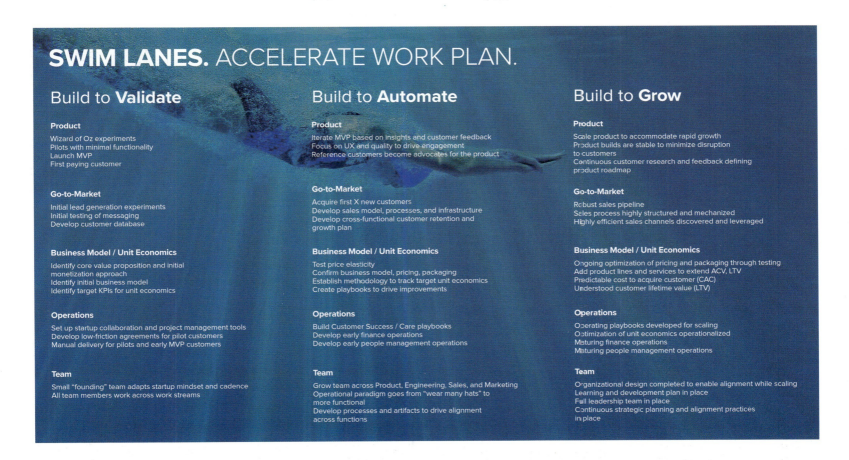

SWIM LANES. ACCELERATE WORK PLAN.

Build to **Validate**

Product
Wizard of Oz experiments
Pilots with minimal functionality
Launch MVP
First paying customer

Go-to-Market
Initial lead generation experiments
Initial testing of messaging
Develop customer database

Business Model / Unit Economics
Identify core value proposition and initial monetization approach
Identify initial business model
Identify target KPIs for unit economics

Operations
Set up startup collaboration and project management tools
Develop low-friction agreements for pilot customers
Manual delivery for pilots and early MVP customers

Team
Small "founding" team adapts startup mindset and cadence
All team members work across work streams

Build to **Automate**

Product
Iterate MVP based on insights and customer feedback
Focus on UX and quality to drive engagement
Reference customers become advocates for the product

Go-to-Market
Acquire first X new customers
Develop sales model, processes, and infrastructure
Develop cross-functional customer retention and growth plan

Business Model / Unit Economics
Test price elasticity
Confirm business model, pricing, packaging
Establish methodology to track target unit economics
Create playbooks to drive improvements

Operations
Build Customer Success / Care playbooks
Develop early finance operations
Develop early people management operations

Team
Grow team across Product, Engineering, Sales, and Marketing
Operational paradigm goes from "wear many hats" to more functional
Develop processes and artifacts to drive alignment across functions

Build to **Grow**

Product
Scale product to accommodate rapid growth
Product builds are stable to minimize disruption to customers
Continuous customer research and feedback defining product roadmap

Go-to-Market
Robust sales pipeline
Sales process highly structured and mechanized
Highly efficient sales channels discovered and leveraged

Business Model / Unit Economics
Ongoing optimization of pricing and packaging through testing
Add product lines and services to extend ACV, LTV
Predictable cost to acquire customer (CAC)
Understood customer lifetime value (LTV)

Operations
Operating playbooks developed for scaling
Optimization of unit economics operationalized
Maturing finance operations
Maturing people management operations

Team
Organizational design completed to enable alignment while scaling
Learning and development plan in place
Full leadership team in place
Continuous strategic planning and alignment practices in place

Product development and achieving product-market fit. Can you build a solution that delivers the benefits customers responded to during the incubation? What pieces can you put together to solve their pain in a way they want it to be solved?

Go to market. Can you find prospects and convert them to users and buyers? What is the best model for acquiring customers? What selling models work?

Business model. Can you get someone to pay, when and how are they likely to want to pay, and how much will they be willing to pay?

Operations or unit economics. Can you deliver the product, solution, or experience to the customer profitably? How will you set up the infrastructure? Will you take advantage of shared services at the Mothership? How? Which ones?

Team. Can you hire—and pay—the team you need across all these swim lanes at every stage?

MISTAKES TO AVOID

Companies that tried to incubate and are now accelerating their ventures with little success often ask us to review, assess, and remediate those ventures. Part of the problem is they failed to incubate properly, so, you know how it goes: garbage in, garbage out. In other cases, the incubation may have been just fine, but when the team moved to Accelerate, it made a series of mistakes all too common among startups:

- Long development cycles before proving a benefit to customers; focusing on building the whole product without doing a series of tests soliciting iterative feedback from customers at every step

- Go-big mentality, usually accompanied by a big-bang release (marketing splash) before having product-market fit

- Scaling user acquisition without a proven business model and path to positive unit economics

So how *do* you give your venture the *best* possible chance for success during the Accelerate phase? Keep focusing on customers, execute the plan you built during the Incubate phase, pivot as you develop new information during the Accelerate stages, and maintain the same humility and growth mindset you adopted while incubating.

→ Objectives and Outcomes of Each Stage of Accelerate

Build to Validate

During this phase, your team needs to learn as quickly as possible what works and what doesn't in a particular area. In the early stages of Accelerate, you need to test key assumptions on a handful of pilot customers. The key objective is *learning*.

You may very well build things that you know you'll eventually throw out or do things that don't scale in order to learn as quickly as possible.

Key Objectives

- Run customer pilots.
- Continue customer development learning.
- Find the cheapest or fastest ways to test assumptions.
- Turn unknowns about mitigating risks into knowns.
- Build a Wizard of Oz version first to find out what customers like; even more importantly find the commonalities among customers, what they like and how to serve them, so the venture doesn't build something bespoke for each customer.
- As automation requirements become clear, build quick enhancements, and insert into the testing cycle.
- Measure and evaluate usage and engagement.

Key Outcomes

- Early customers engaged, actively using the product, and willing to be a reference.
- Deep, granular understanding of the product or service and customer engagement journey.
- Early indication of willingness to pay. In the best case, first revenue recognized.
- Refined go-to-market and business model strategy confirmed.
- Mothership support operationalized. (The NVB must appoint and empower New Venture Advocates to support the venture; more on this in chapter 10.)
- Team self-sufficient and highly functional.
- MVP launched.
- Series "A" Pitch ready to take to NVB (plan and budget).

Once you have achieved most of these outcomes, you know you are ready to move on to the next stage.

A SPECIAL NOTE FROM CLEMENT WANG ON PRODUCT DEVELOPMENT DURING THE BUILD TO VALIDATE PHASE

During the Build to Validate phase, the team is usually engaged with a small number of pilot customers and building the minimum product necessary to make those customers successful. This build may include experiments in which the team is performing many of the functions manually (affectionately known as Wizard of Oz in early-product development because while it looks finished to the end user or customer when you are testing it, many of the product functions are happening manually "behind the curtain"), perhaps supported by minimal builds or prototypes that simulate what an online, automated, or physical experience may look or feel like.

At this stage, the development tends to focus on quick turns and fast iterations, with an emphasis on learning exactly how to make customers successful and fleshing out the specific user experience to support that success. During this phase of development, the teams are not yet practicing traditional product development (agile or otherwise). Even the fastest cycles in traditional product development are too slow and too inwardly focused than what is required here. The team focuses on delivering value to the customer, reacting quickly to feedback, and removing ambiguity on what the product should be, eschewing some of the things that will become more important when the team is ready to move to a more mature product development model such as architecture, scalability, or even quality control. For example, during this phase, the team may throw out some or all of the technical build as it learns—and rapidly zeros in on—an exact spec that can be built and fully automated. During this interval, the venture team needs to find a development partner outside the parent company, or an internal group or individual (whether already an employee or hired for the role) who is philosophically aligned with the Build to Validate ethos. Too many product development firms want a full spec and statement of work, as well as the excessive and premature fees that go with that, too early.

One of the key deliverables of the Build to Validate phase is a detailed understanding of the MVP, based on continuing interactions with pilot customers, including feature prioritization and a road map for the upcoming Build to Automate work streams. We prefer to work with development teams, either internal or external, that believe in continuing the cadence of build sprints delivering rapid, high-quality iterations. We clearly guide teams to withstand the pressure to build a detailed specification at the beginning of the Build to Validate phase. If anything, we want the team to finalize the development schedule for hardening the product only at the end of the Build to Validate work stream.

> While we are focused on Build to Validate, the best development organizations (whether in-house or external) continue to iterate throughout the Build to Automate phase and even as they move to the later Build to Grow stage. The development cycles may slow to weekly or monthly as the emphasis shifts from optimizing for speed, agility, and learning to standardizing architecture, scalability, quality, reliability, and so on, especially as the number of customers increases and the cost of bad quality, outages, and other issues rises as well.

Build to Automate

Now that the team has a deep understanding of what it takes to make early customers successful, it can now turn its attention toward standardizing or automating what it has learned. Across the first handful of customers, patterns will have emerged, and the team can make an informed choice about what to mobilize the company around that is most likely to work with the most customers.

From a product development perspective, usually a playbook emerges that lays out how a customer will experience the product from initial contact through sale, and then through delivery. The team can now start to build out the product; in the case of software, this usually means building out the front end and back end of the product and eliminating the manual processing that has been happening in the background during the Build to Validate phase. In the case of a service, hardware, or physical (food, clothing, etc.) product, this can mean codifying a playbook or building out the standard manufacturing or production and supply chain processes required to deliver the product. It is still important to continue learning and iterating during this phase. But the focus now is on how to standardize the patterns that emerge, rather than creating a custom experience for each customer. One key milestone from this phase likely will be a Version 1 release of the product that is ready to launch into the market.

Key Objectives

- Augment or adapt the Build to Automate plan as necessary, based on milestones achieved.

- Engage product and development leads to deliver a rapid, high-quality build cycle that yields an increasing level of predictability and certainty to customers and other stakeholders with integrated feedback.

- Develop a sales pipeline qualification tool reflecting the buying process.

- Create, test, and verify the "who" and "how" for other key workflows and operational or financial assumptions, such as marketing, go to market, sales, onboarding, service, and so on.

- Continue to hire and develop a high-functioning team that can get a generally available product into the market.

- Connections to the various Mothership functions are operationalized and functioning well.

Key Outcomes

- Product and customer product-market fit is achieved. The MVP is advanced through rapid iteration to a more fully built and launched product or service in the market. There is user growth on a platform ramping up with measurable progress toward product-market fit (one measure we've adopted is measuring that at least 40 percent of users would be "very disappointed" if they could no longer have access to the product, service, solution, experience, or process).

- Go to market. The venture should have a repeatable sales funnel and pipeline and a well-defined playbook for generating leads and closing sales. The venture should also have a solid understanding of messaging by target segment and by channel that the team has tested and validated to drive adoption. There should be indications of customers becoming evangelists or references. Word of mouth is spreading, leading to a level of virality in the customer acquisition process that is demonstrating strong product-market fit by this point as well.

- Business model. Customers are paying for value received, and the venture has developed standard pricing or packaging.

- Operations or unit economics. The venture should have a repeatable way of getting customers up and running on or accessing the product or service. Retention rates should be high, and the sales team should be getting into a position to ultimately upsell the customers. The team is measuring unit economics, and while it may not have positive unit economics yet, it has some good hypotheses about how it might get there and is testing those hypotheses. The team should also be working on setting up the systems and processes associated with the Mothership Gives and Gets as outlined in its business, operations, and execution plan.

Once the team has achieved most of these outcomes, it knows it is ready to move to the Build to Grow stage.

Build to Grow

By the time the team reaches this stage, it has many successful customers. It also has built a repeatable, predictable standardized or automated way for building and delivering the product or service, finding and converting prospects into users, and making those prospects successful. During Build to Grow, you are still focused on continuing to rapidly grow your customer base and optimizing all parts of the business. The main objective is to get to positive unit economics in the business while proving out key growth levers including optimizing the cost of sales and cost of delivery, and tweaking pricing to maximize revenues. There is a seamless transition you may not even notice, moving from Building to Automate and Building to Grow, as the team does the following:

- Codifies all aspects and operations of the business, including building operating playbooks developed to enable you to bring people on quickly and really help the company as it hopefully hits the hypergrowth phase.

- Measures, augments, and corrects processes across:

  – Talent acquisition

  – Customer acquisition, sales, channels

  – Product development

  – Marketing

  – Operations

  – Other departments and functions you have added as needed.

- Watches for scaling challenges that may emerge across the business and quickly corrects or addresses them.
- Makes sure revenue growth levers are widely understood and, most importantly, managed.
- Demonstrates it has operationalized how to leverage assets, capabilities, core competencies, channels, customers, and so on from the Mothership. Successfully engaging the Mothership is what will help you leapfrog traditional startups. (For more on seizing the Mothership advantage with New Venture Advocates, see chapter 10.)

By this time, the business should have a playbook for everything and be operating as a well-oiled machine having done a ton of automation and standardization across all the swim lanes. Scaling is then taking that well-optimized playbook and running the venture as a fully functioning Mothership business unit or division. As a full-fledged line of business, the venture is now entering the stage where large companies excel—Scaling. The objectives of the venture or business unit are now the goals the team and the NVB sets for themselves as a normal operating business, and the outcomes are now the key performance indicators you have agreed on and adopted. At this point, keep going.

→ Maintain the Discipline You Learned during Incubate

Just as there were work plans, scripts, tools, and processes to ensure your venture team was embarking on a repeatable, scalable journey leading to a rigorous and robust business and execution plan during the Incubate phase, so too must you maintain that discipline during Accelerate, only at this point the team needs to be fully functioning and able to run on its own. Each of your ventures will be unique so while we can help you with the phases and stages and give you target objectives and outcomes, the way you work is now on you.

While the stages and swim lanes are constant, your actual activities vary by venture. You have laid out quite a few in your Pitch Day business and execution plan, but in the early days of Accelerate, you need to get more granular and create a work plan with your team that captures the main activities by stage and by swim lane.

Here is a spreadsheet from a real venture we built that outlines the work to do across each swim lane. A number of the activities are similar to those you will need to accomplish, but there are others that will be unique to your venture. The good news is that if you have hired the right team members early on, this is where their operating expertise kicks in and they will know what tasks and activities they need to complete, whether they are the go-to-market lead, the product lead, the finance or operations lead, your HR director, or any other early hire.

Hiring

Task	Week 1	Week 2	Week 3	Week 4	Week 5	Week 6	Week 7	Week 8	Week 9	Week 10	Week 11	Week 12
Design Hiring FT plan: CEO and Product Lead	■											
Define Team Compensation/Incentives with mothership	■	■										
Post CEO and Product Lead roles		■										
Source, Screen and Interview candidates. Work with mothership to complete hires		■	■	■								
HR:												
- Offer letters, EE mgmt				■	■							
- Benefits admin				■	■							
- Stock admin				■	■							
Create briefing deck for new hires/onboarding				■	■							
Design Hiring plan: Additional hires in Months 4-12					■	■						
Define Team Compensation/Incentives with mothership for external and internal hires for new roles					■	■						
Develop candidate pool for key roles (months 4-12)						■	■					
Source, Screen and Interview candidates. Work with mothership to complete hires							■	■	■	■	■	■

Sales & Marketing

Task	Week 1	Week 2	Week 3	Week 4	Week 5	Week 6	Week 7	Week 8	Week 9	Week 10	Week 11	Week 12
Decide on how to use Mothership name with New Venture Brand	■	■										
Register trademark		■										
Update Existing Website to match new trademark and affiliation with Mothership		■	■	■	■							
Briefing Deck about New Venture	■											

Customer & Product Development

Task	Week 1	Week 2	Week 3	Week 4	Week 5	Week 6	Week 7	Week 8	Week 9	Week 10	Week 11	Week 12
Mine Airtable to generate complete view of Pilot targets	■											
Learn rapid iteration testing methodology	■											
Build initial testing frameworks for risk mitigation	■											
Test lead gen approach	■	■	■	■	■	■	■	■	■	■	■	■
Test value props / GTM	■	■	■	■	■	■	■	■	■	■	■	■
Test Product feature / usability	■	■	■	■	■	■	■	■	■	■	■	■
Complete NDA/MOU	■											
Continue discussion with existing potential pilots		■	■									
Get signed NDA / MOU with first 3 Pilots		■	■									
Get CPODs / EMEA Demo		■	■									
Conceptualize / iterate initial wizard of oz product		■	■	■								
Define Data gathering			■	■								
Test Data Delivery				■	■	■						
Test Data Quality				■	■	■						
Generate Test Insights					■	■	■					
Test Existing CPODS / EMEA IP						■	■					
Get signed NDA / MOU with next set of Pilots							■	■				

Operations

Task	Week 1	Week 2	Week 3	Week 4	Week 5	Week 6	Week 7	Week 8	Week 9	Week 10	Week 11	Week 12
Daily Standups	■	■	■	■	■	■	■	■	■	■	■	■
Weekly Synthesis and 1:1s	■	■	■	■	■	■	■	■	■	■	■	■
Weekly Sponsor Meeting	■	■	■	■	■	■	■	■	■	■	■	■
EMEA Share-out Meeting	■	■	■	■	■	■	■	■	■	■	■	■

Accounting, Financing, & Reporting

Task	Week 1	Week 2	Week 3	Week 4	Week 5	Week 6	Week 7	Week 8	Week 9	Week 10	Week 11	Week 12
- Controller: Establish cash control/purchasing	■											
- Cash mgmt, budget/forecast				■				■				■
- KPIs, mgmt reporting, BOD/investor reporting				■				■				■

Governance

Task	Week 1	Week 2	Week 3	Week 4	Week 5	Week 6	Week 7	Week 8	Week 9	Week 10	Week 11	Week 12
Define NVB for Accelerate	■											
Confirm entity for contracts	■											
Board calendar for next 6 months established	■											
Board time commitment and scheduling	■											
Create, socialize first period OKRs	■											
OKR and pivot training for board	■	■										
Finalize OKRs to socialize with NVB		■										
Approve OKRs with NVB		■										
Review and Revise OKR definitions												
Prepare and socialize board package			■	■				■				■
Send board package 72 hours in advance to NVB			■	■				■				■
Monthly Board Meeting				■				■				■

Aligned on the quarterly plan, your team can then dive into the nitty-gritty and lay out an even more precise twelve-week plan so everyone is clear on what each team member is working on.

Continue to do your daily stand-ups, nightly sit-downs, and weekly synthesis, as the pace quickens even more. Given that each of you is likely swimming in your own lane, the need to stay coordinated and connected becomes even more critical.

If you are looking for the very first step, keep in mind that Accelerate starts where Incubate just ended. Remember the Do It on Monday slide we taught you to write for your new venture in the last chapter? Pull it out; the reason you wrote that list was so that once you were funded, you knew what your immediate next steps were going to be—Day 1 of Accelerate. Without that list, the sheer number of tasks that now need to be done can be daunting and overwhelming. Yes, you have your business and execution plan and now you have a detailed work plan, but you also have the first steps. The rest will flow from there, we promise.

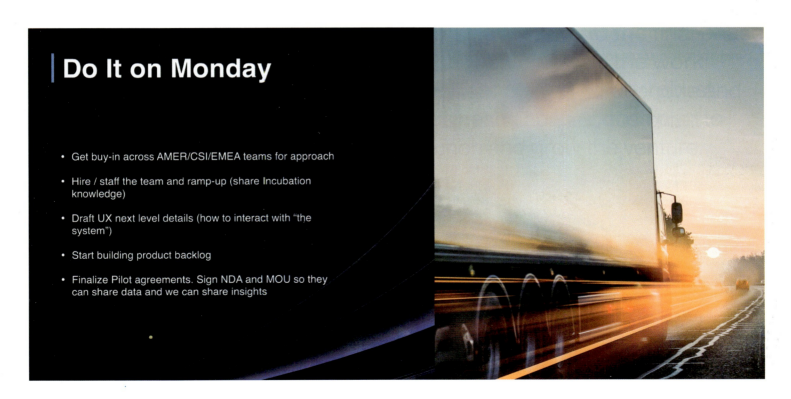

Do It on Monday

- Get buy-in across AMER/CSI/EMEA teams for approach
- Hire / staff the team and ramp-up (share Incubation knowledge)
- Draft UX next level details (how to interact with "the system")
- Start building product backlog
- Finalize Pilot agreements. Sign NDA and MOU so they can share data and we can share insights

→ # Does Your Venture Stand a Chance?

Absolutely! Ventures like yours—born out of the Global 1000—really do become successful companies as you progress through the Accelerate phase, building the venture and leveraging the competitive advantages of the Mothership. If you continue to focus on execution, you too will get to experience the exciting transformation your peers have experienced.

From this image on Pitch Day:

To a launched venture and first revenue during Accelerate:

From this image on Pitch Day:

To a launched venture and first revenue during Accelerate:

While launching one new venture into the marketplace is exciting, for a multinational, multibillion-dollar Global 1000 company, that is just a pebble in the pond. The real benefit comes when the company gets serious about Venture Building and recognizes that perpetual renewal is key to thriving over the long term. That's when a company gets aggressive about managing the Mothership and seizing the advantages it has over any well-funded startup. It takes this repeatable, scalable model, and methodology and builds its own Venture Factory—with its own team—to create a pipeline and portfolio of new ventures to drive meaningful growth.

Let's turn to part 3 and look at how Global 1000s are building their own Growth Engines—institutionalizing disruption by designing and launching a Venture Factory to handle all phases of new venture creation—Ideate, Incubate, Accelerate, Scale.

With methodology, tools, templates, people, and process in hand, let's dive into what else you need to build a world-class Venture Factory.

Part 03

Institutionalizing Growth

Chapter 09

Building Your Own Venture Factory

Institutionalizing Growth for Decades to Come

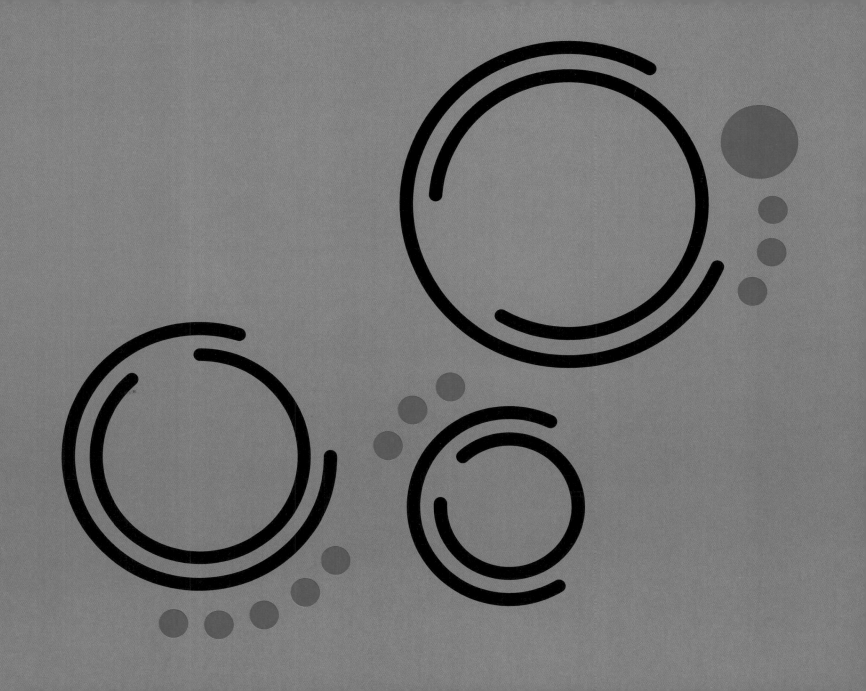

To truly institutionalize growth—and put us out of a job—every company can and should build and run its *own* Venture Factory.

We don't like to call it just an incubator, because as you now have learned, to be successful, you need to master the full spectrum of venture creation—Ideate, Incubate, Accelerate, and Scale.

Building a Venture Factory ensures that the Mothership doesn't just launch one new venture one time, but has the platform, people, methodology, and tools in place to create a pipeline and portfolio of new ventures to drive growth in perpetuity.

A NOTE ON NAMING

In the introduction, we noted that to build a thriving Growth Engine for your company, you need four arrows in your Growth Engine quiver: organic Venture Building through your own incubator/accelerator—your own Venture Factory—*plus* the ability to do corporate venture investing, strategic partnering, and tactical M&A (the latter three are disrupting outside-in topics we must leave for another day). While the focus thus far has been on how to build each venture, we are devoting this chapter to how to build your own Venture Factory. However, vocabulary is a funny thing, and many companies use different names for the Venture Building arm of their Growth Engines. Besides Venture Factory, you will hear people use the terms Accelerator, an Incubator and Accelerator, a Venture Studio, *Company Name*X (after GoogleX's famous incubator), Startup Studio, Playground, Innovation Lab, and more. You can choose your own name, but for clarity we will stick with Venture Factory.

We have invested many years developing a blueprint for building a Venture Factory. So, in sharing this blueprint, not only are you getting lessons learned from those who have gone before you, but you are getting the benefit of our own ideation, incubation, and acceleration work over the years perfecting the model.

To be clear, not every client of ours has built a Venture Factory; but every one of them knows that they can. What has been most interesting to us is how our work has shifted from most companies coming to us focused on creating one or two ventures and then deciding they want to build a Venture Factory to most companies coming to us with the goal of launching their own Venture Factory, leveraging the early ventures as a way for their team to learn by doing. An internal Venture Factory allows you to institutionalize and scale your growth efforts for decades to come.

→ The Benefits of Building a Venture Factory

Among the many benefits to building a Venture Factory, keep these three in mind as prime.

New ventures. A Venture Factory drives growth by creating and launching a portfolio of high-quality new ventures, manages the downside risk by reducing the greatest amount of risk on the least amount of capital, and develops a laser-like focus on solving customer pain.

Talent. Building a Venture Factory sends a message that the company is committed to real innovation and providing creative growth opportunities for its people (not just growth for its shareholders), which in turn enables the company to recruit and retain a pool of highly motivated and often exceptionally talented, internal entrepreneurs. Our Venture Factories often become the darling of the chief human resources officer because they can set up a rotation through the incubator and accelerator for their best and brightest that is sure to beat any of the offerings from their worn-out, twentieth-century catalog of leadership development programs.

Growth-capable executive leadership. By focusing on growth through Venture Building, senior executives are forced to expand their playbook and shift their mindset from being management review board members to adopting the discipline and mindset of top-tier VCs in Silicon Valley and beyond. They learn to execute a portfolio strategy, building many, not just one; to think in terms of seed funding, not overspending too early; to focus on option value, not net present value; and to obsess on customer acquisition and revenue as the early key performance indicators (KPIs) most relevant to a startup, not short-term profit.

WHY CORPORATE INCUBATORS AND ACCELERATORS FAIL

If there were a warning label on this chapter, it would be this: corporate incubators and accelerators have a bad reputation. Sifted, the terrific, new, innovation media platform launched by the *Financial Times*, asked if that negative reputation was deserved. Based on the research it cited by Alex Mahr of Stryber, the answer is yes.* He found that traditional startups have an 11 percent success rate; that increases to 12 percent if the venture had been part of a traditional incubator and accelerator program such as Y Combinator, Techstars, 500 Startups, and

so on, *unless* that startup had been part of a corporate accelerator, in which case only 8 percent succeeded. Sifted asked me to write a response to the research, sharing my perspective on why corporate accelerators failed. I highlighted three reasons:

- **No methodology.** Corporations keep trying traditional VC and startup incubator models—money and mentors. That model doesn't work for large corporations, as VCs and incubators like Y Combinator can afford large failure rates because just one or two successes can return their funds and make their limited partners happy. Corporations need much higher success rates or their Venture Factories will get shut down. Higher success rates come with a customer-driven, repeatable, and scalable methodology for venture creation.

  This book is an antidote to the "no methodology" challenge; please stop throwing spaghetti against the wall and hoping it sticks. Your shareholders don't have that much patience.

- **Mothership friction.** Companies have the ideas, talent, assets, competencies, capital, and customers to create ventures and drive growth. Seizing the Mothership advantage for your ventures helps you beat the startups at their own game. Companies also have inertia, antibodies, and orthodoxies that must be overcome. Corporate accelerators often fail to engage the Mothership to make the from-to shifts in metrics, compensation, procurement, policies, politics, and so on to ensure their ventures can reach escape velocity and thrive. Building an ecosystem of New Venture Advocates across the company can help your newly launched ventures reach escape velocity, especially during the Accelerate phase when they most depend on the shared services of the Mothership.

- **Executive decision-makers fail to grow.** As noted earlier, a big benefit of building a Venture Factory is that it provides an opportunity for your leaders to adapt and learn new skills as well. The flip side of that is if they continue to have a management review board mindset, a quarter-to-quarter bias, and a core-legacy business rigidity, their ventures will fail and, ultimately, so will the company. Just ask the 88 percent of the *Fortune* 500 from fifty years ago that no longer exist.

---

*Maija Palmer, "This Is Why Corporate Accelerators Fail—Your Answers," Sifted, May 12, 2020, https://sifted.eu/articles/why-corporate-accelerators-fail/.

 ## Types of Venture Factories

Venture Factories come in all shapes and sizes. Here are some examples:

A physical Venture Factory set up in Silicon Valley as its own division with real financial objectives by a large industrial company. It has a full staff that handles all aspects of Venture Building:

Ideate, Incubate, and Accelerate for the entire company. Its goal is to incubate and accelerate ten to twenty new ventures a year and grow them into whole new business units. It is incubating ventures sourced from outside the company as well. Turning your Venture Factory into a growth division or strategic business unit has a lot of advantages.

A virtual Venture Factory, launched by a global energy and automation company, that moves from geography to geography, bringing team members and methodology to different parts of the world so ventures can be incubated wherever the company has a presence. In some cases, virtual really means virtual, as all the ventures are incubated by a distributed team in a fully digital environment.

Two Venture Factories with two different teams. Within this financial services institution, one team was set up as a vertical Venture Factory, focusing on new products and business line extensions for a single business unit, while the other was set up as a horizontal Venture Factory to cover those opportunities in the white space, where the customer pain doesn't fall neatly into a business unit but cuts across multiple business units.

A Venture Factory designed to not just incubate new ventures for this multinational conglomerate but to offer incubation services and co-incubate new ventures for, and with, its biggest customers.

A Venture Factory where the internal team doesn't have enough resources to support the full spectrum of venture creation for its parent, a global manufacturing corporation. So, instead, it has decided to own the Ideate and Accelerate phases and is happy to continue to outsource the Incubate phase. Another version of this model emerges when the company doesn't have the *right* resources, as is the case for a large energy company that has learned to ideate and incubate well but doesn't have enough experienced entrepreneurs in-house to accelerate its ventures. In this case a company will typically outsource the Build to Validate phase until it can hire the right talent to run the venture over the long term.

A Venture Factory that serves as a resource to a company's business units or functions that want to incubate a venture or two on their own. It provides the methodology, tools, support, specialists, and training to help the business units incubate their own ventures.

Inevitably, the Venture Factory you build will be unique—designed and structured to fit the reality of your context and your company's culture.

→ How to Build a Venture Factory

To start, here is the actual agenda we cover with our clients during the Venture Factory design phase:

Let us walk you through each category and share the questions you need to answer as part of the design-build exercise. In some cases, we have a point of view on what the answer should be to some of the questions we will pose. In other cases, all we can do is give you the questions to ask, as the answer can only come when

Venture Factory Objective
Venture Factory Basics
    Audience
    Venture Factory Model
    Spectrum of Venture Creation
    Keys to Successful Venture Creation
    New Venture Launch Options
The New Venture Creation Process
    Ideate
    Incubate
    Accelerate
    Scale
Governance
    Mothership
    Venture Factory
    Ventures
Talent Plan
    Venture Factory Team
    New Venture Teams
    New Venture Boards
    Hiring and Compensation

Venture Factory Operations
    Volume
    Cadence
    Calendar
The Venture Factory Experience
    Space
    Tools, Methodology, Technology
    Programming and Inspiration
Communication Plans
    Venture Factory
    New Ventures
Budget / Funding / Metrics
    Costs to Consider
    Fund Estimate
    Metrics and Accountability
    The Venture-Funding Journey
How We Win

DESIGN

LAUNCHING A VENTURE FACTORY

applied to your Mothership's specific context. Also, the order is deliberate, but also iterative, as some decisions you make will impact other decisions you need to make. For example, determining how many ventures a year you want to incubate and accelerate will lead to knowing how many Venture Factory Team members you need.

Remember, as you build your Venture Factory, treat it like a new venture and embrace the iterative process as you go through your Venture Factory's *own* Incubate and Accelerate phases.

Let's start with your Venture Factory's reason for being.

→ Venture Factory Objective

The objective to create, build, and launch new ventures to drive meaningful growth is usually at the core of every Venture Factory. However, there are often other objectives as well:

- Driving the company into new markets
- Monetizing intellectual property or technology that has sat inside R&D for too many years
- Solving global challenges, including demonstrating commitment to environmental, social, and governance (ESG) factors or the United Nations' Sustainable Development Goals
- Co-creating new ventures with partners or customers
- Rebranding, transforming the perception of the company brand and value
- Becoming the "Berkshire Hathaway" for the company as the agile creator of a portfolio of new ventures

There is no right answer, but this is a good time to exercise the new Challenge Framing capabilities you learned in chapter 4. Challenge Framing works for building Venture Factories just as well as it does for defining your ventures.

→ Venture Factory Basics

Who Will the Venture Factory Serve?

At the highest level, you need to start by identifying who the Venture Factory will serve, for example:

- Inside:
  - The whole company
  - Specific business units
  - Corporate functions (strategy, innovation, R&D)
- Outside:
  - Partners
  - Customers
  - External startups

What Incubation Model Will You Employ?

As discussed in chapter 3, you need to decide whether your team will be 100 percent virtual, in person, or a mix. Review that chapter for advice on thinking through the pros and cons of the three models.

Will the Venture Factory Operate Globally?

If the answer is yes, **one** Venture Factory will service the whole company globally, that will impact the previous decision and impact later funding and staffing decisions.

If the answer to that question is yes, but will build **multiple** Venture Factories in different geographic locations, that is fine, but all those Venture Factories should share the same methodology, vocabulary, technology, centralized database documenting the ventures, and so on.

One of our clients is basically a consortium of companies connected but independent around the world. The leader of the North

America New Venture Group realized very quickly that if leaders in other geographies did not work with the same rigor and discipline that she expected from her teams or if they didn't hold the bar as high as she did for ideation, incubation, and acceleration, then they would likely produce unsuccessful ventures.

If their unsuccessful ventures outnumbered her successful ventures, then it was highly likely that the whole concept of Venture Building would get thrown out at some point. So she ran a master class for all her peers and their teams to share the methodology, tools, activities, processes, and templates we had provided them. By the time the group left the class, they were all using the same vocabulary, were aligned on methodology, and were committed to sharing best practices and insights over time.

Will the Venture Factory Cover All Aspects of Venture Creation?

Most Venture Factories manage the Ideate phase (sourcing ideas through multiple channels), own the Incubate phase, and debate the Accelerate phase.

However, unless your business unit executives have metrics rewarding them for innovation or launching ventures, the Venture Factory should keep the venture at least through the Build to Validate phase of Accelerate, when pilots are up and running and generating early revenue. Once you have proved product-market fit and have early revenue, if the leadership requires the ventures to return to a business unit, then at least the sales force and business unit leaders will be excited because there is a new shiny object they can sell. Otherwise, if you throw your ventures over the wall too soon, especially if in the middle of the year and the business unit didn't budget for them, they could be the best ventures on the planet, but they will wither and die because they won't help the business unit make its numbers.

For that reason, and because the ventures need to be measured on different KPIs from a traditional core-legacy business (as we have discussed several times), many of the Venture Factories we are designing are building the capability to grow the ventures until they graduate as full-fledged lines of business several years down the road.

Regardless of which model works best for your organization, you need to think in terms of a dashboard. Realize that once you get the engine going, at any point in time, you will likely have ventures in the Ideate phase, the Incubate phase, and the Accelerate phase and you need to be very disciplined to ensure that all the ventures are getting needed support at whatever stage they are in to be successful (or killed, as factors dictate).

Venture Factory Dashboard

Today — IDEATE, PREP, NVB and NVA | INCUBATE | ACCELERATE

	Q1	Q2	Q3	Q4	Q1
Ideate, Prep and NVB	Ideate Prep and NVB	Ideate Prep and NVB	Ideate Prep and NVB	Ideate Prep and NVB	Ideate Prep and NVB

Build New Ventures

- New Venture 1 — Incubate 1 — Accelerate 1 — Series A ?
- New Venture 2 — Incubate 2 — Accelerate 2 — Series A ?
- New Venture 3 — Incubate 3 — Accelerate 3
- New Venture 4 — Incubate 4 — Accelerate 4
- • NVB Check-in for Ventures 3 and 4
- New Venture 5 — Incubate 5 — Accelerate 5
- New Venture 6 — Incubate 6 — Accelerate 6
- New Venture 7 — Incubate 7 — Accelerate 7
- New Venture 8 — Incubate 8 — Accelerate 8

New Venture Advocate Training

- NVA Training (Q1)
- NVA Training (Q3)
- NVA Training (Q1)

What Will Be Your Criteria for Ending a Venture?

There are obvious reasons why you might kill a venture:

- There is no customer pain.
- The product is not feasible.
- You can't make money.

But there are other reasons why a venture might not work for a company:

- It is too capital intensive; you are looking for asset-light models.
- You need ventures that can demonstrate revenue quickly.
- You don't have enough internal talent; external talent is too expensive.

THE WILL TO KILL. The Venture Factory needs the discipline to kill ventures whenever necessary, at every stage of Incubate …

Month 1
Finding **Customer** Pain

There's no pain.

Month 2
Determining the **Product** or Service

The technology is too far out or can't be built.

Month 3
Designing the **Business**

Will not move the revenue needle or the unit economics don't work.

- The venture doesn't leverage key core competencies or assets the company wants to exploit.

- It can't fulfill ESG goals set by the board.

The bottom line is that you need to understand if there are any guardrails for the ventures you build. Often, because many folks won't know what they don't know, when you launch your Venture Factory, you won't discover all of those criteria until you do the first couple of ventures. That's OK; it's called learning by doing. It may be frustrating, but once you have the first few ventures under your belt, the criteria will be clear.

How Will You Launch the Ventures? What Options Are On or Off the Table?

Another basic question about a Venture Factory is what are the prescribed, acceptable, or likely outcomes for your ventures as they move from the Incubate phase to the Accelerate phase. What options are on or off the table?

- Does every venture need to spin back into an existing business unit?

- Will you set up or manage your ventures as wholly owned subsidiaries or separate lines of business?

- Do you want to spin out your ventures with the ability to take outside funding from other corporations or traditional venture investors?

We ask these questions any time we start incubating a venture because if we know for sure what the company wants as the outcome, then we can adapt the incubation and acceleration models as needed. Honestly, because they want to be perceived as growth stocks, not value stocks, most of our clients don't want to spin them out, but then it is important to think about where the funding will come from if you are launching five, ten, or even twenty ventures a year, as many of our clients are doing. If all three options are possible, that is fine. You just need to work from the future backward and think about what criteria dictate the direction in which each venture goes and how those respective transitions will happen.

What Services Will the Venture Factory Have In-house versus What Services Will the Mothership Provide?

Typically, the answer to this question comes down to economies of scale. If the Venture Factory is going to be doing only a few ventures a year, then it doesn't make sense to duplicate all the Mothership's core functions inside. This is where the New Venture Advocates we will discuss in chapter 10 come in.

However, if you are going to build a lot of ventures, then it makes sense to have certain functions inside the Venture Factory because you will likely move faster if you aren't always having to check in with different departments in the Mothership.

Services the Venture Factory should be able to provide include:

- Legal (corporate legal is hardly ever set up to move at startup speed).

- Marketing (corporate marketing is often concerned with being the brand police).

- Go-to-market early-sales support (there is a *big* difference between a normal core business salesperson and the very first strategic salesperson who figures out how best to sell a new venture's product or service).

- Product (internal product departments almost always want to build too fast, or their transfer pricing to build will blow your cash).
- Procurement (if you have your own budget and you manage it, you should be able to do your own procurement).
- Finance (you need someone who understands startup business models and economics, who can deal with topics like funding and use of funds, and who understands appropriate KPIs for a startup).
- Talent (you will constantly be hiring for the Venture Factory staff and for the ventures, so having someone in-house who understands the specs you need to drive early venture success is invaluable).

Services outside the Venture Factory often include:

- Compliance or regulatory
- Operations or supply chain
- Manufacturing
- IT (though you will need your own IT support, especially if you are incubating ventures in full virtual mode)

Like many of these topics, there is no right or wrong answer, but having clarity is super important, and where you need to leverage the Mothership, please create that ecosystem of New Venture Advocates and make them feel like they are part of your team.

→ The New Venture Creation Process

At this point, you have read an entire how-to guide on the venture creation methodology or process, so we are not going to revisit that in this section. The topic is here as a placeholder, however, because if you are building the Venture Factory before you have begun your Venture Building activity, you want to discuss what methodology to adopt that will enable you to run a repeatable, scalable model for the company.

Ideate

The *how* of Ideate has been covered in prior chapters. The only thing you need to decide as part of your design effort is where to source new venture ideas from. Examples of sources of new venture ideas may include:

- Executives
- Business units
- R&D
- Company employees through a website or regular venture competition
- Partners or customers
- Corporate venture investing group (CVC, if you have one)
- Your Venture Factory Team

Once you determine who can submit ideas to potentially incubate, then you can build the process and infrastructure to manage the submission of those ideas and determine how you will move those ideas to Incubate.

→ Governance

In the next chapter, we discuss the role of executive leadership in the Venture Building process. For the purposes of Venture Factory design, here are the questions you need to ask and answer:

How will the Venture Factory be governed? Will a member of the C-suite govern it or will it have a different sponsor? Ultimately, even if the C-suite is not involved in the day-to-day activities, the CEO and the executive team must be enthusiastic supporters of the Venture Factory and believe that it can become an engine to drive future growth.

Will the members of the Venture Factory Board or governance team also be members of the New Venture Boards? Having the NVB engage in new venture development is a good thing; it keeps the members close to the customer and current on the art of the possible.

Will the Venture Factory have an advisory board? Not every Venture Factory has an advisory board. However, they are useful when you have key influencers who don't own the budget but do have subject-matter expertise or access to some of the core competencies, assets, or capabilities of the Mothership that the incubator and accelerator may need for its ventures. Others you may want to put on an advisory board are those who just love to be naysayers and like to leverage the power of no versus yes. It's better to have those people with you, feeling like they have ownership over your fledgling ventures than crossing their arms, upset because "nobody asked their opinion."

How will the Venture Factory Team work with the various business units and functions and earn their support? For example, per chapter 8, will there be a cadre of New Venture Advocates or Venture Factory Ambassadors appointed and trained across the Mothership to support the new ventures?

Will that extended support network be rewarded or recognized? Among the numerous options are these examples:

- Promotion opportunities
- Increased pay (base or bonus)
- Performance bonus tied to the success of the ventures or the Venture Factory
- Equity or phantom equity in the new venture once it launches

What will be the necessary Gives and Gets between the Mothership and the Venture Factory? As we discussed, during the overview of the Incubate business phase, just as every new venture needs to define the Gives and Gets between it and the Mothership, the Venture Factory needs to brainstorm what each will bring to the other. You can use the Gives and Gets tool in chapter 7. Here is a starting list of items to consider:

→ Talent Plan

There are three types of talent that the Venture Factory is responsible for hiring or curating and managing or organizing:

- New Venture Team members (see chapter 2)
- New Venture Board members (see chapter 10)
- Venture Factory Team members

We are going to focus only on the Venture Factory Team members here. On the Venture Factory staff are typically three types of team members:

- Core team members providing day-to-day support of the New Venture Teams incubating and accelerating.
- Specialists who support the teams at predetermined points in the Venture Building schedule.
- Venture Factory support function personnel.

The number of people you need is primarily determined by the number of ventures you want to build in a year and the types and numbers of activities that the Venture Factory chooses to host on behalf of the Mothership (activities could include running Venture Plan Competitions, trade shows or road shows to highlight great ventures, or master classes for the broader Mothership population, among others. See the Programming and Inspiration section). Regardless of the number of people you need, let's review the roles.

Core team members. There are three key types of core team members to hire onto your Venture Factory Team to support new venture development. (See the sidebar for examples of real spec sheets you could hand to a recruiter, including roles, responsibilities, and qualifications.) These are the team members who will work with the new ventures every day:

EIRs. Entrepreneurs-in-Residence support the overall Venture Building process.

Customer development leads. CD leads drive, train, and provide quality control for the three customer interview processes: pain points, storyboards, and prototypes.

Designers. These specialists support all areas requiring design, including storyboard and prototype development, plus Check-in and Pitch narrative and visual imagery.

SAMPLE SPECS FOR VENTURE FACTORY TEAM MEMBERS

Entrepreneur-in-Residence (Product Leadership)

If you are a creative product leader with a track record of success working for both startups and enterprises, we want to talk to you. Our incubator seeks an Entrepreneur-in-Residence to lead business incubations.

Our incubator is on a mission to help our company succeed with Venture Building. We are disrupting ourselves from the inside out—leveraging our people and assets to build a portfolio of disruptive new businesses. With our help, our company can create and launch dozens of successful businesses.

With our incubators and accelerations as a service, we work side by side with our business unit intrapreneurial teams as they journey from concept through customer validation and prototype development to launch and accelerate. Our approach is dynamic and customer-centric, powered by our work in advanced customer design research and lean innovation processes.

THE ROLE
- Work as a general management leader and product management expert with entrepreneurial teams responsible for creating disruptive new businesses
- Be accountable for New Venture Team success and maintaining a positive work environment. Identify and troubleshoot (or escalate) situations that might derail teams
- Orchestrate incubator resources to train and coach teams on customer interviews, scripts, storyboards, etc.
- Help teams frame and sort through their experiences. Facilitate daily/weekly syntheses, training team to run their own syntheses
- Participate in recruiting, interviewing, and vetting potential entrepreneurial team members
- Establish close adviser relationship with the New Venture Board, helping guide the leader and the team through the incubator's incubation process
- Facilitate workshops and exercises that help establish team norms, methodology, and/or help advance the team toward their goal

Experience
- 8+ years of work experience with demonstrated track record of software and/or digital product management leadership
- 5+ years of experience managing and/or leading teams at an executive level
- Past roles working at or consulting to global enterprises, ideally in a strategic role
- Time spent in customer-facing roles at a senior level (e.g., consulting, sales, sales support, customer service)
- Familiarity and/or experience interviewing customers for market research and/or Voice of the Customer initiatives
- Previous experience working at a startup
- Experience facilitating ideation and solution brainstorming workshops for cross-functional teams

Qualifications
- Exceptional people skills and the demonstrated ability to gain confidence, build rapport, and drive consensus with team members, board members, and partners
- Execution-oriented individual who understands and can apply startup thinking, manage complex projects, and run teams
- Ability to deal with ambiguity in a fast-paced, fluid environment
- Outstanding product management skills with the ability to develop product concept visions, MVP, and road maps at both strategic and detailed level

Customer Development/User Researcher

If you are a passionate, curious, motivated, qualitative research professional, we want to talk to you. Our incubator team seeks a Customer Development/User Researcher to lead teams through the customer-centered research process throughout the incubation.

Our incubator is on a mission to help our company succeed with Venture Building. We are disrupting ourselves from the inside out—leveraging our people and assets to build a portfolio of disruptive new businesses. With our help, our company can create and launch dozens of successful businesses.

With our incubators and accelerations as a service, we work side by side with our business unit intrapreneurial teams as they journey from concept through customer validation and prototype development to launch and accelerate. Our approach is dynamic and customer-centric, powered by our work in advanced customer design research and lean innovation processes.

THE ROLE
As a Customer Development Researcher, you will enable client teams to learn deeply about their end users, uncover user pain, and invalidate/validate hypotheses that typically take the form of open-ended interviews, storyboards, and prototypes. This includes:
- Working with client teams to leverage the incubator's user research process
- Coaching teams on tactics and best practices for conducting effective user research
- Developing research and testing strategies and logistics for entrepreneurial teams by assisting in the creation of interview scripts, storyboards, and prototypes
- Leading research synthesis and translating observations into findings

OTHER KEY RESPONSIBILITIES
- Partnering with designers on the creation of testing stimuli in various degrees of fidelity
- Providing thought leadership on incubator research methodologies such as piloting new tactics, where appropriate, for incorporation into the incubator user research toolkit
- Lead and cohost workshops for client teams of all sizes
- Jumping in and helping out colleagues on other teams, as necessary

Experience
Our incubator is a unique place; as business cofounders inside our company, we are neither like a consulting firm nor like working in a normal business unit. To be successful, we have found the following characteristics to be beneficial:
- Interest in a wide variety of global business topics
- Comfort within a fast-paced collaborative environment with client teams who may be initially uncomfortable with ambiguity
- Desire to mentor others (including nonresearchers) along with the means and patience to do so
- Ability to pivot when necessary
- Adeptness at delivering high-quality research outcomes with time and budget constraints
- Supportive of colleagues when they need a hand to keep projects running smoothly
- Politically savvy when working with our company
- Skilled at knowing when to lead versus when to collaborate
- A curious mind and the ability to make connections between diverse fields and industries

Qualifications
- 5+ years of work experience as a Customer Development Researcher
- Degree in human/computer interaction, behavioral psychology, design
- Experience with a variety of qualitative research methods from foundational (remote and in-person interviewing), generative (participatory design, storyboard testing), and evaluative methods
- Demonstrated experience applying customer research methods in service of conceiving, validating, and building a product
- Previous experience with a startup company is a plus

UX/UI Designer

Our incubator seeks a UX/UI Designer to join our team. If you are a creative problem-solver who understands human-centered design, user research, usability testing, persona creation, and design thinking methods, we want to talk to you.

Our incubator is helping our community build a pipeline and portfolio of disruptive new businesses. We act as cofounders, working side by side with our intrapreneurial teams as they journey from concept through customer validation and prototype development to launch. Our approach is dynamic and highly customer-centric, leveraging our deep experience in customer design research and lean innovation processes. We have helped our customers create and launch dozens of successful businesses and are experiencing tremendous demand for our offerings.

THE ROLE
Help client teams conceive, test, and build new disruptive products by combining work from multiple disciplines: Design, User Research, Usability, Design Thinking. The process begins with Customer Development Research, moves through the brainstorming process, and continues with rapid iteration. Each 12-week incubation is focused on helping project teams define a product concept, vision, and road map that global enterprises can build a business around. The UX/UI Designer and Researcher keeps the customer in the center throughout the incubation process.

Experience
- UX: Information architecture and methods for organizing complex and diverse types of content, low-res prototypes
- UI: Wireframing and high-fidelity prototyping
- Visual Design: Visual hierarchy, grid systems, and typography
- User Research: Script creation, scenario development, qualitative test strategy, persona development, design thinking
- Ability to design and build compelling presentations and pitch decks that communicate boldly and clearly
- Understand team dynamics, communicate clearly, and play nice
- Willing to be flexible and work when the work is needed, sometimes at odd hours (there are lots of peaks and valleys during an incubation)
- Fluency in the following design programs
  - Adobe Creative Cloud
  - Sketch
  - Balsamiq
  - InVision
  - Keynote/PowerPoint

Qualifications
- 3+ years of work experience
- Degree from an accredited university or college in design and/or user experience
- Experience applying customer research methods in service of conceiving/validating/building a product
- Comfort with a fast-paced, collaborative environment with client teams who are often initially uncomfortable with ambiguity
- Politically savvy when working with clients
- Skilled at knowing when to lead versus when to collaborate
- Comfort learning and working within the current Incubator Experience Research process
- Work efficiently in a fast-paced, multi-task environment
- Ability to work effectively with all levels of organizations
- Persuasive written and oral communication style
- Previous startup experience is a plus
- A curious mind and the ability to naturally make connections between diverse fields and industries

Specialist team members. These Venture Factory Team members are not staffed full-time on any particular new venture, but they play a critical role at certain stages of the Incubate and Accelerate phases. Specialists to hire onto your Venture Factory Team include:

Finance or business model expert
- Added to the team around Week 8 when it is starting the business viability phase of incubation
- Helps to drive discipline and decisions on market sizing, business modeling, pricing, budgets, funding requirements, and so on
- Ideally someone with startup finance experience rather than only large company experience

Product or engineering specialist
- Added to the team around Week 6 when solutions to pain are testing well
- May be one or many specialists based on product type (hardware, software, physical product, etc.)
- Balances between conceptual product vision based on customer needs and a technical acumen of the art of the possible
- Leverages connections to help find the right product people for each venture as needed

Go-to-market or sales specialist
- Added to the team for the Week 9 Check-in presentation to learn what the venture team thinks the big opportunity might be
- Helps the team in the last phase to imagine how the product or service can go to market, and what experiments the team might run during the early Accelerate phase to determine the best way to proceed
- Needs a "stay small and scrappy" experimentation mindset best supported by an experienced startup strategic sales or marketing person

Storyteller. Every Venture Factory should have an expert at helping the startups tell their stories. Teams need to think about their pitch decks not as a set of PowerPoint slides but as a *narrative*. The NVB needs to feel customer pain, to get excited by the opportunity, to develop a sense of urgency. To do that you have to tell stories, not just report data. The chief storyteller works with the designers to communicate the new venture to the NVB, the Mothership, and the world.

Subject-matter experts. Hire subject-matter experts for an hour, a day, a week, or for the whole project. Once you know who your team is, if you discover gaps in their expertise or knowledge, you can augment that team with subject-matter experts. For example, one client's venture had 3D printing as a big part of the venture, but it had no 3D printing expertise. So, we hired two people to join the team for three months. That also gave the New Venture Team a chance to see if either person was a good fit to join the team permanently. Another new sustainable mining venture needed someone who understood mining very well, so we hired a mining expert to be on the team for the duration.

Support team members. A Venture Factory does not run itself. And while there are Venture Factory Team members working directly with the New Venture Teams, those team members sometimes need support as well. Typical Venture Factory Team members who can provide needed support functions include:

Incubation leadership. The Venture Factory needs senior executive sponsorship at a minimum and, ultimately, senior executive leadership as well. Obviously, that depends on how your organization is led and managed. The key thing is that the Venture Factory—operating at full scale across the spectrum of new venture creation—is a full-time job.

HR, hiring, staffing. Depending on the number of ventures you will be incubating per year, having someone on staff who can help manage personnel activities is super helpful. The six key things this person does are:

- Define where and how the Venture Factory sources talent and the process it uses to qualify new team members.

- Help hire and develop the Venture Factory staff, making sure the staff member gets training and apprenticeship opportunities (see later for more on this topic).

- Help screen, interview, recruit, and hire the New Venture Team members, both those sourced internally and externally. The HR staff person becomes expert at knowing who has the right characteristics to be comfortable as an entrepreneur and who might not be well suited for the speed, urgency, and ambiguity.

- Help create the programming that can help develop, curate, and refine a pool of highly motivated and exceptionally talented entrepreneurs. Typically, this person works with the Mothership's HR to build engagement with the broader employee base, which actually helps the Mothership attract and retain the best and brightest who might otherwise never join or might leave if there isn't a chance to build something new on the inside.

- Help curate and manage, on an ongoing basis, a network of outside experts and advisers by expertise (whether functional or subject matter) to tap into, should the teams need help for the short term or long term.

- Interface with outside recruiters should the company be open to using recruiters to find the Venture Factory Team, any of the New Venture Team members during the Incubate phase, or the permanent team for the launched new ventures as it begins to hire new team members for the Accelerate and Scale phases as forecasted in the Pitch Day operating plans.

Administration and coordination (COO). The Venture Factory needs someone full-time to manage all the activity of the Venture Factory. One of the main items that person must manage is the master calendar, notably:

- Week 0s
- Week 1 of incubation
- Check-ins, Pitch Days
- Subject-matter expert visits
- NVB Day in the Life visits
- Weekly synthesis sessions
- Challenge Framing sessions
- Portfolio Reviews
- Mothership programming
- New Venture Competitions
- Other events to add to the calendar and manage

A Renaissance person is essential, for whom no task is daunting, and who can stay on top of everything—juggling a thousand things for the Venture Factory Team and every New Venture Team.

If you are moving New Venture Team members from one geography to another for twelve weeks, that involves a ton of logistics. So, this administrative person can also help with housing, transportation, and moving logistics. This person deals with a range of people, from the CEO to customers to frontline staff, so should be extraordinarily organized, supremely professional, and a self-starter who needs no direction and is sophisticated in the mores of the business world. When and if you find one of these people, never let them go.

Facilities or space management. When fully functioning, the Venture Factory could have any number of teams coming and going at any given moment, and all need their space set up and, ultimately, photographed and disassembled once they graduate. Also, these teams are working a lot, and while they don't need a foosball table, they *do* need food and drinks. We send a facilities manager to every geographic location where we are opening a Venture Factory to make sure it has all the right supplies and is set up correctly. The team can use that starting point as the template for keeping the space operating at a high level in perpetuity. Plus, teams run out of supplies, computer cords, whiteboard space, water, so someone needs to handle all that for them so they don't have to stop. After all, taking the time to go out for Post-it notes is five less customer interviews the team can do. If the team members are working virtually, the facilities manager makes sure that each team member's home office is set up for success.

IT and tech support. In chapter 3, we set out the tech stack you need and the different types of tools a team is likely to use (both the full-time Venture Factory Team and the New Venture Teams). Having someone full-time on the Venture Factory staff who can install, maintain, and support team members with all the different technology tools they need is well worth it.

Mothership management. Again, depending on the number of ventures you want to incubate in a year and who the Venture Factory is serving, it may be helpful to have someone whose full-time job is to manage the Mothership. Activities this person covers include:

- Capturing and sharing insights or learnings from incubation and acceleration with the whole company

- Identifying, training, and managing the network of New Venture Advocates inside the Mothership to support new ventures

- Developing a network of internal experts and ambassadors who represent, or can provide access to, the core competencies, assets, and capabilities of the Mothership and calling on them as needed

- Refining the criteria for recruiting, onboarding, and managing the NVB members

- Bridging between the new venture and the Mothership during the Accelerate phase, managing the Gives and the Gets as identified by the New Venture Team in its operating plan as presented on Pitch Day

The number of staff you need in your Venture Factory relates to the number of ventures you want to incubate. Here is a sample organization chart that assumes a company has three Venture Factory hubs and launches eight ventures per location (twenty-four per year). That is a lot of ventures. Many of our Venture Factory clients start with a goal of incubating five or six a year. In many cases, a centralized Venture Factory resource can service multiple hubs because it can work virtually with teams.

VENTURE FACTORY STAFFING. Sample Org Chart.
Ideate. Incubate. Accelerate. Scale. Mothership / Partner Management.

VENTURE FACTORY SUPPORT STAFF
(GLOBAL RESPONSIBILITY)

- COO
- HR
- IT / Tech Support
- Internal Communications
- PR
- Mothership Management
- Venture Challenge Management
- SMEs as needed

VENTURE FACTORY STAFFING
(8 VENTURES PER LOCATION x 3 LOCATIONS)
(PER PHYSICAL SITE — US, EUROPE, AND ASIA)

- 3 EIRs
- 3 Customer Development
- 3 Designers
- 1 Finance / Business Modeling
- 1 Go-To-Market / Sales
- 1 Product / Engineering
- 1 Storyteller
- 1 Facilities / Admin
- SMEs as needed

Onboarding and Training the Venture Factory Staff
Creating a fully functional and effective Venture Factory Team involves a three-step training or apprenticeship model.

Step 1: Learning by Doing
Whenever you bring on a new team member, have them work side by side with more experienced team members as they incubate and accelerate at least one new venture. Full immersion and learning by doing is the best way to train your Venture Factory Team. Even if you have hired former entrepreneurs with real startup experience, while many of them are the ideal candidates, not all of them can teach what they did, so finding people who adopt a growth mindset along with a dose of humility as they go through their first incubation is key to their success.

Step 2: Learning by Designing/Coleading
While working on their first new venture, the new members of your Venture Factory Team can work with the experienced team members to design the Incubate phase for the next new venture. This next venture to incubate is typically drawn from the list of

opportunities identified during a prior Ideate session (Challenge Framing, portfolio assessment, new venture challenge, or any other source of ideas for new ventures you may employ). They should now be able to colead a number of venture team activities.

Step 3: Learning by Leading

Once finished incubating the first set of ventures, a new Venture Factory Team member can now take the lead on running their activity for the next set of new ventures (whether they are the EIR running the whole venture, the customer development expert, the UI/UX designer, or any other specialist). At this point, a more experienced team member could check in from time to time or put aside a set time each day or week to answer any questions or address any issues. Things move very fast, so small challenges can rapidly escalate to a venture team running off the rails if not caught in time. Once you have a cadre of experienced Venture Factory Team members, you will be amazed at how smoothly your factory runs.

> **VENTURE FACTORY TEAM COMPENSATION**
>
> In chapter 8, we discussed the need to think creatively about compensating the members of New Venture Teams, so they can share in the upside. If you have a dedicated Venture Factory Team, it is important that its members don't feel as if they have done all the work helping the ventures launch but never get to share in the glory of their success. A trained Venture Factory Team member is gold, so retaining that person in the Venture Factory is key.
>
> Besides rewarding the team for achieving the metrics you determine are relevant for your Venture Factory, another way clients have given the Venture Factory Team the ability to share in the ventures it helps build is to create a Venture Factory fund into which is added a small percentage of equity (phantom or otherwise) from every venture you launch. Then the Venture Factory Team members get a percentage of that pool, which, like the phantom equity for venture team members, can be vested to encourage retention.
>
> We recommend putting the equity in a pool for *all* of the Venture Factory staff versus giving whoever worked on a particular venture equity in that venture. You want to encourage those helping to run the ventures to be objective. If they aren't hearing customer pain or find that the solution depends on the impossible, you want the Venture Factory staff to help kill the venture. If they only win when their particular venture wins, they instead may be incentivized to keep pushing. You don't want that. Usually it is luck of the draw and timing that determines on which venture the Venture Factory Team member gets staffed, so you don't want to reward that one person who got the lucky venture and penalize those team members whose ventures will never see the light of day. The work they are doing is the same, and thus they should have the opportunity to share in the collective wins of the Venture Factory.

Venture Factory Operations

One of the primary factors determining the size, scope, and budget of your Venture Factory is how many ventures you want to incubate a year. And of those, how many are you likely to accelerate a year? We have clients that want to incubate as many as twenty a year so they can reap the benefit of having a sizable portfolio; in other cases, clients are happy launching four a year. There is no right answer, but the volume dictates the team size more than any other factor.

Once you've made that basic decision, there are other operations-related decisions to consider:

- What will be the annual rhythm of Venture Factory activities and events (idea sourcing, Venture Plan Competitions, demo days, master classes, etc.)?

- Will you host Venture Plan Competitions to source ideas and teams? How often?

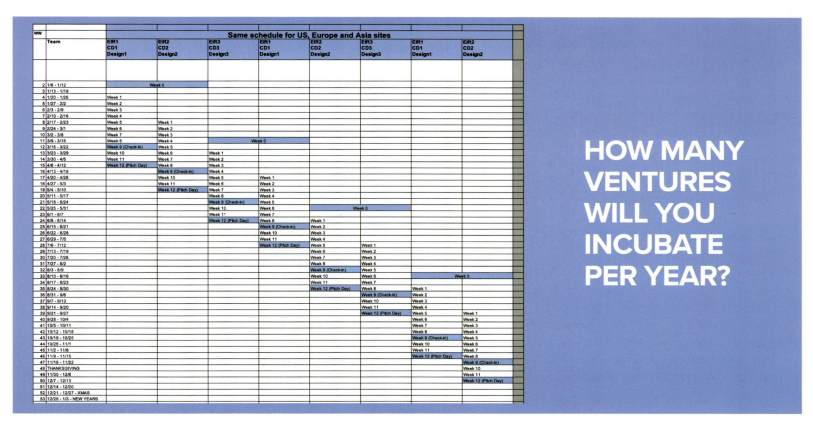

HOW MANY VENTURES WILL YOU INCUBATE PER YEAR?

- Will you allow a venture to come into the Venture Factory at any time, or only at set times during the year?

- Will you run cohorts or classes of new ventures that include multiple ventures all incubating at the same time or will you stagger the starts? The previous image shows a staggered start schedule for eight ventures a year.

While any model you choose works if you have enough experienced resources, staggering the incubation start dates is the most efficient model for several reasons.

Staggering Optimizes Staff Loads
- Staggering allows you to balance EIR and customer development peak loads.
- Designers are most needed Weeks 6 through 12, so you can rotate them more easily and not have to overstaff.
- Specialists are needed for short bursts of intense effort and are better able to support needs with a staggered start, so not every venture needs the finance person or the storyteller at the same time.

Staggering Hedges Against Customer Recruiting Unknowns
One of the most unpredictable aspects of the prep phase is how long it takes to recruit customers so that by Day 1 of Week 1 of the Incubate phase, the team has enough customers to start the customer development interviews.

Staggering the starts accounts for various lead times in recruiting customers—fairly fast for B2C new ventures (so they can be one of the earlier starts), longer for B2B (so those ventures can take one of the later slots).

Staggering Allows for Flexibility in Start Dates
Having slots available throughout the year versus set start dates only twice a year, for example, provides more agility and flexibility to incubate new ventures that may not fall neatly into your predetermined calendar.

→ Designing the Venture Factory Experience

For a discussion on why space matters, both your digital and physical space, check out chapter 3 on Preparing to Incubate.

Finalizing Venture Factory Tools and Technology Stack
Review chapter 3 for an extensive list of the tools and technology we use. More importantly, we have included how and why we use each so you can assess what tech stack your Venture Factory and teams will use in the end, especially since the technology is improving every day. As time goes on, the number of options from which to choose is ever increasing.

Programming and Inspiration
In chapter 1, we discussed the philosophical underpinnings to the methodology—understand customer pain, marry that pain with the art of the possible, use technology and trends to solve the pain, and

place a series of small bets to remove the greatest amount of risk on the least amount of capital. Then fast forward to the Gives and Gets section earlier where we discussed the need for the Venture Factory to give back to the Mothership at the same time it is developing the laundry list of experience, assets, core competencies, and capabilities it needs to get from the Mothership. One of the best ways for the Venture Factory to give back to the Mothership is to help the core business stay current on the art of the possible.

Done right, the Venture Factory serves as the vanguard to help the whole organization:

- Understand its global customers
- Sense and respond to emerging trends
- Uncover new forms of competition and new types of competitors
- Learn how to identify and manage risks
- Introduce new approaches to generating ideas and opportunities

The Venture Factory you are building can help the Mothership build a companywide, global community that is both up to speed on the latest trends and technology and 100 percent focused on leveraging that innovation to solve customer pain and drive growth. The Venture Factory can create and offer programming that inspires, enables, and excites the broader employee base, drives employee engagement, and helps develop future leadership.

Programming can include anything from techniques the team is using such as customer interview tips or storyboard drawing, to trends they are seeing, to insights they are gaining from meeting with subject-matter experts, futurists, VCs, and more. You can build a website, host master classes, offer webinars, create a speaker series, and much more. Some companies use blogs or vlogs, newsletters, or social media. Whatever you can do to give back to the Mothership pays dividends in the goodwill you build across the organization.

The Venture Factory Team and its ventures often develop a global network of venture capita firms, traditional startup accelerators, universities, top-tier startups, CVC firms, a range of Global 1000 companies, and other members of the global innovation and Venture Building ecosystems. They build a network of experts to call on for information, inspiration, and conversation. If managed carefully these networks provide invaluable support, connections, information, and ideas that benefit not just the Venture Building teams but the entire Mothership.

And, as we noted earlier, the best Venture Factories partner with the chief talent officers to provide a venue and program that can be included in the leadership development rotation programs for your best and your brightest.

→ Venture Factory Communication Plan

Hand in hand with the programming and inspiration plan is the Venture Factory communication plan. We highlighted the importance of narrative and design when we discussed the ventures and how they need to tell a story of who and what they are. Likewise, the Venture Factory needs to share its story:

- How will you consolidate corporate support and sponsorship?
- Does it make sense to stay under the radar or to message Venture Factory efforts broadly within the company?
- What (if any) is your external PR plan?
- How can the communications plan for the Venture Factory also satisfy the need for ongoing talent recruitment?

WHAT IS YOUR INTERNAL AND EXTERNAL COMMUNICATION PLAN?

Talking points / key messages

Internal (examples)
- **Benefits** to the Mothership
- Key **learnings** and **insights**
- Investment **highlights**
- Portfolio company **news**
- Interesting **events** to attend

External (examples)
- **Market knowledge** and point of view (demographic, ethnographic, trends)
- **Access to company** customers and partners for pilots and early product validation
- The **company as a customer** to lend brand validation and credibility
- The **company as a channel partner** to sell / market to your customers
- Wide range of **operating expertise** (data, supply chain, sales, marketing, etc.)

Internal mechanisms

- **Regular newsletter** / blog / video / podcasts on CVC activities
- **Solicitation of Mothership and Business Unit ideas** and customer insights
- **Regular sharing on trends**, technology, customer desirability, industry moves
- **Reach out to internal experts** to help startups leverage our global assets and capabilities
- **Board meeting presentations**

External mechanisms

- Website
- Social media
- Newsletter, blog, podcast
- Launch event
- **Ongoing outreach to press**, influencers, think tanks, universities, industry / domain experts with public relations
- **Regular appearances** at events, panels, meetups, entrepreneur forums
- **Joint events** with complementary corporate venturing units, G1000-backed startups
- **Regular meetings with strategic VCs**
- **Outreach to universities** (with campus communications), millennial and Gen Z influencers (sensor network)

- How will you communicate the value you are providing, including useful customer insights that you could use more broadly?

Many companies say they want to build a Venture Factory to learn. But rarely is there anyone in the Venture Factory with the job of capturing that learning, curating it, and disseminating it widely across the firm. Make it someone's job in the Venture Factory to cover the following themes:

Be the Eyes and Ears for the Corporation
- A scout and sensor network in touch with the ever-changing market trends
- The liaison for M&A, helping to connect potentially interested parties

Share Learnings and Successes with Employees and Investors
- Provide early wins and unique insights your senior executives can use to help shift the organizational culture toward organic growth
- Capture and share acquired wisdom from new venture creation
- Spread best practices

Leverage the Venture Factory for Talent Development, Recruitment, and Retention
- Use the Venture Factory as a way to attract undergraduate- and graduate-level recruits
- Build that leadership development rotation to infuse new venture creation thinking into the corporate culture
- Create New Venture Advocates to provide opportunities for team members who aren't interested in being entrepreneurs starting new businesses in the Venture Factory, but who are entrepreneurial—interested in transforming their function or department

Exemplify Positive Messages to Company, Investors, Partners, Recruits
Those messages may include:

- Innovation at your company is not mere window dressing; it's real. You are building a Growth Engine.
- You have no intention of getting disrupted but have every intention of being the disruptor, leveraging all your gifts as a large company—ideas, talent, brand, resources, technology, capital, global reach, channels, and customers—to beat the startups at their own game.
- You are a growth stock, not a value stock.
- You aren't abandoning your core as you continue to work on new products and business line extensions (as well as new ventures) leveraging your Venture Factory methodology.
- You are working on big problems to make a difference in the world.

Craft the message, tell your story; people will find it intriguing and interesting. Just don't be boring.

→ Budget, Funding, and Metrics

When designing your Venture Factory, you need to think about the budget required to build it, the funding needed to build ventures in it, and the metrics by which the Venture Factory will be held accountable.

Budget

To know how much funding you need, you must build a budget. Here are the line items that make up the baseline Venture Factory budget:

Venture Factory Costs
- Venture Factory staff salaries
- Consulting and other specialist SME fees
- Space or rent
- Furniture
- Space IT or telecom equipment
- Staff IT or telecom equipment, software, and SaaS
- Materials
- Food
- Conferences, subscriptions, and other education or inspiration resources
- Internal communications (website, town halls, etc.)
- External communications (attendance at conferences or events, press tours, etc.)

Per Incubate
New Venture Team salaries (Sometimes the Venture Factory covers the salaries of the team members during the Incubate phase and sometimes their home departments cover them for that period. Once the venture moves to Accelerate, its seed funding should cover all salary costs.)

- New Venture Team consulting and other specialist or SME fees
- Housing, travel, and entertainment (if people are traveling)
- Customer recruiting
- Miscellaneous

Per Accelerate
Budgets for the Accelerate phase are included in the funding section of the final business and execution plan.

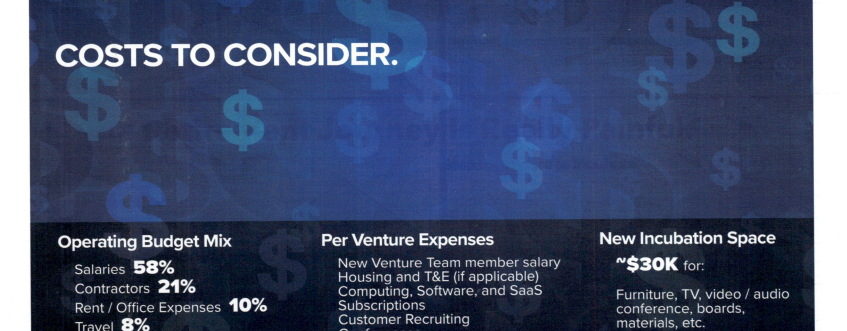

Venture Factory Funding

If you are building a Venture Factory, you need to ask the following questions:

- Where will funding for the Venture Factory come from? Options may include:

    – A discretionary fund that the board has given the CEO

    – HR budget

    – R&D budget

    – Business unit budget

    – CVC fund

    – Other

- How much funding will it receive?

- Will the Venture Factory funding cover Venture Building costs as well? If so, which phases? Will the Ideate and Incubate phases come from a different bucket than the Accelerate phase?

- Will the Venture Factory own the seed fund for the ventures, or will that fund reside elsewhere?

- Will there even be a fund, or will all investment be evergreen or off the balance sheet?

- Will spin out—taking outside funding from traditional VC or CVC or other sources—ever be an option?

Funding Your Ventures

There are three levels of funding for each venture:

- The amount of money you need to support the teams incubating the ventures for twelve weeks.

- The immediate seed funding the venture requires should you decide to launch and accelerate.

- The follow-on funding the venture has reported it needs for each subsequent round, assuming it achieves the metrics and milestones laid out in its business and execution plan and has agreed with its NVB.

Every business and execution plan has an operating plan with a timeline telling the NVB what it will be doing over a range of time and a use-of-funds page highlighting the cost of those activities and resources.

TIMELINE *FIRST 20 MONTHS*

MILESTONES

MONTHS	0-5	6-10 *MVP Completed*	11-15	16-20
Development	Initial Development	Phase 1 – Refine Product	Phase 2 – Retain Users	Phase 3 – Expand Scope
Milestones	• Launched **Online Listings Portal** • Launched **Broker & Owner** Portals • Launched Tour Companion **App**	• 2,000/mo. Occupier **Searches** • 150/mo. Occupier **Tours**	• 10,000/mo. Occupier **Searches** • 600/mo. Occupier **Tours**	• Generated **revenue** from Brokers, Service Providers and Owners • Launched additional occupier features **beyond Find and Acquire**
Test Assumptions	• Can we get brokers to bring the tour companion app into most tours they conduct?	• Can we get occupiers to contribute subjective ratings and photographs?	• Will we lose broker and/or occupier engagement as we share information that they supply to the marketplace?	• Can we get landlord brokers to submit listings on a regular basis? Can we monetize leads to brokers and other pros?
Test Privacy Concerns		• No sharing	• Start experimenting with aggregated release of data	• Start experimenting with providing anonymized individual-level data

While every venture is different, with different budgets and resource requirements, you can make some assumptions to provide the leadership with estimates to determine the money required for both the Venture Factory and the portfolio of new ventures you will create, build, and launch.

Assumptions to make:

- Number of ventures you will incubate each quarter, half year, year—whatever your reporting requirements are

- Number of ventures you expect to make it all the way through to launch and the Accelerate phase

- Number of ventures you expect to make it through each phase of Accelerate:

  – Build to Validate?

  – Build to Automate?

  – Build to Grow?

  – Will you launch your ventures with a partner who will share in the funding?

With a few assumptions and the data and decisions you have determined as part of your Venture Factory design phase, crunching the numbers for the Venture Factory is very straightforward. Your finance or business model specialist is happy to do it for you.

Determining Metrics

As with every venture you build, metrics are an important part of the Venture Factory design because the team must know what it is held accountable for—and rewarded for—over time. During your design work, you need to ask these questions:

- What are the overall objectives of the Venture Factory? What is its reason for existence? For example, in some cases, our clients set up the Venture Factory as an actual division or line of business with revenue goals. In other cases, the Venture Factory serves the other business units across the company, so the goals are related to helping make their businesses or ventures successful. In some cases, the Venture Factory handles the Ideate and Incubate phases but hands off to the business units, which are then accountable (with real metrics) for the Accelerate and Scale phases. There is no right or wrong model; you just need to have an explicit conversation and make the objectives meaningful enough that you can build metrics around them.

- Based on the objectives you agree to, what metrics should be established to evaluate the performance of the Venture Factory? Some examples could include:

  – Incubations and accelerations executed versus planned

  – Additional demand for Venture Factory services from inside and outside the company

  – Top-line and bottom-line financial contribution

  – Financial markets shift in perception from value stock to growth stock

  – Brand value perception impact

  – Incubation or acceleration team and board satisfaction

  – Budgeted versus actual spending

- Talent benefits related to recruiting and retention
- Your venture teams' ability to demonstrate they can mitigate risk
- Percentage of successful ventures, measured by the number of ventures in the market demonstrating product-market fit and achieving first revenue

- Are the metrics aligned with a "small bets, fail fast" new venture creation mindset? We are not looking for "profit" to be a metric in the early years because that is not what you are looking for in your ventures; you are looking for customer acquisition and revenue. Make sure your metrics align with building startups, not running the core and legacy businesses. (See our sidenote on compensation for Venture Factory Team members, as that compensation is tied to the metrics you set.)

Voilà! You have a Venture Factory designed to pump out a pipeline and portfolio of new ventures to drive meaningful organic growth over time. We have covered every important topic but one—who will conduct that growth?

Senior executives, C-suite occupants, and distinguished members of the board, it is time for the spotlight to turn on you.

Your job is to steward your organizations, to disrupt yourselves, to galvanize real innovation, and to drive meaningful, sustainable growth—not just for your company and shareholders, but for your people, your customers, your community, and the world. A precondition for success is an *engaged* NVB. Your job is to *unleash* the Unicorns within. Let's explore exactly what is the role of the NVB throughout the Venture Building process: Ideate, Incubate, Accelerate, Scale. And let's drive home why it is up to you to determine whether you will be the disruptor or the disrupted, the dinosaur or the daring.

Chapter 10

Driving the New Venture Growth Engine

The Role of the C-Suite and Senior Executives

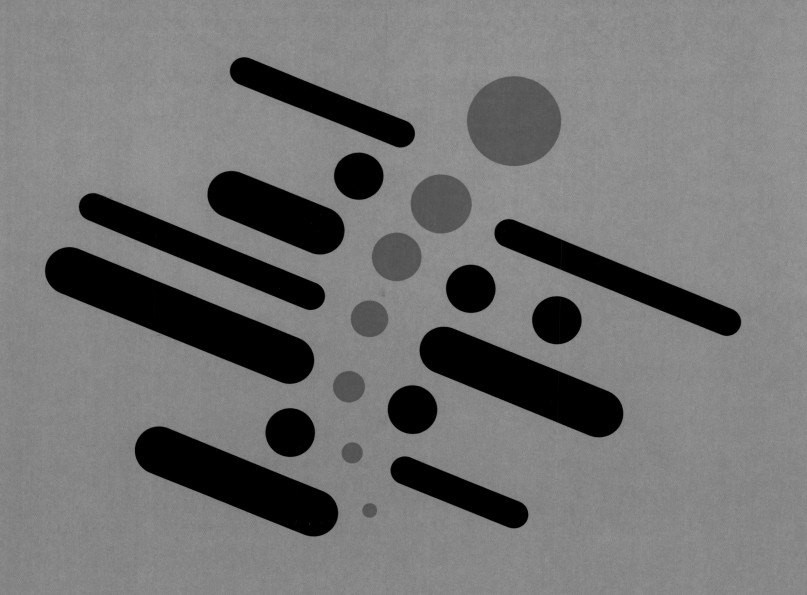

Dear board member, CEO, CMO, CRO, CFO, CTO, CIO, CHRO, chief strategy officer, head of innovation, head of digital transformation, business unit head, and every other senior executive who is tasked with driving the growth agenda for your firm:

We have reserved this chapter specifically for you.

> **IF YOU OPENED STRAIGHT TO THIS CHAPTER, PLEASE DO GO BACK AND READ:**
>
> - The introduction
> - Chapter 1: Before You Start (which includes the preconditions for success you need to commit to or, frankly, don't bother Venture Building)
> - Chapter 9: Building Your Own Venture Factory
>
> **Followed by:**
>
> - This chapter
> - The conclusion

Launching and leading a Venture Factory must be driven from the top down. The CEO and top executives must:

- Believe creating a pipeline and portfolio of new ventures represents a significant opportunity to drive innovation and growth
- Be willing to learn to operate like top-tier VCs, not traditional, big company, management review board members
- Understand that revenue and customer acquisition take precedence over profit in the short term

Otherwise, forget about it. Without this top-down strategy and executive support, your new ventures will die on the vine. We can give you all the methodology, tools, templates, activities, and process in the world, but if the C-suite has no guts, there will be no glory.

As John Chambers, former chair and CEO of Cisco, has warned large companies who don't stay current: "If I'm not making you sweat, I should be, because I am sorry to say but 40% of you in this room will be out of business in 10 years because 70% of you will attempt to go digital but only 30% of you will succeed."[1]

→ What You Are Up Against

In an attempt to offer a more upbeat message on how to improve those lousy odds, we have been traveling the world giving keynotes to CEOs and C-suite members of every flavor as well as to members of their boards about how to drive meaningful growth through Venture Building and Venture Investing (building CVCs). While most C-suite members are well intentioned, vehemently nodding their heads as we highlight the opportunities to beat the startups at their own game, far too many are merely checking the box for their board of directors.

And those boards aren't much better. In a talk in front of two hundred board members of *Fortune* 500 companies, I asked how many had conducted an interview with a customer during their tenure on the board. Very few hands went up. It seems they are too busy exercising their fiduciary duty, which somehow doesn't include talking to customers. They all talk the talk, but very few walk the talk.

That said, it's often not their fault. They are driven by the financial markets, and the financial markets are completely archaic. If the big investment banks and their market analysts who sit on high, judging corporates, are so smart, why have they left billions of dollars on the table in fintech startups they took public but, frankly, could have created? It's easy to be a critic; it's not so easy to be a doer. We have lost patience with industry experts who want to pontificate, but not activate.

Rather than obsessing on dividends, they should be encouraging companies to invest in their future. Rather than NPV, they should be rewarding option value. Rather than focusing on the next quarter, they should assess what the pipeline and portfolio of new ventures could mean as they relate to continuous relevance, reinvention, and returns for the long term.

Ironically, the Street does reward startups that go public with great revenue potential—and zero profits. Why shouldn't more established companies, often with incredible leadership, experience, track record, and talent—launching their own startups from within—get rewarded with growth stock multiples in the same way? Bottom line, honestly, they should.

The markets should absolutely recognize companies trying to build Venture Factories—companies that adopt a portfolio mindset and model to driving organic growth—as it means those companies will be:

- Closer to the customer
- Current on the art of the possible—the technology and trends driving and enabling the future
- Better at attracting and retaining talent wanting more entrepreneurial opportunities
- More agile and easier to pivot
- Disruptors themselves, not the disrupted

And while we do believe building a Growth Engine that includes launching ventures, creating a Venture Factory, and doing world-class corporate venture investing, strategic partnering, and targeted startup M&A (not just big company corporate development) are the C-suite's responsibility to lead, we don't believe a company needs *innovation transformation* to be successful.

In fact, we are not big believers in massive transformation programs at all. We don't think they work, as the effort is often too broad and abstract. We do believe that if you focus on execution and send enough speedboats out in the form of new ventures and tether them to the Mothership—and if those speedboats are worth $100 million, £200 million, €300 million, which could yield 2 to 3 billion in whatever your currency in market cap, the Mothership will turn. Leadership will start to ask, what are those from-to shifts you said we might have to make to ensure these ventures reach escape velocity? "Transformation" is expensive; placing small bets to remove the greatest amount of risk on the least amount of capital is not. Venture Building is driven by those *inside* the company, providing them with creative opportunities, while big-T transformation is too often driven by people outside the company, often leading to lots of resentment.

So while you don't need massive culture-change projects to innovate and drive meaningful growth through Venture Building, you do need the oversight of an *engaged* New Venture Board.

→ The Imperatives of an Engaged New Venture Board

As we discussed in the first chapter, there are five preconditions for success. Without these, you shouldn't launch a venture or build a Venture Factory. As a reminder, one of those preconditions is an engaged NVB.

While the CEO needs to drive the growth agenda and support Venture Building, the NVB is in charge of engaging with the new ventures on a daily basis. The NVB is the decision-making body governing the new venture. In essence, the NVB members serve as the project's venture capitalists.

The NVB members are usually senior executives from inside the company. If a company has a Venture Factory, a member of the Venture Factory Team would be on the NVB, as they will have a portfolio view across all ventures currently being incubated and accelerated and the institutional memory of ventures that have been incubated and accelerated by the company in the past.

Depending on the nature of the venture, the Venture Factory Team member may be partnered with other business unit leaders or functional heads who generated the new venture idea or who are sponsoring the idea either with talent or funding. Regardless of where they are sourced from, the NVB should include four to six leaders with the ability to do the following with a sense of urgency and speed.

Imperative 1: Make Definitive Go/No-Go Decisions

If you want to build startups, from Day 1, NVB members need to learn to behave like top-tier venture capitalists. To help them, we often put one of our VCs-in-Residence on the Venture Board during the Incubate and Accelerate phases. They serve as a Board Member-in-Residence working side by side with the internal NVB members so they can learn by doing alongside a real VC.

There are three key go/no-go decisions a team may put in front of the NVB (notice we don't call these the "endless maybe" decisions):

Week 3 or 4. While there is no formal presentation to the NVB until about Week 9, if by Week 3 or 4, the New Venture Team is not hearing significant enough customer pain, the team may let the NVB know it recommends either pivoting to a newly discovered source of pain or shutting down the venture immediately. The NVB *must* become adept at killing ventures. If it doesn't kill ventures in a timely manner, it puts the entire Venture Building agenda at risk, as the bad apples will keep spending money at the expense of the good apples.

Week 9. The Check-in meeting is the first formal report the New Venture Team makes to the NVB. The agenda for this meeting is focused on pain, customer personas, early hypotheses around product, and the big opportunity. By design it is not focused on the business model because if there is no pain to solve or feasible product or solution to build there is no point to continue. However, the Check-in meeting is when the NVB should be very explicit about the questions it wants answered during the business viability phase and addressed in the Pitch Day business plan.

Week 12. Pitch Day is when the ultimate go/no-go, fund/no-fund (and to what level of funding) decisions get made. Assuming you decide to launch the venture, a series of launch-related decisions will also need to be made during Pitch Day (we discuss these additional decisions later). Post–Pitch Day, the NVB can either remain the same or be reconfigured to meet the needs of the newly launched venture and emerging market. (We discuss the decision to maintain, change, or augment the NVB when we talk about governance.)

Imperative 2: Deliver Funding

As the intermediary between the parent company and the venture, the primary fiduciary responsibility of the NVB is to act as the manager and conduit of the larger company's investment into the smaller one. Its first such duty is to approve the venture's incubated business plan, provide the first tranche of funding, and set the enterprise on its way as a new company. Its ongoing duty includes ensuring that the new venture achieves its predetermined performance milestones before unlocking subsequent rounds of funding. (See the sidebar "Different Ways to Fund a Venture" for more new venture and Venture Factory funding considerations.)

DIFFERENT WAYS TO FUND A VENTURE

While the NVB's job is to manage and deliver the funding, the decision about where that funding comes from must be predetermined as a condition for success *before* the new venture starts incubating. And, again, it must be driven from the top: by the CEO or C-suite.

Remember, the ventures that are incubating are real companies from Day 1, so if customers are getting excited about the venture, they start raising their hands to be beta sites or pilot customers. That means that at the end of Week 12, the team could have twenty customers lined up who are not going to wait for the NVB to do a full court sprint to find money at the last minute.

The goal is to place small bets and run de-risking experiments, so you should ask for early-stage Seed-level venture dollars, not full-scale, Series A, B, or C dollars.

Typically, if funding is coming exclusively from the Mothership, there are a number of potential (and creative) sources for that funding.

CEO Discretionary Fund or Specified Seed Fund

When budgets are set in advance, it is very hard to ask a business unit to add expenses on the fly, especially if that business unit's head is expected to deliver a certain number to their boss's budget, who must roll up to another budget, or the company's bottom line.

It is often much easier (and frankly better for the venture) for a CEO to create a seed fund to launch ventures until they achieve first revenue than to get the business units to adopt them before the ventures have achieved product-market fit and early revenue. Once the ventures demonstrate they can generate revenue, business unit heads often are eager to roll them back in, because now they have become a source of new revenue and growth.

Business Unit Budgets

In many cases, having a companywide seed fund attached to a Venture Factory that can provide a platform for the whole company makes the most sense. However, in some cases, business units are multibillion-dollar entities in and of themselves with discretionary funds they can invest and—in some enlightened companies—are *expected* to invest in growth opportunities, including launching new ventures. While as we noted above, it is often hard to spend business unit budget dollars on new initiatives after budgets have been set, if the CEO and C-suite are *really* focused on growth through Venture Building, they typically allocate a certain percentage of business unit budgets to these activities, *in advance*, as part of the annual budgeting process.

Talent or HR Leadership Development Budgets

Because Venture Building provides invaluable learning by creating opportunities for team members, HR can provide a source of funding at least for the Incubate phase. Especially in countries such as France, which require corporations to spend a certain percentage of their budgets on personnel development and capability building, Venture Building is a great way to spend those dollars because the company can be creating a new venture while at the same time meeting its personnel development requirements. It can develop its people, as well as retain them, because those employees don't need to leave the company to have access to entrepreneurial opportunities. So many heads of talent complain that they are stuck with nineteenth-century catalogs of leadership development programs that we find they become huge fans of Venture Building, as becoming New Venture Team members and New Venture Advocates provides great learning and promotion opportunities for high potential employees.

R&D Budgets

Often R&D budgets are huge but carefully guarded. A company may not want to touch that sacred cow, or deal with the politics, yet just siphoning 2 percent to 5 percent of the R&D budget to an internal incubator and accelerator can be more money than the Venture Factory or new ventures will need, and the ROI may be much better over time across multiple dimensions (not just the financial return). We are working directly with more and more R&D groups who are finding themselves under pressure to demonstrate they have the ability (and desire) to produce customer-driven solutions that can be monetized and commercialized.

Stop Paying or Reduce Dividends and Reinvest in the Company

Prove to your investors that you can make more money for them than they can make for themselves. Obviously, this transition is not as easy as we are making it sound, but dividends and dinosaurs too often go hand in hand. Fast-moving Silicon Valley companies don't pay dividends. Growth stocks don't pay dividends. Why should you?

Imperative 3: Ensure Access to Customers, Channels, and Markets

This requirement underscores the need to select board members who have superior access to the marketplace, prospective customers, and that market's infrastructure (supply and distribution channels, potential partners, etc.). It is access to the often millions of customers a large global enterprise already has that gives the company's new ventures the competitive advantage over *any* well-funded startup.

Key is that the NVB members must not only be *able* to provide access but be *willing* to provide that access. If you have a huge number of customers but can't get those who own those customers to share them, then they are of no use to you. A great board committed to providing access to customers—even if only to interview them—can give the new venture a powerful running start. Once customers have completed the first interview, they are usually so impressed by the fact that the team wasn't trying to sell them anything, but rather was really listening to their pain and sincere about solving that pain, that they will sign up for the next set of interviews because they see that as an opportunity to help you help themselves.

Imperative 4: Provide Access to Core Competencies, Assets, Resources, and Capabilities

Remember, one of the exercises the New Venture Team engages in early on is the Asset Jam—identifying everything the Mothership can bring to the table.

However, identifying these benefits and being able to deliver them to the new venture as needed are two different skills. The need to immediately get the company's global supply chain expert or the head of talent in Bolivia on the phone to answer a question or provide support quickly is the reason that the NVB should be composed primarily of parent company executives. Ultimately, for all their other virtues, the ability of board members to get the help that the new venture needs may be the most valuable.

Imperative 5: Remove Mothership Friction to Ensure the New Ventures Can Reach Escape Velocity

The fact that most of the NVB members are senior executives chosen for proven competence at the parent company, and who enjoy the trust of the broader organization, means that when the venture needs to move quickly and a functional area or bureaucrat is standing in the way, the NVB members can break the logjam to maintain momentum. Not only do you need to be able to do that once, but you need to be cognizant when friction occurs over and over again as that points you to where some fundamental from-to shifts may need to take place.

Imperative 6: Build an Innovation Ecosystem of New Venture Advocates to Help with Imperatives 4 and 5

Only you—board member, CEO, C-suite, and senior executive—can build an ecosystem of innovators, disruptors, and provocateurs across the organization who are empowered, rewarded, willing, and able to help your ventures seize the Mothership advantage and thrive. (We go into more detail on the role of the New Venture Advocate toward the end of the chapter.) Not only do they help your ventures drive meaningful growth for the company, they become the antidote to the hardening of the arteries and the bureaucracy detested by Warren Buffett—if only you will unleash them as well.

Imperative 7: Determine the Appropriate Governance Model That Works Best for Both the Mothership and the Venture

The NVB needs to make a decision on the path forward for each new venture it launches: set up the new venture within an existing business unit (spin-in), set up the new venture inside the organization as a separate legal entity or business unit (wholly owned subsidiary), or establish the new venture as a separate legal entity and leverage investment from outside entities, for example, traditional VCs, CVCs, PE firms, or other funding sources (spin-out). (We go into more detail on this topic later in the chapter.)

DRIVING HOME THESE POINTS AND THE IMPORTANCE OF YOUR ROLE

We are huge acolytes of the Oracle of Omaha, the genius investor Warren Buffett. We often find ourselves quoting him when talking to our C-suite and board member clients about the need for them to grow and adapt, the imperative to not just strategize but execute, the cancer of corporate friction, and how to ensure their ventures can thrive and reach escape velocity. He frequently talks about the "ABCs of business decay." In a recent letter he wrote: "My successor [to the board from which he was stepping down] will need one other particular strength: the ability to fight off the ABCs of business decay, which are arrogance, bureaucracy and complacency.... When these corporate cancers metastasize, even the strongest of companies can falter."*

The Berkshire chief went on to highlight General Motors, IBM, Sears Roebuck, and US Steel as examples of corporate titans that once appeared to have unassailable grips on their industries. "The destructive behavior I deplored above eventually led each of them to fall to depths that their CEOs and directors had not long before thought impossible," he said.

Buffett noted in the letter that he structured his company to minimize red tape. Berkshire's decentralized web of autonomous subsidiaries, underpinned by a culture of trust, acts as the "ideal antidote to bureaucracy," he said.

"We would rather suffer the visible costs of a few bad decisions than incur the many invisible costs that come from decisions made too slowly—or not at all—because of a stifling bureaucracy," Buffett said.

---

*Theron Mohamed, "Warren Buffett Warned the Bill & Melinda Gates Foundation's CEO About the 'ABCs.' The Investor Has Flagged Those Threats Before," *Markets Insider*, July 10, 2021, https://markets.businessinsider.com/news/stocks/warren-buffett-bill-melinda-gates-foundation-ceo-abcs-philanthropy-dangers-2021-7.

→ The New Venture Board Sponsor

Every NVB needs to appoint one of their own to be the New Venture Team's Sponsor. The Sponsor serves as the main conduit between the team, the NVB, and the Mothership, and thus plays a more hands-on role than most other board members.

There is no secret sauce to determine who becomes the Sponsor. It is either obvious—they are the present or future backer of the venture, have supplied the people or the customers, are the top subject-matter expert, or someone volunteers. Sponsors may be selected for a variety of reasons and from any number of sources:

- The executive whose group generated the idea and to whom the venture may return once launched

- An executive with access to a particular group of customers or stakeholders critical to the new venture
- A representative of the Venture Factory, if the company has one
- A member of the company's CVC fund
- A former entrepreneur with operating experience, who is now an executive at the company

Besides participating in all the activities required of the rest of the NVB, the Sponsor also:

- Makes sure the NVB members supply the team with customers to interview.
- Attends the synthesis sessions the team holds every week.
- Aids the team in leveraging the assets and removing roadblocks from the Mothership.
- Arrives early for the NVB Check-in and Final Pitch Day sessions to help the teams prepare their presentations and preview their messaging.
- Consults the team on what content and cadence would be best for keeping the Mothership informed on the new venture, both to other executive teams and to anyone in the company at large who may be interested in following the team's progress and learning.
- Drives the NVB to be ready to act, so that the new venture does not lose momentum after Pitch Day.

→ New Venture Board Incubate Activities

An *engaged* NVB is one that commits to participating in eight Incubate phase touch points that are important for the success of the venture. We don't ask for a lot of their time over the twelve weeks, but each touch point is important. We tell clients when we work with them that participating in these activities is part of the preconditions for success they need to commit to, or we won't work with them.

Ideation (time required—one day to one week). As we discussed in chapter 4, regardless of how you source venture ideas, the NVB needs to sign off on what the New Venture Team will be incubating. You may be serving as a judge for the New Venture Competition; participating in the Portfolio Review of ideas that are being considered for incubation; approving the output of the Challenge Framing session including the Stakeholder Map of potential customers the team is going to target for interviews; or setting or reviewing the guardrails for what might be in or out for the venture (for example, types of business models, level of capital investment intensity, geographic reach, etc.).

New Venture Team selection (time varies by venture based on the number of team members and need to look for external team members versus internal staffing). If an idea has been generated that does not have a team associated with it already, then the NVB needs to staff the New Venture Team.

Typically, the NVB, led by the Sponsor, selects the New Venture Team members based on the experience, skills, and expertise required for each new venture. Further, the NVB decides whether recruiting external members to the team is important to fill obvious

EXECUTIVE INTERVIEW
EXPLORING VENTURE OPTIONS

PURPOSE

This guide is for use when clients have identified a broad venture area but haven't started on it yet or have some domains they want to explore. This guide can be used across multiple stakeholders to identify important themes that cut across them, as well as enablers and impediments, so that our work is designed to address these factors.

This guide is not suitable for:

- Asking detailed questions about a venture they're already working on and they want us to support or remediate—if that is the case, use the Existing Initiative guide

- Assessing a portfolio of ideas in consideration

This document contains two sections:

- A script for the conversation with *[italicized notes in square brackets]* for the interviewer to probe at particular points

- A guide that you can download and send to the interviewee in advance of the interview, so they can prepare their thoughts

1: SCRIPT FOR THE CONVERSATION

BACKGROUND TO THE INTERVIEW

[Introduce yourself]
[Do a check on time allocated to the session]
[Ask about their background and experience]

Thank you for supporting our interviews to understand leadership's perspective on innovation and growth.

By asking open-ended questions, we seek to gather useful feedback and insights to help guide your growth program going forward.

Our goal is to uncover genuine attitudes and beliefs to help advance the agenda for your growth program and to properly understand the organization's current capabilities and challenges.

After the interviews, we will identify important themes that cut across stakeholders, as well as enablers and impediments, so we can begin addressing these as we further design and execute your growth and execution agenda. We will be sure to take these into account as we move forward with the New Venture Team, New Venture Board, and other key constituents of the program.

DETAILED QUESTIONS WE AIM TO COVER

General Strategy and Overview

What are some of the organization's most important strategic initiatives? What are the innovation aspirations of the organization? Are you particularly excited about any specific scenarios for the organization's future?

What does your organization value: revenue, growth, profit, cash/balance sheet, capability building, learning by doing, shifting culture?

Who "matters most" to the future of your company? (e.g., stakeholders, partners, customers)

What keeps you up at night, and where is disruption coming from?

What domains do you believe the company should explore to drive disruptive growth? Are there domains to be avoided? If so, which ones, and why?

Are there specific ventures that you would love to see incubated?

Innovation and Execution

Can you tell me a story about a successful innovation program, new venture, or new business that has been launched here? What made it successful, and what does success mean to you?

Can you run me through a case example of failure? What led to that?

Who is responsible for delivering on new products, services, and growth today?

What is the tolerance for risk and failure in your organization? Are the lessons of failure ever celebrated?

Core Competencies, Assets, Capabilities

What are your core strengths as an organization? What assets, capabilities, and competencies can you leverage to help your new ventures reach escape velocity?

What are your weaknesses or blind spots? What are you not good at as a company?

Governance

How do decisions get made in your organization? Are there different levels of empowerment?

Where does friction come from in your organization? (e.g., regulatory, risk, compliance, legal, procurement, marketing, HR)

[Probe: Will we need to create New Venture Advocates in other departments or functions that the venture will depend upon to reach escape velocity? For example, who in the legal team is going to write the one-page term sheet, not the forty-page term sheet? Who in purchasing is going to get a new vendor on your system in six hours, not six months?]

How do people overcome challenges? How do things really get done?

Communication

How do you communicate as an organization? How do you share strategy, aspirations, ideas, learning, successes?

Closing Questions

Are there other people with whom we should speak?

Is there any material you'd like to share with us to help our understanding of what you've described today?

Any questions for us?

At the end of the session, we'll share next steps with you. *[Describe the relevant next steps, e.g., challenge framing, NVB onboarding.]*

2: THE INTERVIEW GUIDE

BACKGROUND TO THE INTERVIEW

Thank you for supporting our interviews to understand leadership's perspective on innovation and growth.

By asking open-ended questions, we seek to gather useful feedback and insights to help guide your growth program going forward.

Our goal is to uncover genuine attitudes and beliefs to help advance the agenda for your growth program, and to properly understand the organization's current capabilities and challenges.

After the interviews, we will identify important themes that cut across stakeholders, as well as enablers and impediments, so we can begin addressing these as we further design and execute your growth and execution agenda. We will be sure to take these into account as we move forward with the New Venture Team, New Venture Board, and other key constituents of the program.

DETAILED QUESTIONS WE AIM TO COVER

General Strategy and Overview

What are some of the organization's most important strategic initiatives? What are the innovation aspirations of the organization? Are you particularly excited about any specific scenarios for the organization's future?

What does your organization value: revenue, growth, profit, cash/balance sheet, capability building, learning by doing, shifting culture?

Who "matters most" to the future of your company? (e.g., stakeholders, partners, customers)

What keeps you up at night, and where is disruption coming from?

What domains do you believe the company should explore to drive disruptive growth? Are there domains to be avoided? If so, which ones, and why?

Are there specific ventures that you would love to see incubated?

Innovation and Execution

Can you tell me a story about a successful innovation program, new venture, or new business that has been launched here? What made it successful, and what does success mean to you?

Can you run me through a case example of failure? What led to that?

Who is responsible for delivering on new products, services, and growth today?

What is the tolerance for risk and failure in your organization? Are the lessons of failure ever celebrated?

Core Competencies, Assets, Capabilities

What are your core strengths as an organization? What assets, capabilities, and competencies can you leverage to help your new ventures reach escape velocity?

What are your weaknesses or blind spots? What are you not good at as a company?

Governance

How do decisions get made in your organization? Are there different levels of empowerment?

Where does friction come from in your organization? (e.g., regulatory, risk, compliance, legal, procurement, marketing, HR)

How do people overcome challenges? How do things really get done?

Communication

How do you communicate as an organization? How do you share strategy, aspirations, ideas, learning, successes?

Closing Questions

Are there other people with whom we should speak?

Is there any material you'd like to share with us to help our understanding of what you've described today?

Any questions for us?

At the end of the session, we'll share next steps with you.

subject-matter or skill gaps. If the company wants to launch a Venture Factory internally (see chapter 9), it can select the Venture Factory Team members in advance as well and add them to the New Venture Team.

We often work with heads of talent and chief human resource officers to help them build a process for identifying and tracking a pool of potential internal entrepreneurs who they can tap as necessary to build ventures or staff a Venture Factory. Rotating through the Venture Factory is a great professional development opportunity.

Executive Interview (time required—one hour). A savvy New Venture Team always interviews each member of the NVB to understand any history, interests, biases, customer insights, or other information or background relevant to the new venture each NVB member might have.

There are two types of executive interview scripts—one for when you are dealing with a brand-new venture or domain that has not yet been incubated or explored and one for situations where there is a venture already in flight. We always tell the team leads to send these guides to the executives we are going to interview in advance so they can be prepared, allowing the team interviewing them to have a more substantive conversation.

NVB Onboarding Session (time required—ninety minutes). This session ensures the NVB members understand what happens during the Incubate phase and what to expect and not expect when incubating a new venture. The members need to understand their role—that is, not to behave as if this is a management review board, but rather to learn to be venture capitalists.

We typically share what the team needs from the NVB over the next twelve weeks and beyond, with a preview of the "Looking Forward to Accelerate" Pitch Day decisions agenda, which includes all the decisions the board ultimately needs to make after the Pitch Day in three months (see pages 280–281). The onboarding session should be scheduled during or before the venture team's Week 0.

Day in the Life of the team (time required—three hours to a half-day). Sometime between Week 3 and Week 8, the NVB members should schedule a half-day to visit (in person or virtually) the teams as they do their work. They can plan it at their leisure, and they may choose to drop in more than once, but the idea is that they engage with the teams in the thick of the action (the teams do not prepare a presentation for the NVB members for these visits). The team may be doing customer interviews or insights synthesis or product or service brainstorming and testing, and so on. One goal is for the board members to hear the voice of the customer.

Another goal is for them to understand how rigorous and robust the process is before the NVB's first formal Check-in. That way, every board member can enter that first Check-in meeting with the voice of the customer in their head as opposed to their own, potentially uninformed opinion. They also enter that meeting believing in the process, so they can be focused 100 percent on the new venture rather than wondering what the team has been doing.

Many NVB members enjoy the sessions so much that they have canceled plans and stayed longer or made a return visit just to be able to engage with the team and the customers more deeply.

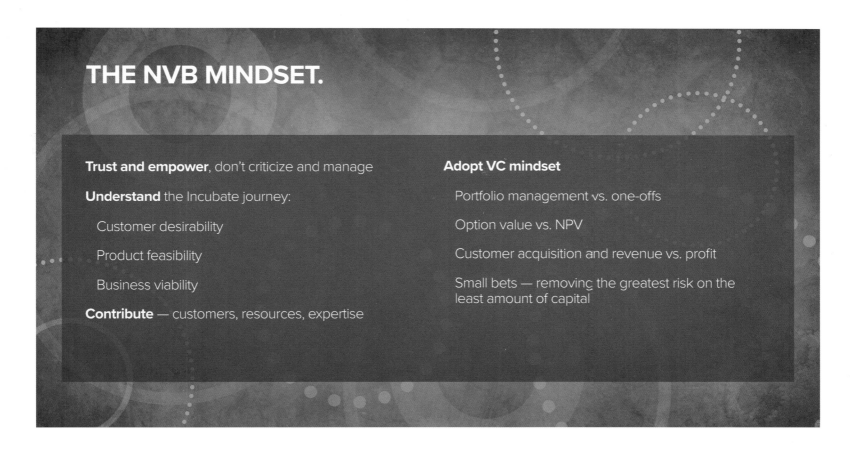

Weekly synthesis sessions (time required—two sessions for one hour each). Each week, the New Venture Team holds synthesis sessions to assess what it has learned during the week and then prepares the questions to answer the following week. While NVB members are welcome to listen in on any of these sessions, we ask that they engage remotely in a minimum of two of the sessions over the course of the Incubate project.

New Venture Board Check-in meeting plus executive session (time required—three to four hours). In Week 9, the team should hold the first formal Check-in meeting. In these meetings, team members present summaries of their customer pain findings from open-ended interviews and the early solutions they are considering based on customer storyboard interviews. Now that the pain, the opportunity, and the venture are becoming more real, the NVB should once again review the "Looking Forward to Accelerate" Pitch Day decisions agenda during an executive session so it is prepared to make decisions that maintain the new venture's momentum after launch. If a venture has made it this far, it is almost guaranteed that the venture will launch, because at this point, there is a huge amount of pain and a product or service solution that is feasible.

If the team has not heard enough pain to suit the NVB at this point, the new venture should shut down. It will be a difficult experience, but the teams and the NVB have to get comfortable killing ventures and moving on to the next one. By the way, this is much easier to do when you are working with a portfolio of ventures versus incubating and accelerating one at a time. No Silicon Valley VC has only one startup in their portfolio. (Chapter 9 discussed the need to develop the criteria to use to launch versus kill ventures as part of designing your Venture Factory.)

Pitch Day plus executive session (time required—four hours). Pitch Day is when the New Venture Team presents its final business, execution, and operating plan to the NVB and asks for funding to launch and accelerate. It is make-or-break time: either the venture is funded and gets underway or the plan is found wanting, and the new venture fades away or is put on hold.

Unlike a new business plan typically presented blind to a venture capitalist, the NVB has a good idea of what's coming. After all, the individual board members have been involved with the team, to various degrees, from the beginning; and during Check-in four weeks earlier, it had the opportunity to look at the team's plans and make comments and suggestions.

Still, that is no guarantee the NVB will sign off on what it sees now. Did the team take seriously the board members' suggestions during the Check-in? Has the team used those intervening weeks to resolve the issues the board presented? And what new thing has the team done that it has now added to the story?

At this point, the team has given its heart and soul to this new venture plan—it has conducted enormous amounts of research; it has lived this project day and night; and it has fallen in love not only with its plan, but with the plan's *prospects* for the months and years ahead. Team members see their future in this new venture, their best chance to make their mark on the world.

Now it comes down to a few hours of presentation.

Pitch Day, no matter how developed the relationship between the team and the NVB, is a *formal* process. As you saw in the detailed outline in chapter 7, the team members' presentations need to be professional, complete, and detailed—and they must answer any questions board members asked during the Check-in session accurately and precisely.

The NVB members don't have it any easier. They have gotten to know the team members, lived with them, and shared their dreams. In many cases, they may have even contributed to the team's vision and strategy. Now they must judge the venture and decide—Go or No Go, Fund or No Fund—based on customer desirability, product feasibility, and business viability. But the NVB does no favors to the team, the parent company, or itself, if it is not objective in its decision.

As for the parent company, the stakes couldn't be higher. It is pursuing the prospects of this new venture—and others in the pipeline—because it may represent the future of the Mothership itself. An investment in something outside the company's comfort zone may

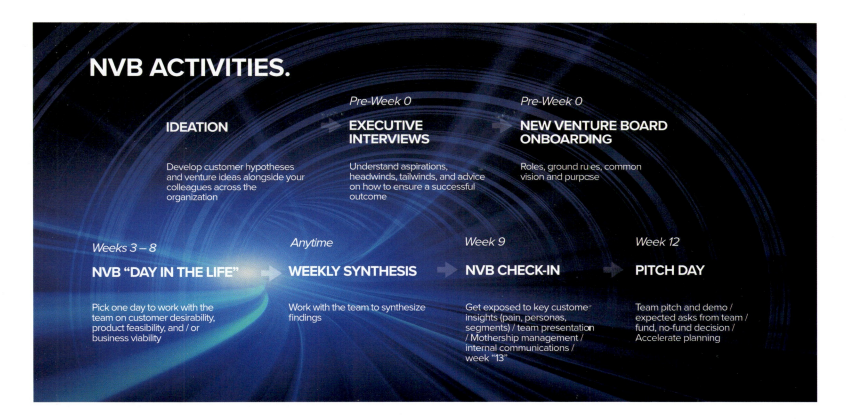

be on the line. And it may also be the last chance to keep top talent with the company, people who will otherwise depart if the venture isn't funded. That's a lot to have on the line.

Precisely because of the rigorous and robust twelve weeks of work, the number of customer interviews the team has conducted, the methodology the team has followed, and the regular participation by the NVB during the Incubate phase, once we get to Pitch Day, the chance that the new venture will *not* be launched and moved to the Accelerate phase (with initial funding) is exceedingly small. If you follow our model and kill early any ventures that can't find customer pain, can only solve the pain with an impossible solution, or can't see a way to make money, you are likely to fund the venture.

Pitch Day is usually followed by a celebration for both the New Venture Team and the NVB—a week or at least a weekend off after twelve weeks of long days and high intensity, followed by, most exciting of all, the first day of the Accelerate phase and life as a funded startup. Many team members tell us that Pitch Day was one of the most important and rewarding days of their careers.

PITCH DAY DECISIONS

The NVB must make a number of decisions on or shortly after the NVT presents their final business and execution plan on Pitch Day. To make sure they are prepared, we start sharing this agenda as early as the first NVB onboarding session; we review it during the Check-in session and we ensure the NVB is ready to act, come Pitch Day.

LOOKING FORWARD TO ACCELERATE

PREVIEW OF PITCH DAY DECISIONS ON THE HORIZON

- **Fund vs. No-Fund**
  - Do we have the right GM/business owner, product lead, and/or other critical roles in place to make maximum progress in the Build to Validate phase?
  - Do we have alignment on Build to Validate success milestones?
  - If future milestones are successfully met, what is the process to secure funding and what lead times are required?
  - Who else will have a voice in the fund/no-fund decision? Do they need to be prepped sooner rather than later?
  - Given that the venture will likely have customer pilots identified, are we prepared to launch the company immediately? If not, what is the likely timing?
    - Ideally, we can keep the team together and moving at Incubate pace.

- **Spin-In vs. Spin-Out**
  - What criteria will the New Venture Board/Mothership use to determine whether to spin in or spin out?
  - Who will own future investment/funding decisions in either case?
  - What will be the brand association?
  - If spun out, who are likely partners and when should they be approached?

- **Options for Execution (build, buy, partner, invest)**
  - Recommendations will be in the business and execution plan.

- **Future for Existing Team**
  - Immediate:
    - What is happening vis-à-vis their current compensation?
    - Assuming successful contribution to incubation, what type of company recognition will they or can they receive?
    - Have metrics been adjusted for the fact they will be working on something unique for three months that probably does not fit into their current performance plan?
  - Post-Pitch Day options for incubation team members:
    - For existing incubation members, will they be part of go-forward team?
      - Are they true founders or members of the team?
      - What role will each existing team member who stays play in the new venture?
    - If not part of the accelerating team:
      - Will they work on incubating the next new venture, either as a full-time or interim team member?
      - Will they help build the Venture Factory for the Mothership?
      - Will they move back to their former roles and share learnings with the home team?
    - Who will communicate roles and/or transitions to the team?

- **Team Composition Beyond Existing Team**
  - Accelerate will likely see additional hires plus outside development partners in early months.

- **Compensation**
  - Do we have an aligned incentive plan in place with the existing team and required new hires for Week 13 and beyond? Options may include:
    - Spin-In (either as a wholly owned subsidiary or as part of an existing business unit).
      - Careful consideration of additional hires needed from outside, if any.
      - Traditional compensation currently in place?
      - Salary plus bonus tied to results?
      - Salary plus synthetic or phantom equity tied to results?
    - Spin-Out.
      - Careful consideration of additional hires needed from outside, if any.
      - What will it take to recruit required team members from the outside?
      - What will it take to have consistency for team members?
      - How can compensation structures appropriate for early-stage entrepreneurs be implemented?

- **Governance**
  - Will the venture be a new company, a new line of business, or part of an internal company Venture Factory?
  - Who will the new venture report to and/or who will be on the new venture's board?
    - Possibilities: C-suite executive, appropriate business-line executive sponsor, possible external funding source (traditional VCs or CVCs), experienced target market, industry and/or domain experts.

- **Legal**
  - Entity formation.
  - Pilot agreements.
  - Nondisclosure/invention assignments.

- **IT/Security Plan**
  - Maintaining continuity from Incubate to Accelerate.
  - How to set up infrastructure that allows the venture to be nimble.
  - How to set up security requirements that balance the need to protect the Mothership vs. the team's need to run fast and iterate.

- **Location of the New Venture**
  - Where will the new venture be headquartered?
  - Will team members have to move?
  - Who can be virtual?
  - What experience does the GM/business owner have in running virtual operations?

- **Will the venture be able to use external services, or will it use the shared services available at the Mothership?** (e.g., accounting, finance, communications, procurement, channels, etc.)
  - If shared services, have New Venture Advocates been appointed and trained to serve as the new venture's liaisons to ensure the new venture can maintain momentum?

- **Identification/Introduction**
  - Connect with partners who can help build the MVP and/or develop channels (partner, buy, invest).

- **Gives and Gets**
  - What will be the mechanism to manage the interaction with the Mothership to leverage the core assets, capabilities, competencies, channels, customers, networks, and brand to help the new venture accelerate faster?
  - What from/to shifts does the Mothership need to make to provide incentives to core business leaders and/or management to ensure the new ventures can succeed? (e.g., metrics, comp., resourcing, procurement, governance, etc.)
  - How will the Mothership gain benefit and realize value from the new venture?

- **Funding Launch and Accelerate**
  - What will be the Accelerate path forward? Options include:
    - Team accelerates on its own.
    - Team accelerates with specialist support (finance, go-to-market, product, customer success, HR, etc., until full-time hires are in place and the venture is fully functional and able to stand on its own).
    - Team accelerates with a Board Member-in-Residence to mentor the team.

→ Key End of Incubate NVB Decisions

Before the NVB can fully move the venture into the Accelerate phase and the new activities that come with that transition, it must make two particularly critical decisions: governance and compensation.

Governance

Until Pitch Day, the NVB has been the governing body for the new venture. However, once the business is about to launch, several decisions need to be made that relate to governance. These decisions in turn will determine your ongoing role as an NVB member.

First, the NVB needs to decide which of the following three options it will pursue for the venture:

- Spin out the new venture, taking outside funding and accepting governance determined by those outside funders

- Create a wholly owned subsidiary, keeping the venture inside the Mothership but setting it up as its own line of business and allowing the venture team to go outside for services, such as accounting, legal, HR, marketing, and so on if it needs to for speed or specialized services

- Spin in to an existing business unit, requiring the new venture to leverage shared services of the Mothership to obtain economies of scale

If the decision is to spin the venture into an existing business unit, then that will likely dictate the governance model for the new venture. The same people governing the business unit will now govern the venture. That said, it is normal and useful for at least some members of the existing NVB to stay on for continuity while the venture develops momentum.

If the venture remains a wholly owned subsidiary and is not spun into an existing division with a preordained governance structure, a number of secondary choices need to be made, including:

- Keep the existing New Venture Board

- Add new internal board members who may provide additional support or subject-matter expertise as well as access to key core competencies or assets that the new venture needs to accelerate

- Add external board members who also may provide (among other contributions) subject-matter expertise, access to customers or markets, and experience the team can leverage

The best boards are built like the best teams: first you determine the roles, experience, or support the new venture requires; then you recruit board members who meet those specifications.

Here are a few more details to consider for each model.

Spin-Out

As we have discussed several times throughout the book, most of our clients do not want to spin out their new ventures and take outside funding because they want to retain the new markets, customers, and revenue for themselves. By doing so, they hope to get the credit they deserve—to become recognized as growth stocks, not value stocks. There are, however, two primary reasons the NVB might decide to spin out a new venture:

- The venture represents a big new opportunity that requires wider expertise than the company currently possesses or has access to that the additional funding partners could provide.
- The venture requires a lot of capital (think new infrastructure, new drugs, new hardware, new manufacturing facilities, or entertainment venues), and the company may not want to fund the venture on its own. It may decide it is better to share the upside with others, who are in turn willing to share the risk.

Should the NVB decide it wants to spin out the venture as a stand-alone startup for which it wants to raise additional capital from external funders, it needs to help the New Venture Team prepare a pitch deck that it can present to VCs, CVCs, or other funding sources. Our VC-in-Residence prepares the team members for the questions they are likely to be asked, and Mach49 helps identify potential candidates the team can approach. Our VC-in-Residence also educates the NVB on the "rules of engagement" when partnering with outside investors. The NVB members should also be prepared to leverage their personal and professional networks to provide contacts to the new venture. In some cases, it is helpful if the NVB demonstrates its support of the venture by participating in pitch sessions to outside funders.

Spinning out as a stand-alone enterprise means the new venture will need to set up all the internal functions and operations that well-established departments in the Mothership would otherwise provide. The NVB should be prepared to help the venture make that transition to independence. Activities may include:

- Setting up the structure and establishing the legal entity (legal, financial, capital structure, etc.)
- Reviewing the organization structure
- Assessing the board structure and board member recruiting
- Hiring and staffing, which may include contractor support
- Finalizing compensation and equity
- Technology development and support
- Investor networking, including VC and CVC introductions
- Marketing and branding leverage
- Attending road shows and supporting external PR

Ultimately, if professional investors such as traditional venture capitalists fund the venture, they will take the lead. An error, however, often made by parent companies that decide to spin out their new venture is that they treat their spin-out new ventures as a fait accompli—the parent company assumes its work is done, the new company is now on its own, and the parent company can wash its hands of the matter or, at the very least, it can rely on the new investors to be solely on point.

The reality is that this scenario is almost never the case. In fact, one of the main reasons an external funder may get interested is specifically because the parent company promises to be an engaged strategic investor providing key ingredients like access to customers, channels, and expertise, complementing the capital and startup operating experience the outside investors provide.

For that reason, while the outside investors control the monthly board meetings and agenda, the parent company should assume that it needs to stay engaged even after the venture becomes independent.

Wholly Owned Subsidiary

Given that most of our clients don't want to spin out their ventures, they still have to decide which governance model to use for the ventures they keep inside. Will these ventures be new businesses that are wholly owned but operating independently of the Mothership functions and business unit structures or will they need to leverage the shared services of the parent company to achieve economies of scale?

The NVB and the C-suite should be very honest with themselves. Where the NVB believes that the friction of dealing with the Mothership will be too great and would slow down the momentum of the new venture as it launches, though spending money on outside resources is not the ideal because it increases the venture's cash burn, the opportunity to avoid friction, maintain the momentum, and get the new venture into the market generating revenue faster will often overcome that concern.

If going outside for resources, Mach49 often steps in and helps the New Venture Team develop a plan for identifying, interviewing, and selecting those external resources. The NVB can easily do the same, leveraging its management experience and networks to play a similar role. Given that you may have individuals who haven't hired outside service providers before, the NVB members may need to participate in the interviews and first meetings to ensure the relationships are initiated successfully. Such resources may include:

- Legal
- Accounting
- Marketing
- Customer support
- Sales and sales support
- Product development
- HR or recruiting
- IT
- Others as required

In the wholly owned subsidiary model, the NVB is still the board and in control. It may have added to its numbers or changed a few of the folks sitting around the table, but the New Venture Team still answers to it as the board. This contrasts with the spin-out scenario where the New Venture Team now answers to the new board made up of the new investors. Depending on the Mothership's ownership vis-à-vis the new investors as determined by the funding round, at most only one member of the original NVB is likely to be an active board member. If the Mothership has kept only a minor holding in the venture, that person will likely only be a board observer.

Spin-In

As noted above, spin-in typically means taking the venture and moving it into an existing business unit. It is our least favorite option for early-stage ventures because most business unit heads are not compensated to pay attention to a startup that is not going to move the needle on their metrics. On top of that, often the timing of a new venture launch is terrible, coming somewhere in the middle of a budget year when funding for a startup was not anticipated and may represent an unwelcome cost.

Most of the Venture Factories (incubator and accelerators) we build are keeping the ventures with them through the entire Build to Validate stage of Accelerate and often into the early Build to Automate phase to ensure that the venture is not starved of oxygen inside the walls of what might be a multibillion-dollar, euro, yen, or pound business division. Once the venture starts generating revenue, then the traditional lines of business often get excited because it gives them a new shiny object to add to their sources of revenue. Until then, unless the venture was sponsored by the business unit in the first place, we recommend keeping it outside the day-to-day operations of the core and legacy business.

SHARED SERVICES

A Shared Services model is the one that most of the new ventures our clients launch end up adopting. That means that unless the new venture is part of a Venture Factory built to offer its own services to the ventures during the Accelerate phase, the newly funded and launched ventures are expected to rely on the shared services (HR, IT, legal, procurement, marketing, etc.) provided by the Mothership.

The only difference between the Shared Services model and the Independent Services model is that the Mothership has determined it wants to leverage the economies of scale of the parent company—bringing the assets, functional support, and scale that the Mothership can effectively provide to the ventures. This model makes total sense from a cost-management perspective—although watch those transfer pricing costs; we had one new venture client whose internal product development team was going to cost it *three times* and take twice the time that an outside provider offered—but you must mind the potential for friction that will slow the venture down.

Stanford Business School professor Huggy Rao and Stanford Engineering School professor Robert Sutton wrote an excellent book called *Scaling Up Excellence*. Now they are writing a book that we believe will have even greater impact and is hugely important to ensuring new ventures reach escape velocity: *The Friction Trap: How Smart Companies Make the Right Things Easier, the Wrong Things Harder, and Do It Without Driving People Crazy*. In Bob and Huggy's words*:

> "Since we wrote *Scaling Up Excellence* in 2014, my co-author Huggy Rao and I have been deluged with stories about how organizations stymie and exasperate their executives, front-line employees, customers, and so many others.
>
> The beleaguered people who we teach, participate in our research, and reach out to us often provide disturbing details. They explain how getting smart and necessary things done where they work requires convoluted, unnecessary, time-consuming, and soul-crushing gyrations—which get worse as organizations grow, age, and become more complex. This burden distracts them from more crucial matters. It undermines their performance and creativity. And it frustrates, discourages, and exhausts them."

> So, if you want to use a Shared Services model, that is fine—but as the NVB launching a venture from within, you have two additional jobs:
>
> - Help your new ventures avoid the same mistakes you may experience in the parent company.
> - Make sure the friction of the Mothership does not slow your new ventures down.
>
> We have found the best way to overcome that friction is for the Mothership to invest in creating the cadre of New Venture Advocates we introduce in this chapter in every department from which the new venture needs support. If you truly grant them the power to make exceptions to the standard rules and procedures, they will be the group that helps the ventures seize the Mothership advantage, continue to be laser focused on the customer (versus internal politics), and accelerate and scale much more quickly.
>
> ---
>
> *Bob Sutton, The Friction Project, https://www.bobsutton.net/friction-project/.

Compensation

One of the stickiest issues the NVB must deal with post–Pitch Day is *how to compensate* New Venture Team members.

On the one hand, you can argue that the company has a compensation plan that the team members are used to and therefore there is no reason to change the model. However, on the other hand, the new venture will likely need to recruit additional team members from the outside who are very tuned into the classic venture model, which includes sharing in the upside through some form of equity.

In addition, as noted, when we launch these new ventures, we want the Mothership to place a series of small bets, removing the greatest amount of risk on the least amount of capital, so we don't want you to overfund the fledgling ventures. With limited seed funding, the New Venture Team will appreciate that, like their peers running venture-backed startups, they must manage their burn rate. The only way to manage that burn rate is to not have to pay market rates on compensation, and the only way to do that is to offer *equity*.

If the new venture is a spin-out, that model is easy, because the new company will be set up with a normal cap table with equity for the founders, equity for the investors, and a pool for additional employees.

If the new venture is remaining as a wholly owned subsidiary, the NVB has to think about how to compensate the team. One model has worked very well—it revolves around creating a *phantom stock plan*. Phantom stock plans are fairly straightforward and tied to the venture hitting certain milestones negotiated between the NVB and the venture team. They operate in the same way as a real equity plan, except in this case, rather than the valuation being tied to an IPO or other exit event, it is tied to achieving targets. One of the interesting adaptations we made was to create two compensation levers. One is normal base pay plus a bonus lever, which looks exactly like the company's normal compensation model. The other is a phantom equity lever. New Venture Team members coming from the inside can adjust the mix based on their needs.

This option is attractive because it opens the opportunity to be part of an internal startup to people who might be incredible entrepreneurs and perfect for a New Venture Team but can't afford the risk due to their current life situation (kids in college, elderly parents, new baby). Using this model, they don't have to take the risk, but of course, then they don't get the upside either. For many of them, that is OK just for the sheer pleasure of getting to launch a new venture and doing something completely new and creative.

On the other hand, if you have a younger employee who is at risk of leaving because they *can* afford to take a risk and join a startup, the company now has a mechanism to retain that employee as a member of the venture team by offering them upside in that venture. While the return might not be quite as high as it could be in a real startup, the risk is also not nearly as high.

The phantom stock model, or a variation on this theme, also enables the new venture to recruit the talent and startup experience it may desperately need from the outside startup ecosystem—individuals who might not otherwise consider working for a perceived "dinosaur."

Our experience is that once these veterans of Silicon Valley or other startup ecosystems see that there is strong upside potential with less risk and the opportunity to build a startup without having to go hat in hand to the VCs every time they need money, they are intrigued. Once they realize that not only do they get to deal with just *one* investor, but that investor also comes with millions of customers, global reach, and tons of core competencies and experts to tap into, all of a sudden, ventures generated from within look *very* attractive.

→ Launch and Accelerate NVB Activities

The Incubate phase is over; you have decided to fund and launch the venture. Now is when the real fun begins; now is when you as senior executives and NVB members become true VCs as you shift into startup governance—and once you have funded several ventures—portfolio management mode.

As we move into the Accelerate phase, probably the best way to capture the shift from NVB Incubate activities to NVB Accelerate activities is to share the standard email that twenty-five-year veteran VC, now Mach49 senior vice president and Board Member-in-Residence Bill Kingsley crafted as our standard NVB "Welcome to Accelerate" transition letter.

Dear NVB,

[Your Name of the New Venture team] is making progress in its first days of Acceleration.

My understanding is that each of you will continue as New Venture Board members of the venture. You may also want to engage observers to the NVB, for leadership development, access to other subject matter expertise or cross-initiative/company pollination. Adding others as observers is a great way to grow experience for your colleagues. If possible, I would limit the number of observers for the first few meetings until you develop your own board meeting culture and cadence as these are likely to be very different from your traditional management meetings.

As far as time commitment, if you are going to continue as Board Members for this venture, as best practice, you should commit to attend regularly and be fully present for ALL board meetings. Per the schedule below, some of those meetings will be in person while others will be conducted by video conference.

Similar to how top tier VCs work with startups in their portfolios, board meetings for the venture should occur approximately every 4 weeks and will generally last 60 minutes. Two to three hours will be requested for meetings immediately prior to milestone reviews. A strawman list of potential dates is provided at the bottom of this note, corresponding to reporting schedules that exist within the Mothership. A specific schedule will require some back and forth with you and/or your assistants. I recommend that calendar holds be created as soon as possible covering the next 12 months and communicated to the venture team.

Regarding content and preparation for board meetings, here is what we don't want the New Venture Team to do: Spend the entire meeting going through board decks slide by slide as they might in a regular management review meeting. Instead, the expectation is that each board member (and respective observers) will have reviewed the materials ahead of time and have reasoned questions coming into the meeting. We want such valuable time together focused on strategic considerations that can leverage the board member and further develop the business. This is a critical muscle to build up front for each of the ventures.

What to Expect from Accelerate Board Meetings

As noted, the NVB will prepare for monthly one-hour board meetings. The team lead's goal is to get all board members (and observers) materials three days in advance. A typical board meeting at this early stage looks like this example:

1. Board materials Q&A (15 minutes)
2. Strategy, milestone, customer topic (15 minutes)
3. Upcoming milestones, plan needs, help (10 minutes)
4. Board minutes, wrap-up, and next steps (5 minutes)
5. Executive session with board only (15 minutes)

In the first fifteen minutes, the team lead should get participants to ask clarifying questions about the materials. Answers and discussion should be short. Items requiring follow-up should be noted and scheduled for further review. We install objectives and key results (OKRs) and govern the venture to a series of milestones matching the operating plan developed for Pitch Day, unless subsequently revised.

While NVB members may transition in and out over time as the needs of the venture ebb and flow, the goal is to preserve some level of continuity over the long term, and where transitions do need to happen, ensure they are seamless.

→ Seizing the Mothership Advantage—Building an Internal Innovation Ecosystem

As board member, CEO, or C-suite member, one of the most important activities that you will focus on during the Accelerate phase—now that you realize your organization can indeed create, build, and launch great ventures from within—is to build the internal innovation ecosystem to support those ventures that we have alluded to throughout the book. As noted from the start, we are not talking about transformation, but about unleashing a cadre of New Venture Advocates (NVAs), housed outside the Venture Factory in your various functions and divisions, to help the new ventures reap the competitive advantage that comes from being launched by a big company. By seizing those Mothership advantages, you can beat the startups at their own game.

There are three key Mothership drivers to launching successful ventures and Venture Factories:

- An engaged New Venture Board
- A passionate, full-time, committed New Venture Team
- A trained, empowered, and entrepreneurial cadre of New Venture Advocates

THE SILICON VALLEY INNOVATION ECOSYSTEM.

The innovation ecosystem to support new ventures.

We have discussed the first two, but what is this third group?

To help illustrate, whenever we give a speech—whether to large groups of executives or to the NVB during its onboarding session—we show two slides.

The first slide (on the previous page) shows an image of the Silicon Valley ecosystem. If you think about Silicon Valley, it revolves around startups and entrepreneurs. All of the players were founded and grew up in service to the startups, so they evolved in fundamentally different ways than their peer companies in other places. Our law firms, Wilson Sonsini Goodson & Rosati, Orrick, DLA Piper, and Fenwick & West LLP, among others, do not look like big law firms in Minneapolis or Paris. Silicon Valley Bank does not look like any of the big banks anywhere else in the world; each of these firms and their peers are 100 percent geared toward servicing startups.

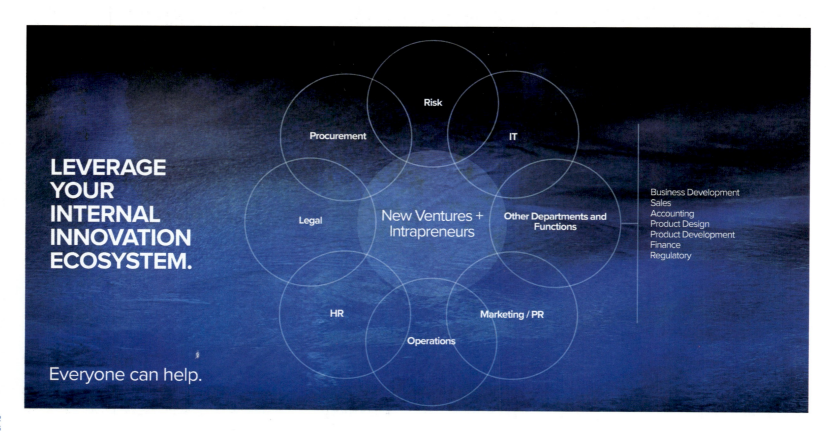

So, while we don't believe in transformation or changing the whole company, we do believe you need at least *one* entrepreneurial-minded team member in every function who will be the go-to person for the new ventures. That person, the New Venture Advocate, must be empowered to work with the sense of urgency and speed required for the ventures to succeed. As early as the prep phase we detailed in chapter 3, one of the topics we start talking to clients about is how they are going to bring the Silicon Valley inside. In other words, how are they going to build an internal innovation ecosystem to remove friction and support their new ventures?

For example, as you look at the second slide (on the facing page):

- Who in legal will write the one-page term sheet for the pilot a customer wants to run with the venture (not the forty-page term sheet)?
- Who in procurement will get the new vendor that the startup needs to partner with on your approved list in a week versus ninety days?
- Who in HR is able to write the spec for that growth hacker they have never heard of before or fast-track employees needed to build the new venture who don't look like your typical employee? Or, more challenging, implement that phantom share plan the venture needs to attract great team members.
- Who in marketing is going to challenge the traditional brand police and help the new venture develop momentum in the market? (One of our very successful ventures is a wholly owned subsidiary of the Mothership. It was going to use the wholly owned brand of the Mothership as *approved by the top executives in the company*, and the brand police still wasted six weeks, delaying the venture's launch, saying, "That's not possible, you can't use that brand.")

And so on through all the departments likely to see requests from your new ventures as they accelerate and scale.

What is really cool about building a cadre of NVAs is that it will be another major milestone in the Mothership's efforts to truly institutionalize disruption. Creating a cohort of NVAs provides an opportunity for people in every function—who might not want the lifestyle of an entrepreneur—to be *entrepreneurial*, to drive change in their department or functions. NVAs can help identify the from-to shifts that departments or functions need to make to stimulate growth. Even better, often the mechanisms and decisions they make on behalf of the ventures end up being of tremendous value in reinvigorating the legacy business as well. Think of each of these pioneering individuals becoming a catalyst or revolutionary cell inside their organizations, holding up the mirror to the systems and processes that may have made sense at one time in the Mothership's history but don't have a reason to exist anymore.

The reason the NVB should think about the three governance options (spin-in, wholly owned subsidiary, spin-out) up front during the Preparing to Incubate phase is because if the Mothership knows for sure it wants to leverage a Shared Services model, then the NVB and the New Venture Team will want to identify, interview, and start working with NVA candidates early so they can be involved in as much of the incubation process as possible. Early involvement gives those NVAs the feeling of ownership over the new ventures and gives them time to start imagining the challenges a new venture may pose to the Mothership's standard operating procedures and rules.

If the goal is indeed to build a pipeline and portfolio of new ventures to drive growth (with or without a Venture Factory), the NVB should keep that in mind as it is determining the number of NVAs it might need to engage, train, and empower.

Here are the activities that NVAs may want to participate in to prepare them for supporting future venture launches. While you may not need their help during the Incubate phase, they can make a world of difference as the venture moves to the Accelerate and Scale phases where access to Mothership resources and support can determine how fast the venture can grow.

NVA Activities during the Prep Phase

- Identify NVAs from the critical set of corporate functions that can accelerate (or conversely, impede) new venture or business creation and access to Mothership capability. Those can include (but are not limited to):
  - Human resources
  - IT
  - Legal
  - Risk management
  - Procurement
  - Marketing
  - Government and regulatory
  - Finance
  - Sales
  - Operations
  - Manufacturing and supply chain

- The NVA team should include an NVA Sponsor, a single point of contact who can act as NVA liaison. That person may even be a member of the NVB. The NVA Sponsor needs to have the respect and clout within the organization to help the NVAs progress and overcome obstacles in their departments. This Sponsor could, as an example, come from the office of the CEO, COO, CAO, a well-respected CHRO, or even the chief of staff, among others.

- Interview and onboard the NVA team members just as you would onboard the New Venture Team and the NVB. Brief them on overall context, need, and their role going forward. Make sure they know that they are empowered and expected to speak up, challenge, shine a light on the friction the company may unintentionally create, and fight for the new ventures.

- Understand the rules of engagement with each of the core functions. Which of their activities, rules, and processes can be modified to support the pace of the new venture versus what are immovable policies? Beginning this dialogue early helps everyone involved figure out how to leverage what the Mothership has to offer in the most efficient and effective way.

NVA Activities during the Ideate Phase

- Invite NVAs in during the Ideate phase of the work, so that they:
  - Are a part of creating early ideas and venture hypotheses. That also gives them the full context of where the venture ideas came from and their underlying logic, especially relative to the customer pain the New Venture Team is trying to solve.
  - Begin creating relationships with the New Venture Team and the NVB right from the start of the work effort.

- Can begin, as early as possible, the work of contemplating actions that assist with impediment removal for new ventures and businesses.

- Conduct an NVA-focused working session during the Ideate phase that allows the NVAs to think through the from-to shifts that must occur in each of their departments for successful venture realization. In many cases, from-to shifts may need to occur in a number of departments to support not only the spin-in and wholly owned subsidiary models but also the spin-out model (for example, legal helping to push an outside funder's term sheet over the line in a timely manner). During the working session, participants should ask the following questions, keeping the current venture idea in mind:

  - What do we have to do today (in each function) to support the ventures?

  - What do we need to add, change, or do differently in the future to enable new venture(s) as we incubate and/or accelerate them?

  - Who or where might that support come from (inside, outside, etc.)?

Summaries of these working sessions should include the New Venture Team and the NVB, so the teams can begin to create the relationships, shared assumptions, and collective mindset conducive to Mothership management and the NVAs' work going forward.

- Have the NVAs prepare hypotheses for what they might do to improve the experience of New Venture Team members who need to work with their departments or functions. Then have them write a Challenge Statement that they can share with both their department and the NVB about their vision for how their function or department could help the new venture reach escape velocity and solve their customer pain faster, cheaper, and smarter. Here are some simple worksheets NVAs can use.

**EXERCISE:
HYPOTHESIS**

**We believe [type of person]
needs to solve [problem]
while performing [task]
which will give them [new ability].**

**We believe that [type of customer]
have a [problem/lack of knowledge/behavior]
that leads to [consequence]
and that if we tried [solution]
it would lead to [improvement/results].**

Hypotheses

**EXERCISE:
CHALLENGE QUESTION**

How might we [goal or result]
for [stakeholders]
in a way that [approach]
so that [benefit or impact]

Questions

**EXERCISE:
MOTHERSHIP MANAGEMENT FROM-TO SHIFTS**

Preconditions for Success

Show Guts
- Fully embrace trends and digital disruption.
- Get serious about unleashing your talent.
- Tolerate risk and failure.
- Continuously fund a portfolio of small bets.

Move Fast
- Free entrepreneurs to make customer-driven decisions quickly.
- Leverage core assets and competencies.
- Urgency—12 weeks is all you need to incubate new ventures and make a fund/no-fund decision.

Be Engaged
- Set up a New Venture Board to ensure startup success, with executives who can:
  - Deliver funding and make go/no-go decisions.
  - Ensure the new venture can get access to customers, channels, and markets.
  - Provide access to core competencies, assets, and capabilities of the organization.
  - Remove Mothership friction to ensure the new venture can reach escape velocity.

Think Fresh
- What is getting in the way of creating and launching new ventures?
  - Metrics
  - Governance
  - Compensation
  - Resource Allocation
  - Procurement
  - Policies
  - Procedures
  - Politics

From   **To**

Ultimately, the NVAs drive these hypotheses and Challenge Statements down to a set of from-to shifts they believe the Mothership as a whole and, more specifically, their departments have to make to support new venture creation and acceleration.

NVA Activities during the Incubate Phase

- NVAs work individually and as a cohort to develop early plans to address Mothership management and the from-to shifts and actions they can see are necessary.
- NVAs should be invited to attend any of the weekly synthesis sessions they wish as observers to stay up to speed on the New Venture Team's progress.
- NVAs should be invited to attend or listen in on the Week 9 Check-in with the NVB (live or recorded).
  - NVAs should attend or listen in on the Check-in to keep up with current venture status and to hear NVB questions, considerations, and recommendations. NVAs can adjust and add to their from-to shifts list, provide updates to their department or function heads, and enlist the rest of their team to highlight early naysayers or challenges. They can then either request help from the NVB or other senior executives to help remove potential friction or adjust their efforts accordingly.
  - The New Venture Team may also want to host a meeting specifically for the NVAs to share their Gives and Gets page, which highlights areas where the Mothership can help ensure the new venture can take advantage of all the Mothership has to offer.
- NVAs also attend or listen in on Pitch Day, with plans and approvals in place to start interacting with the new venture once it is launched.

NVA Accelerate Activities

The venture has launched and now is moving into the Accelerate phase. Now the NVAs kick into gear and are available to answer questions and access resources, expertise, core competencies, and assets the venture might need—in other words, to provide the support for which they have been preparing. Inevitably, there are challenges, but that's OK. Just as the new venture is going through the Accelerate phases of Build to Validate, Build to Automate, and Build to Grow, so too does the role of the NVA evolve.

Early on, focus areas for NVAs might include (but are not limited to):

- Marketing (brand owner coordination or affiliation, customer momentum activities)
- Sales (account knowledge or coordination)
- Human resources (fast-track employees, compensation mapping)
- Digital or IT (linkage with existing digital strategies)
- Legal support (either inside counsel or working with venture-experienced external counsel)
  - Term sheets, contractual support, licenses, IP, corporate actions, governance
- Procurement (approve vendors, get on approved lists, leverage Mothership buying power)

→ The Three Ps

In the end, seizing the Mothership advantage, institutionalizing disruption, and ensuring the company's new ventures can scale and reach escape velocity comes down to how well the NVB and the NVAs can overcome the perpetually present three Ps preventing peak performance:

Policies. Established companies have established rules and policies. They do that to maximize efficiency, reduce costs, limit legal risk, and control renegade (which is usually the exception, not the rule) behavior. Companies such as Netflix have taught us that most of these policies are outdated in today's business environment. And they are exceptionally useless to new ventures, which are not supposed to be efficient and cost effective. Rather, they are supposed to be *successful*. Forcing the new venture to follow the same rules as the parent company essentially puts it in a straitjacket that hurts its chances of survival.

Procedures. Similarly, mature companies develop universal systems and processes that define organizational communications, filing paperwork, applying for internal job openings, and so on. Compared to the corporate organizational pyramid, a new venture is an impossibly flat organization. In a startup, the entry-level team member talks directly to the CEO daily, and that CEO, when everyone else is busy, may end up scheduling the daily stand-ups or making the coffee.

That's not to say there are no rules and procedures in a new venture, but there are very few, and most deal with who speaks to customers and the parent company. Internally, it is almost a pure democracy, and any premature attempt to structure that behavior will either be ignored or slow the venture's ability to react quickly to market changes.

Politics. In many ways, politics is the greatest institutional threat to a new company venture. Within a mature company where the rules of success and career advancement are well established, a maverick operation like a new startup, not least because it gets special treatment from senior management, can be perceived as a real threat—a virus that needs to be attacked by corporate antibodies.

This resistance is almost always sub rosa and all but invisible. But, suddenly, requests from the new venture go unanswered or are responded to too slowly or incompletely as threatened or jealous peers quietly conduct sabotage on the intruder.

Neither is senior management immune. Top executives may have their own agendas; initiatives that they want to pursue that don't include a new venture, if successful, may help the career of a rival or take resources from their own pet project (even though that project has no validated customer pain to justify it). When politics at the executive level happens, suddenly promised resources to the new venture dry up and its talent is raided for other projects. These threats are truly pernicious, because they usually don't become obvious until the new venture is crippled and likely doomed.

The only remedy to this type of destructive company politics is to make it too costly to maintain. And that can only begin at the top—with the CEO and board of directors. They must be committed to stand by their new ventures through thick and thin—at least at the beginning—and not abandon a venture the first time it hits a rough patch. Moreover, the CEO and board must communicate that commitment throughout the organization, and anyone who attempts to sabotage, slow-walk, or divert resources is part of the past, and *not* part of the company's future.

The three Ps are not inevitable, they are not your company's destiny, and they can be overcome, one New Venture Team member, one Venture Factory member, one NVB member, and one NVA at a time. The work is exciting, creative, fulfilling, *and* fun. The energy, enthusiasm, engagement, and renewed sense of purpose the NVAs display—because they have an opportunity to help drive growth, to immerse themselves in truly *meaningful* work—is palpable and contagious. You are not just providing opportunities to your internal entrepreneurs; you are providing entrepreneurial opportunities to everyone in the firm who raises their hand. By unleashing the NVAs, you help them help you unleash the Unicorns within.

Finally, NVB members need to have a growth mindset and to adopt the demeanor of a top-tier VC versus a classic management review board member. VCs lean into their investments and do whatever they need to do to accelerate those ventures and make them successful. The best VCs are typically C-level startup veterans: they've been down this path before and can provide wise counsel.

Moreover, top investors typically have huge networks they can call upon to provide the highest levels of specialty expertise to aid the new company. And, if worse comes to worst, because of their investment, they hold sufficient equity in the company to intervene and, if necessary, replace the new venture's top management with veteran outside talent. All these characteristics should describe an NVB member and their role across all three stages of the Accelerate phase: Build to Validate (equivalent to seed funding), Build to Automate (Series A), and Build to Grow (Series B).

Soon you too will become experienced startup board members. You will develop a sixth sense for common pitfalls and challenges. You will always be on the lookout for these challenges so you can ward them off before they become terminal. A great board and a great team can work miracles together as long as the NVB members stay engaged. As you move through the Accelerate phase and on into the Scale phase, an engaged NVB is still a precondition for success.

So, what are you waiting for? It's time to get started. *Now* is your opportunity to unleash the Unicorn within. But first let's pull it all together for you as we sum up the journey and share one final thought. It can be the first poster for your Venture Factory wall:

The Ten Principles for Building Your Growth Engine and Beating the Startups at Their Own Game.

Conclusion

Unleashing the Unicorn Within

The Ten Principles for Driving Growth and Beating Startups at Their Own Game

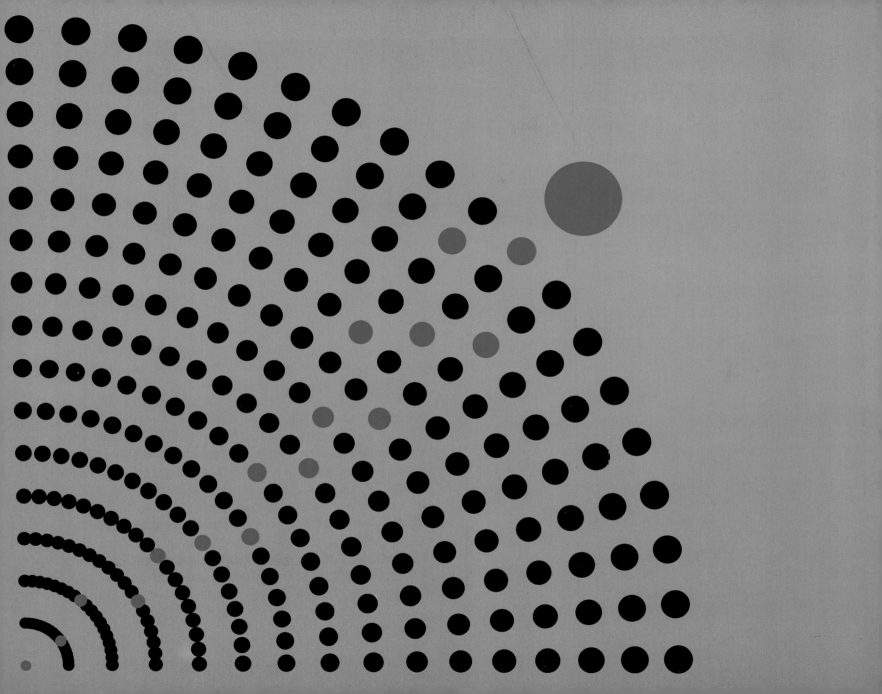

Over the course of tens of thousands of words and scores of charts, we have covered hundreds of different items related to guiding a startup venture from its earliest conception to the moment it is ready to burst on the scene, challenge its market competitors, and delight its new customers.

We've also shown you how to manage the Mothership, to deal with the changes these new ventures bring, and ways to seize the Mothership advantage—and we've shared how to construct your own Venture Factory, giving you the ability to repeat the new venture creation process over and over into the future.

We hope that, given the complexity of these processes, you will revisit the pages of this book for reference many times. As you do, take a few minutes to revisit this chapter as well. It will help you, amid all the detail of new company creation, to remember the big picture.

Let's put it all together.

1. Frame the Challenge
Creating, building, and launching successful new ventures always begins with an aspirational challenge related to the customer pain you are trying to solve. This challenge should be broad enough to generate disruptive ideas, yet still be bounded by well-defined value propositions to real customers and stakeholders, that is, to the people who matter most.

2. Unleash Your Internal Talent
Organizations that wish to remain relevant and thrive in the digital economy need to unleash their Intrapreneurs and give them the time and space to focus and work full-time on new ventures. In identifying these individuals, the parent company needs to step away from its usual evaluation rules and metrics and look for those people whose intrapreneurial personalities may have limited their careers or labeled them as mavericks or troublemakers in the company. Further, the parent company should recognize that not all internal entrepreneurs are the same—their strengths and skills become crucial at different points during the Incubate and Accelerate phases—and should be leveraged at the appropriate phase.

3. Embrace Risk and Failure
Why, despite enjoying tremendous assets and an army of talented Intrapreneurs, do many large companies find it difficult to design

and launch new ventures, especially new ventures that can disrupt existing markets and create important new ones? It's simple: they don't embrace risk and failure as part of their culture. Smart organizations are now redefining the way they assess their people. In those companies, taking the risk to innovate has become a badge of honor, rather than a blemish on one's career.

4. Add Method to the Madness

Successful Venture Building requires three factors:

- A team that is passionate about its new venture idea and allowed to work full-time for at least twelve weeks can handle the pace and ambiguity inherent in entrepreneurship, and brings complementary talents (superpowers) to bear to realize that idea. If a multibillion-dollar, multinational company cannot free up four to six people to work on a new venture for twelve weeks full-time (and hold their old jobs in case there is no customer pain), that company isn't serious about innovation.

- A portfolio of tools, frameworks, and methodologies to ensure the company has a repeatable and scalable process to enable New Venture Teams and the Mothership to work at the greatest speed and with the greatest predictability and efficiency. Only with a real methodology can a large company maximize each new venture's probability of success and ensure it can build a pipeline and portfolio of new ventures (not just one). You need a portfolio of new ventures to drive meaningful, move-the-needle growth.

- The outside inspiration, experience, and mentoring needed to move smartly and minimize mistakes. The best Venture Factories provide their startup teams with a broad range of expertise—former entrepreneurs, VC investing experience, customer development professionals, UX or UI experts, go-to-market gurus, product developers, technology architects, marketers that love storytelling and design, and C-suite whisperers to help the Mothership embrace the from-to shifts needed to ensure their new ventures thrive.

5. Find Real Customer Pain

The best startups always exhibit *radical customer empathy*. They understand that surveys, focus groups, and hearsay are *never* substitutes for direct customer and stakeholder interviews. Surveys are statistically significant, but strategically irrelevant, because you have merely outsourced your visceral understanding and empathy for the customer to someone else, who will repackage it and sell it again. By outsourcing your understanding of customer pain, you miss valuable opportunities to learn the nuances of culture, philosophy, style, and personality that matter most to delivering a compelling customer experience. Whether it is B2B, B2C, or B2B2C—regardless how technical and complex what you are building is—to sell it requires a customer to buy it.

Needless to say, if your venture is going to conduct the interviews, that team must first want to talk to customers and, second, have the training, discipline, and dedication that exceeds the professionals. Keep in mind that most independent startups don't have the budget to hire professionals—and they are definitely not more trained—they just have less baggage and more courage to just do it. Most of all, the team must be armed with the right questions about what it is trying to learn as it moves from pain point interviews to storyboards to prototypes—always listening for nuances every step of the way.

6. Master the Art of the Possible

All great startups can identify opportunities at the nexus of customer pain, the latest technologies, and emerging business models. And they have the imagination to move from there to the creation of a monetizable product or service that solves that pain. Having the vision to leap from pain to product to market is the magic moment for all great startups. Given the pace of change, large companies and their internal entrepreneurs must stay current on the trends and technologies they can access and adapt—even create and use—to delight their customers over and over again.

7. Work from the Future Backward

The best way to determine where you are going is to first decide where you want to be; the destination defines the direction. You need to establish your business and product offerings in the context of an opportunity framework—an executable vision—that is sufficiently significant to drive Mothership growth and a product road map to achieve that aspiration. With this bigger picture in mind, you now work back to the nearest future during which you can determine success. That is, you start with the minimum viable product: an MVP that can be tested quickly and inexpensively to learn, find traction, and ultimately establish product-market fit that can scale.

8. Prototype and Pilot: De-Risk, De-Risk, De-Risk

The Accelerate phase may be even more important than the Incubate phase. You want to incubate right to avoid the garbage-in, garbage-out problem, but Accelerate is when you drive to product-market fit and real revenue. Finding product-market fit requires an agile, yet rigorous approach to prototyping, piloting, and when necessary, pivoting. Regarding the last: don't fall in love with your product or service; many of the world's greatest companies were founded with very different product plans or business models than what led to their ultimate success. Be willing to turn on a dime in a new direction based on what you learn from customers. And whether it is technical, market, business model, or governance risk, your goal is to remove the greatest amount of risk with the least amount of capital.

9. Seize the Mothership Advantage to Reach Escape Velocity

Corporate startups have a unique advantage over typical VC-backed startups. The Global 1000 should avail themselves of those advantages, not least because they completely differentiate you from the disruptors dismissing you as dinosaurs. We are convinced that we are only in the early stages of seeing the current Disruption Economy evolve worldwide. For large companies to survive and thrive in this time of radical change, the name of the game is *growth*. To grow exponentially and cast aside the startup gnats buzzing you, the C-suite needs its own disruptor, its own chief growth officer. And this CGO needs a platform to drive growth—an internal Venture Factory with *one* job: to build a pipeline and portfolio of new customer-obsessed ventures, businesses, and products on a regular basis, in perpetuity, and across the globe.

The success of the CGO, the Venture Factory, and the ventures—and, therefore, the company—depends on their ability to leverage the Mothership's established customers, channels, talent, technology, brand, supply chain, and capital to ensure its new ventures reach escape velocity into the marketplace far more quickly, and more robustly, than any independent startup against which the company competes. You must understand your core assets, capabilities, and competencies, and then you *must* remove the friction—the orthodoxies, antibodies, and inertia that kill good ideas or, at a minimum, starve them of oxygen. You need to get all that is *great* about your company in the hands of your internal entrepreneurs and New Venture Advocates. And you must create your own "Silicon Valley inside" to let your ventures thrive.

10. Do Good, Have Fun

There are two altruistic reasons to start a new venture and frankly why we founded Mach49. First, people are living longer and longer due to improved health care and technological advancements. That means they will be working longer and longer. As much as we celebrate startups, most people are employed by large companies, and they need purposeful, meaningful work for their ever-longer careers. Launching new ventures is one way to allow people in your organization to be entrepreneurial and creative, to feel alive, and yes, to have *fun*. We are blessed to be alive seven days a week, not just on the weekends. Life is meant to be lived, and the kind of work you feel good about can be extraordinarily fulfilling and rewarding. And, if you can excise the fear of failure from the lexicon of your workforce, then even ventures that don't work still become valuable growth experiences that can improve the core business.

The second reason is to tackle the big, complex challenges we face on this planet. Climate change, education, disease, poverty, racism and bigotry, wildfires, hunger, water, disappearing species, and other challenges need our big companies to lean in—willing and able to disrupt them. Whatever your values, your duty is to build ventures that reflect the change you want to effect in the world.

Big companies have the ability within their power to address every one of these challenges. If we fall into the trap of finding the challenges too overwhelming, we risk doing nothing. If we think "that's not our job," that it's government's task to fix that problem, and that we personally are helpless, we are *wrong*, and deeply so. Each and every one of us has within us the capacity to drive profound change.

New ventures can be bold. They are a way to place the small bets we need to test solutions. They can move with speed and agility and, when managed right, are unbounded by the status quo. Even if your new idea isn't destined to solve anything so grand, the way you go about building your venture can do good in and of itself. You, your Venture Factory, and your ventures can be role models in the way you hire, use resources, treat people, interact with partners, engage with the environment, accept differences, respect human rights, and play for the long term, not just the quarter. You *can* do well by doing good and you can have fun along the way, whether you are in the C-suite leading the way or the entrepreneur making it happen. Each and every one of us can drive positive, sustainable, meaningful growth for ourselves, our customers, our companies, and yes, absolutely, our planet.

The time to start is *now*.

The moment is here.

Build your Venture Factory.

Do great things.

Unleash the Unicorn within!

Notes

Introduction

1. Sarah Krouse, "Dimon Sees Threat from Silicon Valley," *Wall Street Journal*, February 26, 2014, https://www.wsj.com/articles/BL-MBB-17071.
2. Hans Greimel, "Toyoda Warns Toyota Faces 'Life-or-Death' Battle," Automotive News, May 13, 2018, https://www.autonews.com/article/20180513/OEM/180519904/toyoda-warns-toyota-faces-life-or-death-battle.
3. HEC Paris, "40% of Companies Will Be Dead in Ten Years," November 15, 2019, https://www.hec.edu/en/news-room/40-companies-will-be-dead-ten-years.
4. CB Insights, "$1B+ Market Map: The World's 936 Unicorn Companies in One Infographic," December 9, 2021, https://www.cbinsights.com/research/unicorn-startup-market-map/.
5. Dan Primack, "Why the Startup World Needs to Ditch 'Unicorns' for 'Dragons,'" Axios, April 31, 2021, https://www.axios.com/unicorn-startup-privately-held-valued-1-billion-c64e66cb-ec22-4c68-9aaf-db7f71431704.html.
6. For other sources, see Bobby Chernev, "What Percentage of Startups Fail? (67+ Stats for 2020)," Review 42, February 25, 2021, https://review42.com/resources/what-percentage-of-startups-fail/.
7. Maija Palmer, "This Is Why Corporate Accelerators Fail—Your Answers," Sifted, May 12, 2020, https://sifted.eu/articles/why-corporate-accelerators-fail/.
8. Palmer, "This is Why Corporate Accelerators Fail."

Chapter 1

1. Many people, including Marc Andreessen, credit Andy with introducing this idea.

Chapter 6

1. Steve Blank, "Why Build, Measure, Learn—isn't just throwing things against the wall to see if they work—the Minimum Viable Product," blog post, May 6, 2015, https://steveblank.com/2015/05/06/build-measure-learn-throw-things-against-the-wall-and-see-if-they-work/.

Chapter 7

1. Oliver Gassmann, Michaela Csik, and Karolin Frankenberger, *The Business Model Navigator: 55 Models That Will Revolutionise Your Business* (Harlow, UK: Pearson Education Limited, 2014).

Chapter 10

1. Julie Bort, "Retiring Cisco CEO Delivers Dire Prediction: 40% of Companies Will Be Dead in 10 Years," *Business Insider*, June 8, 2015, https://www.businessinsider.com/chambers-40-of-companies-are-dying-2015-6.

Index

ABCs of business decay, 272
Accelerate phase, 206–225
    being prepared for, 30–33
    Build to Automate in, 214, 215, 219–220
    Build to Grow in, 214, 215, 220–221
    Build to Validate in, 32, 175, 214, 215, 217–219, 280
    discipline in, 221–223
    industry veterans in, 211
    mistakes to avoid in, 216
    NVAs in, 295
    NVBs in, 287–288
    objectives and outcomes in, 217–221
    potential for success in, 224–225
    preconditions for, 210–211
    stages and swim lanes in, 214–216, 221–222
    tips for, 211–216
    what happens in, 208–210
    work plan for, 221–222
acceleration, 10
    road map for, 19
    in startups versus Venture Factories, 14
administration and coordination, 247–248
advisory boards, 36, 211–212, 242
agendas, "Looking Forward to Accelerate," 30, 32–33, 280–281

agility, 13
Airbnb, 8, 17, 29
Airbus, 88
Airtable, 60–61, 113, 164
Altman, Sam, 210
altruism, 303
Alvarez, Cindy, 121
Amazon, 8
anchors, 94
apples to oranges comparisons, 120, 178–179
Apple TV, 60
Archer-Daniels-Midland, 88
Asset Jam, 82, 84, 94, 171
    Gives and Gets based on, 198
assets, access to, 271
assumptions, about superstars, 38
automation, building for, 214, 215, 219–221

Balsamiq, 62–63, 165
Benchmark Capital, 28
Beriker, James, 209
Berkshire Hathaway, 272
bias, 106, 118
big-bang releases, 216
Blakely, Dave, 172, 173
Blank, Steve, 172, 210
Blink: The Power of Thinking Without Thinking (Gladwell), 180
Blockbuster, 17

Board Members-in-Residence (BMIRs), 213, 266–267
body language, 129
brand building, 97
brand equity, 84
budgets
    concept suitability and, 76–77
    in operating and execution plans, 193
    planning for Incubate, 56
    for Venture Factories, 256–260
Buffett, Warren, 272
buildable products, 152, 169–171, 200
Build to Automate, 214, 215, 219–220
    iteration in, 219
    work plan for, 221–222
    work streams for, 218
Build to Grow, 214, 215, 220–221
    iteration in, 219
    work plan for, 221–222
Build to Validate, 175, 214, 215, 217–219
    milestones in, 32, 280
    work plan for, 221–222
Burn, Mike, 94, 171
burn rate, 193
business and execution plans, 178–179
business case, 180–192
    business model in, 190–192
    customer journey in, 187–188
    on customer pain, 184–185
    describing the opportunity in, 185–186

    go to market and monetization in, 190–192
    market section in, 182–184
    product vision and MVP in, 189
    tech road map in, 189
    where you've been in, 181–182
    who you are in, 180
business decay, 272
Business Model Navigator, The (Gassman, Frankenberger, and Csik), 190
business models, 216
    Build to Automate, 220
    business plan on, 190–192
    experts on, in Venture Factories, 246
    list of, 191
Business phase, 176–205
    building the business case in, 180–192
    operating and execution plan in, 192–205
    responsibilities in, 178
business units
    funding ventures from, 269
    working with, 243
    See also spin-in ventures

calendars
    for customer interview scheduling, 61
    NVT, 55, 56
    for prototype interviews, 155
Calendly, 61

capability, concept assessment for, 69, 78–79
cash flow, 193
CB Insights, 9
celebrations, 208
central hubs, 59–60
CEO-in-Residence, 96
CEOs
   discretionary funds of, 269
   finding the new venture's, 212–213
Challenge Framing, 68, 81–82, 94, 98–99, 237, 300
   approving output of, 273
   in building Venture Factories, 236
   in exploring venture options, 274, 275
   finding ideas with, 237
   managing, 247
   in New Venture Competitions, 104
   NVBs and, 273
Challenge Question exercise, 86, 294
Challenge Statements, 81–82, 86, 92
   describing in the business case, 181
   Domain Exploration and, 99
   elements of, 86
   examples of, 87
   framing, 94
   NVAs and, 293–295
Chambers, John, 8, 265
Charpie, David, 209
Check-in meetings
   customer interview quotes in, 63
   designers for, 244
   focus on customer pain in, 184
   go/no-go decisions and, 267, 268
   market or sales specialists for, 246
   NVB, 267, 276, 277–278
   NVT presentations, 49
   Product phase, 167

chief financial officers, 95
Chime Bank, 8
choice-supportive bias, 118
Cisco, 8, 265
collaboration, technology for, 63
commoditization, 153
communication
   early messaging, 146
   NVT to Mothership, 57
   positive messages in, 255
   technology for, 60, 63
   in Venture Factories, 254–255
   See also business case
company-identified and company-organized teams, 37
compensation, 78, 286–287
   in "Looking Forward to Accelerate," 32
   Venture Factories and, 243, 250
Competing for the Future (Hamel and Prahalad), 12
competition, operating and execution plans on, 199–202
complexity, 153
compliance, 241
concepts, for new venture
   assessment of, 69–80, 94
   capability for, 69, 78–79
   desirability of, 69, 70–71
   feasibility of, 69, 72–73
   ranking, 80
   suitability of, 69, 76–77
   viability of, 69, 74–75
confirmation bias, 118
consistency bias, 118
consultants, 211
context, in storyboard, 136
core competencies, 9, 17
   access to, 48, 271

Asset Jam and, 171
   concept assessment based on, 69, 78–79
corporate venture capital (CVC) funds, 27–28, 169, 228
costs, 257. *See also* budgets; funding
cost structure, 84
cost to manufacture, 153
cover slides, 180
Cowboy Ventures, 9
creativity, 42, 57–58
credibility, 112
CRM (customer relationship management), 60–61, 113
Csik, Michaela, 190
curiosity, 28
customer development
   continuous process of, 149
   customer interviews in, 113–114
   definition of, 112
   importance of, 113–114
   leads for, 42
   Portfolio Review Days and, 96–97
   in the Product phase, 152
   prototype interviews in, 153–155
   storyboard interviews in, 135–148
   Venture Factory leads for, 244
customer interviews
   bias in, 118
   describing in the business case, 181
   documenting, 113
   how many to do, 113–114
   improving interview techniques for, 128–129
   ins and outs of, 114–121
   note taking in, 63, 121, 128
   pain point, 114, 121–135
   planning approach for, 56

   practicing for, 46
   prototype, 114, 153–155
   question types for, 119
   recruiting customers for, 46, 47, 114–118
   scripts for, 118–119
   storyboard, 114, 135–140
   technology for, 61, 63
   tips for, 127, 129
   traps in, 120–121
customer journey, 187–188
customer pain, 13
   business case on, 184–185
   commonality of, 185
   concept desirability and, 70–71
   credibility and, 112
   distinctiveness and, 185
   finding real, 301
   hypothesis creation on, 85
   hypothesis testing on, 113
   Incubate phase I, 110–149
   interviews for, 26–27
   kill decisions based on, 182, 267
   killing off ideas based on lack of, 135
   matching with trends and technology, 27–28
   operating and execution plans, 199
   understanding, 26–27
   validating global nature of, 129–131
customer personas, 93, 128, 146
   in the business case, 184–185
   developing, 147–148
customer relationship management (CRM), 60–61, 113
customers, target, 70
   access to, 270–271
   Day in the Life of, 187–188
   number of, 41
   operating and execution plans on, 199

customer segments, 87, 93
    based on customer pain, 129–131
customer testing, 14
CVC. *See* corporate venture capital (CVC) funds

Danner, John, 16
dashboards, incubator, 237, 238
data, 14
data flow, 173
Day in the Life of the customer, 187–188
Day in the Life of the team, 276
deliverability, 152
design
    for New Venture Plan Competitions, 102–103
    technology for, 62–63
    Venture Factory, 234–235
designers, 42–43, 244
desirability, 69, 70–71
detractors, 145–146
development cycles, 216
devil's advocates, 38
Dimon, Jamie, 8
discipline, 221–223
disruption, institutionalizing, 291, 302–303
disruptors, 8, 40
distribution channels, 84, 270–271
diversity, in New Venture Teams, 36–37, 40
dividends, 270
documentation
    of customer interviews, 26–27, 113, 121
    of pain point interviews, 124–125
    of prototype scores, 164
    of storyboard interviews, 139
    technology for, 60–62

doing good, 303
Do It on Monday lists, 204–205, 223
Domain Exploration, 98–99
Dorf, Bob, 210

Ecosystem Mapping, 98–99, 210
ecosystems, internal innovation, 288–295
Efficiency Experts, 39–40
empathy
    creating in the business case, 185, 188
    exhibiting radical customer, 301
    in NVT members, 42
engagement of NBV members, 48, 49, 266–272
engineering specialists, 246
Entrepreneur-in-Residence, 244
entrepreneurs
    networking for, 211–212
    in Portfolio Review Days, 95, 97
    resources for, 209–210
entrepreneurs, internal, 9
    keeping them happy, 103
    lifestyle of, 37
equity compensation, 250
execution, 178
    in "Looking Forward to Accelerate," 32
executive interviews, 94, 99, 274–275, 276
exercises
    Asset Jam, 84
    Challenge Question, 86, 294
    Customer Pain Hypothesis, 85
    Developing Personas, 147–148
    Hypothesis, 293
    Hypothesis Statement, 123
    Identify Who Matters Most, 88–91

    Mothership Management From-To Shifts, 294
    What Matters Most?, 83
expertise, 17
    access to, 48

facilities, 248
failure, embracing, 300–301
feasibility, 69, 72–73
    product design and, 169–171
feedback
    in Build to Validate, 218
    on New Venture Plan Competitions, 100, 101
    from pain point interviews, 134
    from storyboard interviews, 139
financial services, 241
Financial Times, 15, 231
Fortune 500 companies, longevity of, 8–9
Foundation Capital, 12, 70
Frankenberger, Karolin, 190
The Friction Trap: How Smart Companies Make the Right Things Easier, the Wrong Things Harder, and Do It Without Driving People Crazy (Rao and Sutton), 285–286
fun, 303
funding, 17
    approval of, 204–205
    identifying sources of, 30
    levels of for ventures, 258–260
    in "Looking Forward to Accelerate," 32–33
    NVBs in providing, 48, 268–270
    operating and execution plans on, 193, 195–196
    small bets and, 28
    for spin-outs, 283

    in startups versus Venture Factories, 14–15
    for Venture Factories, 256–260
future, working backward from the, 30, 45, 102, 104, 240, 302

Gainey, Mark, 12
Galle, Greg, 94, 171
Gassmann, Oliver, 190
General Motors, 272
Gives and Gets, 197–199, 243
Gladwell, Malcolm, 180
Global 1000 companies, 16, 172
global challenges, 236, 303
Gmail, 62
go-big mentality, 216
go/no-go decisions, 15, 16, 17, 48, 266–267
    based on customer pain, 135
    criteria for in Venture Factories, 239–240
    inflection points for, 182
good, doing, 303
Google, 209
    AdWords, 117
    Calendar, 61
    Drive, 61–62, 113, 164
    Sheets, 60–61
    Slides, 62
go-to-market options, 190–191
governance
    choosing models for, 48, 282
    determining appropriate, 271
    in "Looking Forward to Accelerate," 32–33
    NVB decisions on, 282–286
    operating and execution plans on, 197
    in Preparing to Incubate, 291
    for Venture Factories, 242–243

Graham, Paul, 210
Griffith, Erin, 9
growth
    building for, 220–221
    institutionalizing, 20, 226–261
    leadership capable of, 231
    pipeline for incubating, 11–12
    principles for driving, 298–303
    Venture Factories in, 234–235
Growth Engines
    challenges facing, 265–266
    imperatives for, 266–272
    incubate activities for, 273–281
    key decisions for end of incubate, 282–287
    launch and accelerate activities for, 287–288
    Mothership advantage for, 288–295
    policies, procedures, and politics in, 296–297
    requirements for, 228, 261–297
Growth Geniuses, 39
growth mindset, 28, 37, 297
G Suite, 61

Hamel, Gary, 12
Hare, Chelsea, 138
Harman, Drew, 27, 112
Hastings, Reed, 12
hear no evil interview trap, 120–121
high performers, 38
hiring, 216, 247. *See also* talent plans, for Venture Factories
hiring plans, 194
Holland, Paul, 12, 70
How to Start a Startup class, 210
human resources, 247, 270, 291, 295
hypotheses
    NVAs and, 293–295
    for pain point interviews, 122–124
    testing, 69

IBM, 272
ideation, 10, 66–109
    concept assessment in, 69–80
    getting started with, 109
    New Venture Plan Competitions and, 100–109
    number of ideas and, 68–69, 81
    NVAs in, 292–295
    NVBs in, 273
    sources of ideas and, 241
    in startups, 13
    strategy and, 68
    in Venture Factories, 241
imagination, 16
Incubate phase
    Business phase in, 176–205
    customer focus in, 110–149
    NVAs in, 295
    NVBs in, 273–281
    outsiders in, 45
    preparing for, 50–63
    process in, 47
    Product phase in, 150–175
    Week 0, 46–47
    workstreams in, 112
incubation, 10
    assembling teams for, 82
    coming up with ideas for, 98–109
    dashboards for, 237, 238
    idea that's ready to incubate and, 81–93
    leadership for in Venture Factories, 247
    managing the Mothership and, 15–17
    methodology for, 16
    Portfolio Reviews for, 94–97
    road map for, 18–19
incubation models, 236
incubation plans, 181
incubators, Venture Factories versus, 228, 231–232
innovation
    full-time teams for, 29, 44
    internal ecosystems for, 288–295
    transformation and, 266
inspiration, 301
intellectual property, 87
international teams, 54
    language barriers in, 61, 155
    logistics for Venture Factory, 248
    Venture Factory, 236–237
    video conferencing and, 59–60
interviews
    customer, 26–27, 113–140
    executive, 94, 99
    pain point, 114, 121–135
    planning approach for customer/stakeholder, 56
    prototype, 114, 153–155, 158–161
    stakeholder, 56, 122
    storyboard, 114, 135–148
    surveys versus, 26–27
Intrapreneurs, 39, 209–210
introductions, personal, 115–116
InVision, 62
IT departments, 59, 241, 248, 295

Jobs, Steve, 14, 58, 153
Joby Aviation, 8
JPMorgan Chase, 8

Kana Communications, 12
Keynote, 63
key performance indicators (KPIs), 231, 237
key results, 288
killing ventures, 15, 16, 17, 266–267
    criteria for in Venture Factories, 239–240
    inflection points for, 182
    pain point interviews and, 135
Kingsley, Bill, 209, 287–288
know-how, 87
KPIs. *See* key performance indicators (KPIs)

Lammers, Patrick, 172
Lampert, Russ, 183
landing pages, 62
    customer recruiting with, 117
    prototype, 155–156
    for prototypes, 165
launches, 240, 287–288
leaders and leadership, 261–297
    development of, 253
    failure of to grow, 16–17
    fear of disruption by, 8
    growth of, 232
    politics and, 296–297
    in Portfolio Review Days, 95
    for Venture Factories, 231
leading the witness, 120
Lean Customer Development: Building Products Your Customers Will Buy (Alvarez), 121
lean startup methodology, 172
learning
    by designing, 248–249
    by doing, 248
    by leading, 249
    sharing with employees and investors, 255

Lee, Aileen, 9
legal services, 240, 291, 295
LinkedIn, 57, 116–117
logos, 56–57, 180
"Looking Forward to Accelerate" agenda, 30, 32–33, 45, 280–281
lunatic fringe, 37
Lyft, 169

Mach49, 12, 13
    Accelerate phase at, 208–209
    Board Member-in-Residence, 213
    on industry veterans for Accelerate, 211
    in Portfolio Review Days, 95
    "Welcome to Accelerate" letter, 287–288
Mahr, Alex, 15, 231
management review board mindset, 231, 232
manufacturing, 241
marketability, 153
marketing, 201, 291
    in Build to Automate, 220
    NVAs and, 295
    services for Venture Factories, 240
marketing channels, 84
markets
    access to, 270–271
    in the business case, 182–184
    business model and, 190–192
    experimentation framework for, 210
    experts on in Venture Factory teams, 246
    going to, 216
    kill decisions based on, 182
    segmentation of, 146
    size of, 74, 182, 183–184, 200
    strategy for, 154
    testing, 14
mergers and acquisitions, 228, 255
methodology, 232, 301
metrics, 12, 15, 300
    for Accelerate, 280
    evaluating potential and, 225
    for New Venture Plan Competitions, 98
    in operating and execution plans, 192
    risk mitigation and, 26, 199, 202
    for spin-ins, 284
    for Venture Factories, 237, 250, 261
milestones, 12, 14, 192
    Accelerate, 209
    accountability and, 175
    Build to Automate, 219
    Build to Validate, 32, 280
    celebrating, 208
    for customer interviews, 114
    funding and, 195, 258, 268
    operating and execution plan, 192–193
    phantom stock plan, 286
    reviewing, 288
    risk mitigation and, 28
mindset, 231, 232, 277, 297
minimum viable product (MVP), 11, 33, 42
    in Build to Validate, 218
    business case on, 189
    defining, 43, 169
    definition of, 172
    feasibility and, 72
    market segmentation for, 146
    in New Venture Plan Competitions, 108
    product design based on, 172
    prototypes and, 166, 167
    risk and, 175
    system architecture and, 172–174
Miro, 63
monetization, 190–192
Moore's law, 152
Mothership
    concept alignment with, 76–77
    drivers to successful ventures, 289–291
    engaging in Build to Grow, 221
    friction with, 16, 232, 271
    Gives and Gets with, 197–199
    management from-to shifts, 294
    managing the, 15–17, 28–29
    NVT communication with, 57
    NVT name/logo and, 56–57
    readiness of, 94
    risk and competition and, 201
    transfer pricing and, 196
    Venture Factory management of, 248
    Venture Factory services and, 240–241
Mothership advantage, 10, 20, 28–29, 209, 232, 302–303
    Gives and Gets and, 199
    importance of seizing, 16, 18, 26
    innovation ecosystems and, 271, 288–295
    NVBs in seizing, 286, 288–295
    scaling and, 10
motivation, 78
MVP. *See* minimum viable product (MVP)
Myers-Briggs Type Indicator, 46

Netflix, 17
net promoter scores, 144–146, 164
networking
    for customer interview recruiting, 115–117
    to stay current, 170
    to support new ventures, 211–212
    types of people for, 212
    for Venture Factories, 243
New Venture Advocates, 36, 243, 271, 289–295
New Venture Boards, 17, 30, 181
    in access to customers, channels, and markets, 270–271
    in challenge framing, 81
    customer access through, 115
    Day in the Life of, 49
    executive interviews with, 99
    funding and, 48, 268–270
    go/no-go decisions by, 266–267
    growth mindset for, 297
    imperatives of, 266–272
    Incubate activities of, 273–281
    members of, 266
    mindset for, 277
    policies, procedures, politics, and, 296–297
    in Portfolio Review Days, 94–95
    reviewing, retaining, removing, or revising for Accelerate, 212
    role of, 48
    roles in, 36
    selecting great, 48–49
    Sponsors for, 272–273
    in support networks, 211–212
New Venture Plan Competitions, 100–109, 237, 251
    Challenge Statements in, 99
    competition journey and timing of, 104–105
    judging, 106–109
    preconditions for, 101–103
    scoring sheet for, 108

New Venture Teams, 29, 34–49
    after the 12 weeks, 45–48
    budget for, 56
    calendar for, 56
    celebrations in, 208
    Check-in presentations, 49
    chemistry in, 40–42
    communication with Mothership, 57
    compensation for, 286–287
    describing in the business case, 180–182
    finding talent for, 37–40
    full-time teams for, 29, 44
    great versus bad members in, 41
    hybrid, 55
    inspiration for, 57–58
    leads for, 30, 42, 44–45
    mode and venue for, 53–55
    naming, 56–57
    NVBs in selecting, 273, 276
    onboarding, 46–48
    physical, 53–54
    in Portfolio Review Days, 94–95
    preconditions for, 44–45
    Product phase Check-in for, 167
    role of NVBs with, 48
    roles in, 36, 42–44
    selecting, 36–42
    skills and traits for, 43–44
    split for the Product phase, 152
    staying current, 170
    steps for after decision to launch and fund, 204–205
    supplies for, 58
    system architecture for, 172–174
    technology for, 53, 54, 59–63
    types of, choosing, 37
    virtual, 53

note taking, 63
novelty, 153
NVAs. *See* New Venture Advocates
NVB. *See* New Venture Boards
NVT. *See* New Venture Teams

objectives, 288
office space, 54
onboarding, 248–249, 276
"One Number You Need to Grow" (Reichheld), 144
one-stop shop interview trap, 120
Open-Ended Pain Point Interviews, 121–135
operating and execution plans, 178, 192–205
    asking for money in, 195–196
    critical numbers in, 193
    Gives and Gets in, 197–199
    governance in, 197
    hiring plans in, 193, 194
    organization charts in, 193, 194
    phases and milestones in, 192
    risk and competition in, 199–202
    "Why us?" in, 203
operations, 216
    in Build to Automate, 220
    Venture Factory, 241, 251–252
opportunities
    the business case on, 185–186
    finding the big, 169
options, exploring, 274–275
option value, 16
organization charts, 193, 194, 249
Otter.ai, 63

pain point interviews, 114, 121–135
    hypothesis for, 122–123

    improving interview techniques for, 128–129
    note taking in, 128
    scripts for, 122, 125–127
    summary and synthesis of, 132–135
    See also customer interviews; customer pain
Palmer, Maija, 231–232
partnerships, 84
    in Build to Validate, 218
    co-creating ventures with, 236
    rules of engagement for, 283
    strategic, 228
passion, 301
passives, 145–146
peers, in support networks, 211–212
personality profiles, 46
personas. *See* customer personas
phantom equity plans, 250, 286–287
pipelines, 178–179
    sales, 219
    for Venture Factories, 234–235
Pitch Day, 278–281
    business and execution plans for, 178–179
    decisions based on, 280–281
    go/no-go decisions and, 267–268
    "Looking Forward to Accelerate" and, 32–33
    New Venture Plan Competitions and, 100, 104–109
    NVAs in, 295
    NVBs in, 49, 278–281
pitch decks, 178, 283
planning, 52, 185
    for Accelerate, 42
    for Incubate, 50–63
playbooks, 219, 220, 221, 231

policies, 295–297
politics, 296–297
Portfolio Review Days, 94–97, 273
portfolios, 178–179, 301
portfolio strategy, 16
possible, art of the, 27–28, 170, 302
Prahalad, C.K., 12
Predictive Index, 46
present value, 16
Price, Julie, 121
pricing, 190–191, 196
Primack, Dan, 9
procedures, 296–297
procurement, 241, 291, 295
product design
    business case on, 189
    can you build it and, 169–171
    customer and market fit in, 220
    early, 168–175
    first step in, 172
    operating and execution plans on, 200
    risk and, 175
    specialists, 246
    system architecture and, 172–174
    who builds it and, 171–172
product development, 216
    in Build to Validate, 218–219
productivity, G Suite for, 61
product leads, 42
Product phase, 150–175
    early product design, 168–175
    kill decisions based on, 182
    prototype interviews in, 153–155
    questions to answer in, 152–153
    timeline for prototypes in, 166–167
profit, 16
profitability, 74
program managers, 42

programming, 252–253
projection bias, 118
promoters, 145–146
promotions, 243
prototype interviews, 114, 153–155
    scripts for, 158–161
    tips for, 158
prototypes, 155–175
    benefits of, 154
    for hardware or hard goods, 165
    high-resolution, 164
    low-resolution, 162
    mid-resolution, 163
    sample, 162–164
    scoring tests of, 164
    starting point for, 155–156
    timeline for, 166–167
    what to build, 156–157
Pure Software, 12

Rachleff, Andy, 28, 175
Rao, Huggy, 285–286
R&D budgets, funding ventures with, 270
rebranding, 236
recruiting, 231
    agencies for, 118
    plans for, 194
regulatory services, 241
Reichheld, Fred, 144
reinvestment, 270
releases, 216
reliability, 153
resistance, 295–296
resources, 271
retention rates, 220
revenue models, 200
revenue streams, 193

risk, 16
    embracing, 300–301
    feasibility and, 72
    operating and execution plans on, 199–202
    product design and mitigation of, 175
Rocket Mortgage, 8
rockets, 94
Ross, Ed, 59

sales
    NVAs and, 295
    services for Venture Factories, 240
    in Venture Factory teams, 246
sales forecasts, 193
sales pipeline qualification tools, 219
SAM. *See* serviceable available market (SAM)
Scaff, Marvin, 59
Scale phase, 10, 153, 221
    preconditions for, 216
    in startups versus Venture Factories, 14
    validating global nature of pain and, 129–131
    watching for challenges in, 221
Scaling up Excellence (Rao & Sutton), 285
scripts
    for customer interviews, 118–119
    for executive interviews, 274–275, 276
    for pain point interviews, 122, 125–127
    for prototype interviews, 158–161
    for storyboard interviews, 141–143
Sears Roebuck, 272
security, 59

seed funds, 269
self-organized teams, 37
serviceable available market (SAM), 184
serviceable obtainable market (SOM), 184
Shared Services model, 285–283, 291
Sifted, 15, 231
Silicon Valley, 8, 9
    competing against, 12
    innovation system in, 289
    mavericks in, 37–38
Singh, Sukhjinder, 172
Sketch/Figma, 62
Slack, 60, 128
small bets, 28
    business model and, 190–192
    metrics aligned with, 261
    minimum viable product and, 175
    with technology, 59
social desirability bias, 118
social media, in customer recruiting, 117
Solve Next, 94
SOM. *See* serviceable obtainable market (SOM)
space management, 248
speakerphones, 60
spin-in ventures, 48, 197, 240, 282, 284–286
spin-out ventures, 48, 197, 240, 282, 283
    compensation and, 286
Sponsors, 272–273, 292
stacks, 173
staffing plans, 193, 247
staggered start dates, 252
stakeholder interviews

pain point, 122
planning approach for, 56
Stakeholder Maps, 81, 88–91, 94
    in the business case, 184–185
    Challenge Statements and, 92
    Domain Exploration and, 98–99
    NVBs and, 273
stakeholders
    in the business case, 184–185
    identifying who matters most, 88–91
stakeholder segments, 41
standardization, 178–179
Stanford University, 175
start dates, 252
Startup Owners' Manual, The (Blank and Dorf), 210
startups
    benefits of corporate ventures versus, 13–15
    established companies' advantages over, 9
    principles for beating, 298–303
    resources on, 209–210
    statistics on failure of, 13
staying current, 27–28, 170, 265
storyboard interviews, 114, 135–148
    characteristics of good, 140
    creating storyboards for, 138
    product development based on, 146–148
    rating and ranking, 144–146
    script for, 141–143
    what you should earn from, 140
storytellers, 42–43
    in building the business case, 180
    in Portfolio Review Days, 96
    in Venture Factory teams, 246

storytelling
  in customer interviews, 118–119
  encouraging in pain point interviews, 129
  Keynote for, 63
  power of, 136
  storyboard interviews and, 135–140
Strategos, 12, 37
strategy
  concept suitability and, 76–77
  ideation and, 68
Strikingly, 62
Stripe, 8
Stryber, 15, 231
subject-matter experts, 42, 246
success
  foundational elements of, 26–29
  of independent versus incubated startups, 13–15
  preconditions for, 29–31
suitability, 69, 76–77
summary and synthesis sessions, 132–135, 277
supplies, for NVTs, 58
supply chains, 87, 241
support, internal, 76–77, 201
support networks, 211–212
surveys, 26–27
Sutton, Robert, 285–286
swim lanes, 215–216, 221–222
Sybase, 12
synthesis sessions, 132–135, 277
system architecture, 172–174

tag lines, 180
talent, unleashing your internal, 300
talent development budgets, 270

talent plans, for Venture Factories, 231, 241, 244–250
TAM. *See* total addressable market (TAM)
Tandem, 63
team chemistry, 40–42
teams, Venture Factory, 244–250. *See also* New Venture Teams
technology
  business case on, 189
  feasibility and, 72
  NVAs and, 295
  for NVTs, 53, 54, 59–63
  in Portfolio Review Days, 96, 97
  staying current with, 27–28, 170
  support for Venture Factory, 248
  for Venture Factories, 252
  video conferencing, 59–60
telepresence robots, 60
TMO. *See* total market opportunity (TMO)
tools
  capability assessment, 78–79
  desirability assessment, 70–71
  feasibility assessment, 72–73
  suitability assessment, 76–77
  viability assessment, 74–75
total addressable market (TAM), 183
total market opportunity (TMO), 183
Toyoda, Akio, 8
Toyota, 8
training, 248–249
transfer pricing, 196
TV, 60
"Tyranny of the Large Denominator," 16–17

Uber, 17, 27, 29, 169
uncertainty, comfort with, 41

Unicorns
  current number of, 9
  definition of, 9
  principles for creating, 298–303
  road map for creating, 18–20
  systematic process for developing, 10–12
  unleashing within your company, 9–10
  why yours should win, 13–15
unit economics, 200–201, 216
  in Build to Automate, 220
United Nations' Sustainable Development Goals, 236
urgency, 13
user experience, 200
  in Build to Validate, 218
  playbook for, 219
US Steel, 272

value, option versus present, 16
Venture Building, 10
  elements of success in, 26–29
  people for, 34–49
  preconditions for, 24–33
  preparation for, 52
  systematic process for, 10–12
venture capital, 15, 16, 28, 283
Venture Factories, 13, 20
  basics for, 236–241
  benefits of building, 231–232
  building, 227–261
  communication plans for, 254–255
  compensation and, 243, 250
  designing, 252–253
  executive leadership for, 261–297
  governance for, 242–243

  how to build, 234–235
  incubators versus, 228
  new venture creation process for, 241
  NVT members in, 45–46
  objectives of, 236
  onboarding and training for, 249–250
  operations in, 251–252
  physical, 232–233
  specs for team members in, 244–245
  talent plans for, 244–250
  types of, 232–233
  virtual, 233
Venture Factory Ambassadors, 243
viability, 69, 74–75
video conferencing, 59–60
visas, 54

Wang, Clement, 208–209, 218–219
WebEx, 208
websites, 56–57, 62
"Welcome to Accelerate" letter, 287–288
wholly owned subsidiaries, 48, 197, 240, 282, 284, 286
Wilde, Oscar, 58
wireframes, 62–63, 155–157
witness leading, 120
Wizard of Oz development, 218–219
Wordly, 61

Y Combinator, 175

Zoom, 59, 61
Zuora, 96, 208

Gratitude

What you hold in your hand or are perusing online is not just a book; it's a venture. Like the startups we build and invest in with our amazing clients, it has gone through the whole spectrum of venture creation, from Ideate to Incubate to Accelerate—and now, with the help of so very, very many people, it is poised to Scale. Thus, the section you are reading now is more than merely acknowledgments; it is the one place in the book where I get to express my deepest, most heartfelt, and most profound gratitude for the people who have not just shaped the book, not just created Mach49, but have *made* me—helping me to learn, love, laugh, care, grow, pray, imagine, wonder. I have been so extraordinarily blessed: Paul, Kylie, Devon, Piper; family, friends, faith; colleagues, mentors, clients—many who fall into more than one of these categories. To all of you, thank you!

Let's start with the book itself, which could not have happened without an incredible team led and curated by the incomparable Jim Levine, principal, Levine Greenberg Rostan Literary Agency, who was a friend before he was my agent. Paul and I met Jim, really the ultimate Renaissance man, because of his amazing philanthropic work founding The Fatherhood Project. More than an agent, Jim has been a friend, mentor, and sherpa, leading me through this entire journey, including getting six publishers wildly interested in the book and then helping me choose Harvard Business Review Press as the publisher.

Wow! What an extraordinary experience working with HBRP has been. It all starts with the amazing Kevin Evers, my editor, guru, guide, coach, cajoler, cheerleader, and, when he needed to be, comedian. I told him I would need to write a whole chapter to acknowledge him, so I am at least going to devote this paragraph. If this book is readable and relevant, thank Kevin for that. While I composed the book the way we do Venture Building with clients in real life, Kevin organized it in the way a reader would find useful. When I had way too many visuals, artifacts, samples, and tools, he reined me in with analogies you couldn't dispute: "I see this book as similar to a musical. Do we want scenes that wow people and take a more visual-first approach? Yes! That's what chapters 3, 4, 5, 6, 7, and others are for. Those are your Fred Astaire and Ginger Rogers dances. But we also need dialogue scenes and exposition scenes. It can't all be dancing." When the page count was too high, he made me cut it down—because we didn't want the book to turn from "how to do this" into "how the hell will I ever find time to do this?" When I learned that a paperback, regardless of how many copies I had already presold (a lot) could not even qualify for two of the (shall not be named) bestseller lists (and digital copies don't count either, in the twenty-first century—talk about an industry ripe for disruption), he held up the mirror and reminded me of our own methodology, driving home what it's all about: customer/user experience. He wrote, "I'm also bullish on paperback because of the user experience. I don't want the book to be a heavy tome that sits on people's desks. We want teams to read it together and dog-ear the pages. As such, the book should be readable, transportable, light, bendable, durable. In our experience, readers prefer paperback in this format. And I don't want to sacrifice the user experience to hit a list." Besides his expertise, I must thank Kevin for his patience and endurance as I missed deadline after deadline until he finally said (always with a smile): "That 12/1 deadline is as immovable as Christmas Day. That's when we need to lock up the interior. If we miss it, we all get coal in our stockings." Kevin, you are the best, and I am so lucky you became my editor and will forever be a friend.

In addition to Kevin, I have to thank Stephani Finks for her incredible creative direction. Evidently, I have written the most difficult book to produce in the history of HBRP, but Stephani was the calm in the storm, bringing her unique blend of design, creativity, and book-business superpowers to ensure we created not just something useful but a manifestation of another Mach49 mantra: design matters! Equally stellar and expert is Jen Waring, the book's senior production editor, whose experience manufacturing books in every form, for myriad functions, combined with her rigor, aesthetics, and attention to detail, is second to none. Ably assisted by the wonderful and laser-focused Alicyn Zall, and copyeditor, Jane Gebhart, I have finally met my match in the fine art of editing for perfection. Others I must add to the list of HBRP shout-outs and for whom I am incredibly thankful include fearless leader and publisher Erika Heilman, Julie Devoll (marketing), Felicia Sinusas (PR), Lindsey Dietrich and Jordan Concannon (both direct sales), Jon Shipley (UK team; foreign rights), Sally Ashworth (UK; publicity and events), and Rick Emanuel (manufacturing manager).

Jim introduced me to others who have played critical roles in the creation of *The Unicorn Within*, including Michael Malone, another multitalented human, author, educator, journalist, novelist, and now podcast producer. Since I was CEO of Mach49 and we were in hypergrowth mode, Jim thought it would be best if I had someone help me write the book, and Mike was to be that co-collaborator. Mike and I quickly realized that unlike a biography or academic treatise, if you are going to write a how-to guide you need to have actually done it—over and over again—so we swapped roles. And yes, I wrote the book, but Michael helped me in so many ways: editing, questioning, provoking, and bringing a flair, edge, and style that we hope makes this book not just useful but fun; not just a manual but a manifesto.

A manifesto needs a movement, which is why I am so excited to be working with Mark Fortier, founder and president of Fortier Public Relations, as our publicist. Mark, Dan Rovzar, and their team are literally the world's leading experts in the business book industry, and I am humbled by their interest, excitement, and massive engagement in ensuring that not just the book but its messages of growth, action, optimism, empowerment, responsibility, disruption, design, inclusion, and change-the-world opportunities get out into the world.

Thank you to Rodrigo Corral and his team for the beautiful cover and design work. A special thanks to Adriana Tonello, who became the behind-the-scenes arms and legs. She worked closely with Brad Sharek, chief creative officer at Mach49, to whom I owe the greatest debt of thanks for taking on the design of the book; also, the many artifacts we included are ones he has created over the years. Besides being one of Paul's and my best friends for over thirty years, Brad is responsible for how beautiful the book has turned out to be.

Thanking Brad leads me to the next set of people without whom this book has no reason for being, the Mach49 family. Little did I know when I founded the company how truly blessed I would be by knowing so many incredibly talented people. I am grateful to every single one of you who has joined me on this grand adventure. I wish I had space to acknowledge each of you by name, but please know I love and appreciate all of you. I do want to call out the people who have been with me since the beginning, who believed in the potential of what Mach49 could become and, most important for all of you reading the book, who crafted everything you find between these covers. They invented the methodology and even helped write several of the sections. Here's to Russ Lampert and Brad, who both joined me day one—Russ as CFO, keeping me out of trouble and bringing venture business modeling and economics to our clients, and Brad, who for thirty years has been able to take what I imagine and bring it to life visually.

Thank you to David Charpie and Clement Wang, who have also been with me since the beginning, bringing their vision, superpowers, and prior startup-CEO and head-of-product experiences and success to a truly blank sheet of paper. They built and still run Mach49's global venture-building, Disrupting Inside Out practice—the success of Mach49 and this book is due to their extraordinary talent at building ventures, working with large companies, and making the process teachable, repeatable, and scalable. Dave Blakely soon joined that merry band, after twenty-seven years with IDEO, bringing his rare mix of design thinking and deep technical and engineering prowess. Bill Kingsley, in his VC-in-Residence role, drove a whole new practice around the senior executives and the New Venture Boards. When Ed Ross joined as an Entrepreneur-in-Residence (EIR), he helped us stop reinventing the wheel every time and start documenting and codifying what we were doing. Paul Holland, who was supposed to "retire" but as yet another demonstration of why he is the most amazing life partner on the planet, jumped in to invent and run the Disrupting Outside In practice of venture investing and building world-class corporate venture capital (CVC) funds. Julie Price brought her years of experience in user research to help us invent what we now call customer development. Chelsea Hare and Mercedes Arenas were our first designers; they put exclamation points on finding customer pain and building narratives and stories to communicate value.

In this book, you will learn how to get into the market quickly—placing small bets, piloting, and experimenting in real time—and soon you will have access to a digital platform (code-named Mach149), thanks to Monifa Porter. Those of you in other countries who find that the material is designed for global audiences can thank our founding Europe, Middle East, and Africa (EMEA) team, led by the amazing Clare McKitrick and Steve McCarthy. James Beriker brought an entire cadre of experts, leveraging his network and multiple successes as a Silicon Valley–startup CEO to develop the Accelerate phase. Others who have been at Mach49 since the earliest days, including gracefully navigating the uncertainty of the pandemic, and who have helped incubate the methodology, tools, technology, practices, scripts, activities, and more that you find in this book, include Atif Hussein, Bobby Lalwani, Chris Tacy, Griff Resch, Kevin Ye, Marvin Scaff, Michele Chambliss, Mimi Gay, Mo Weinhardt, Nick Sohriakoff, Scott Seethaler, Shauna Arora, Shelby Hertzog, and my incredible sister Sharon, who, while thankfully keeping us organized at home, joined Mach49 to do the same for the firm and our venture teams. Two people who are exploring new ventures but are still part of the Mach49 family and played a critical role in the content development core to *The Unicorn Within* are wunderkind Collin Hartigan, whose name we tore off a flyer on the wall when we needed a designer and who grew rapidly to become EIR extraordinaire, and Drew Harman, incredible intellect, extraordinary entrepreneur, brilliant board member, and phenomenal friend, who helped develop the earliest methods and coined our now-iconic phrase: "Customer insights are the currency of credibility; everything else is uninformed opinion."

Last on the Mach49 list but definitely not least, my everlasting thanks to Linda Liguori, my executive assistant and Mach49 director of administration. Loo, seriously, I could not live (and certainly wouldn't know where to be) without your diligence, wisdom, creative scheduling (the book was late, but it would still be in the works now if she hadn't found time for me to write and vigilantly guarded that time), organization, client acumen, management prowess, Dudley (M49 team dog), and perpetual positive attitude. Most importantly, thank you for being my friend.

To the people I have learned from, who have mentored me, believed in me, and inspired me—who gave me opportunities at very young ages and throughout my life that allowed me to grow and develop, to lead and build, to aspire and care—you too can take credit for this book, because without you, I would not be where I am today. The wonderful Jon Megibow might be surprised to find himself at the top of the list, but in chronological order, he is first: he was my University of Virginia adviser, literally there for me during the first of many Robert Frostian road-not-taken moments that have yielded untold opportunity and joy in my life (I met Paul shortly after embarking down that first path, and Mach49 is the result of another). Stu Francis gave me my first real job in investment banking after college and stands high above the crowd in terms of integrity, ethics, and grace. He made me think I might want to learn golf someday, which I have—and love.

Fred Sturdivant, fearless leader of the SF Mac Group office, who believed in me and gave me opportunities way beyond my years, continues to be my role model and my idol. You, along with Lucy Reid, Jennifer Bol, Mark Johnson, and Pierre Loewe (we have lost these last two and still mourn them), taught me the importance of a culture built on excellence, caring, inclusivity, curiosity, vision, merit, and fun. You all have superpowers to which I continue to aspire!

Gary Hamel and C.K. Prahalad (another great one who has passed) literally pioneered the field of corporate innovation with the publication of *Competing for the Future*, and then Gary gave me a front-row seat to the development of the entire field by offering me the opportunity to become CEO and cofounder of Strategos, the company we started in 1995. Gary is one of the great intellects, visionaries, and speakers of our time, and I owe a tremendous amount of gratitude to him for getting me into this field in the first place and for giving me the incredible foundation on which I have been able to build. And to my Strategos cofounders, colleagues, and friends, especially Peter Skarzynski, Jim Scholes, Chris Tchen, and Jon Lamb, I hope you are proud of how the field you literally helped create has evolved!

To Reed Hastings, good friend and ultimate disruptor, who nominated me for the Henry Crown Fellowship at the Aspen Institute; to Keith Berwick, Ben Dunlap, and Skip Battle—our HCF mentors extraordinaire, who more than practice what they preach; and to my entire High Five Class: you all taught me the true essence of values-based leadership, what integrity and ethics really mean, and why our entire lives should be devoted to changing the world. The altruistic reasons I founded Mach49 and the last two paragraphs of the book—encouraging venture teams and senior executives to do well by doing good—are for you. I hope the many ventures we have helped our Global 1000 clients build that are truly double-bottom-line make you proud.

Huge thanks to Tim Dyson and the entire leadership team at Next15, including Peter Harris, Jonathan Peachey, and Mark Sanford. Little did you know what a renegade you would be acquiring when you saw the incredible potential of Mach49 and realized you could leverage us to launch Next15 into the growth stratosphere. You truly believed in us and gave us a platform to grow that has enabled us to become a rocket ship and unquestionably reach escape velocity. We had turned down four prior acquisition offers, and it was the knowledge that HBRP was publishing this book that led you to throw your hat in the ring; it has turned out to be a stellar match. Thanks for sharing our values and letting us continue to be who we are, run independently, and bring this work to the world.

To the incredible minds and mentors who have gone before in all aspects of this field and whose ideas have sparked many of our own, including the faculty partners who have been there every step of the way—HUGE THANKS. It is on the shoulders of your incredible research and work, your provocative questioning, your challenges, your insights, your inspiration, and your client engagement that this book stands. To Huggy Rao, Stanford Graduate School of Business, who *knows* the Mothership and can get under the skin of the C-suite better than anyone on the planet, and Rick Kolsky, brilliant lecturer at Kellogg, who has been my mensch and mentor my entire professional career: without your respective encouragement, enthusiasm, and expertise, Mach49 and this book would not exist. As the first two academics I consulted (as well as great friends I knew wouldn't just tell me what I wanted to hear), you continue to help drive ever more rigor into the Mach49 process, yielding ever-greater results, including our new research developing Mach49's Growth Readiness Assessment™ to ensure companies are prepared to build their growth engine in the first place. Early on, Cindy Alvarez provided us with critical content and experience captured in her fantastic book, *Lean Customer Development, Build Products Your Customers Will Buy*. Whenever we had Cindy speak to New Venture Teams, they stopped thinking they knew it all and walked away hyperfocused on finding customer pain.

To Greg Galle and Mike Burn, founders of Solve Next and long-time members of the Mach49 family, your design-thinking expertise and world-changing Think Wrong methodology are second to none and continue to benefit so many of our clients. Readers can thank Greg and Mike for helping us build many of the tools you find in this book. I also have to thank the wonderful David Kelley, because without the work that he and his brother, Tom, spearheaded when they developed the whole field of design thinking at IDEO and that David continues to share with the world through the d.school at Stanford, Mach49's methodology would lack a cornerstone.

Our relationship with Vijay Govindarajan, at Dartmouth's Tuck, who early on saw the synergy between his excellent Three-Box Solution work and Mach49's execution experience and expertise, has yielded a great friendship and tremendous collaboration, for which we are incredibly grateful. To Rita McGrath, your book *The End of Competitive Advantage* sounded the alarm bells and kicked the G1000 into gear, sending them searching for execution-oriented solutions that actually helped them grow rather than just talk about growth in a pretty set of slides. John Danner, University of California, Berkeley and Princeton, your genius, passion, wit, and deep expertise regarding corporate innovation, leadership, and entrepreneurship are ensuring that we take this work to an even higher level as we embark on the next layer of research, studying corporate growth engines across the globe and, more importantly, teaching the financial markets how to value the Unicorn within.

Finally, another entrepreneur turned academic to whom we owe a heap of gratitude is Steve Blank, who seeded the entire field of venture building, including corporate venture building—emphasizing the need to focus on the Mothership by famously noting that internal startups must "fight a two-front war, not just a one-front war." Steve, we have you to thank for our beginning and our future. When we came to the ranch to share our ideas and sit at the feet of the venture-building master, you were supremely encouraging. You also said, as only you can, "You should build a platform." With those words you made sure we were thinking from the future backward as we embarked on a very intentional journey to democratize what we do. This book is a major milestone along that path. Inspired by you almost ten years ago, the next step will indeed be to launch our digital platform, Mach149, to make this work accessible to the masses. Our goal was always to create a teachable, repeatable, and scalable model to build client capability so that we could work ourselves out of a job. Now that we have proven the model, with client after client evangelizing our work and their venture-building and venture-investing success, we hope you are proud of how we have leveraged your insights, focused exclusively on execution, and are answering your original challenge.

I must turn now to our amazing clients, the many "founding" New Venture Team members, the senior executive and C-suite New Venture Board members, the Venture Factory "Mach49 Inside" teams, the CVC fund leaders, the New Venture Advocates—you inspire us every single day. You are the vanguard—leading the charge, focusing on learning by doing, taking real action, and providing the examples and role models that the internal entrepreneurs, growth geniuses, and efficiency experts reading this book will learn from and leverage. Your ideas, talent, competencies, brands, customers, and courage have enabled you to drive meaningful growth for your customers, your companies, yourselves, and the world. There are now too many of you to name (I live in fear of leaving someone out), but you know who you are, and when we finally throw our Mach49 client alumni parties around the world, I will thank you profoundly in person! The greatest blessing for me is that many of you have become lifelong friends. Please know that we are always here for you and incredibly grateful.

Speaking of blessings, while I am sure this isn't the norm, pretty much everyone who knows me knows that spirituality and faith are core to who I am. While I am acutely aware and an outspoken critic of the failings of the Catholic Church, it doesn't detract from the incredible humans, the priests and nuns, whose thoughts, words, readings, homilies, and Monk's Chronicles have inspired me, pushed me, carried me, encouraged me, and challenged me to strive to be better, more caring, more giving and forgiving, more understanding, and more inclusive; to pray, to be an activist, to strive for positive change and peace, to love others as He loved us—not just in my personal life but in my professional life. Some I have known my whole life; others I just follow. Some are now gone: Father John Olivier, Father Tom Moran, Father Egon Javor, Father Pius Horvath, Father David Ayotte, and Sister Anne Cronin have all passed but touched my life in both big and small ways. Others still light the way, holding up the mirror every week: Father Martin Mager, Father Matthew Leavy, Father Maurus Nemeth, Monsignor Lloyd Torgerson, Father David Guffey, and Father Eric Hollas. Readers, you don't know these people, but if you are moved by certain parts of the book or find hope and humanness in it, you have them to thank.

I must also thank my friends. Paul and I have been supremely blessed with a lifetime of extraordinary friendships that continue to this day. The words of Joseph Parry's poem—*Make new friends, but keep the old; those are silver, these are gold*—ring true for us. You know who you are... from childhood to college BFFs, to UVA (where Paul and I met), to San Francisco, to Stanford, to Amsterdam, to Palo Alto, to Portola Valley, to Ormondale, to Nueva, to the golf course, to Fun with Friends and the ILC. What you are is a kind, spirited, adventurous, thoughtful, live-life-to-the-fullest, upbeat, global group—all who have made our lives joyful and fun! Thanks for sticking with me as I have grown Mach49 and written this book; you have been nothing but incredibly encouraging despite the long hours, missed events, abandoned tee times, or too-short phone calls. I love and cherish each of you. A special thank you to Gladys Morales, who has been part of our family for almost twenty-five years and who has taken care of all of us in so many ways; forget the book, our lives don't function without Gladys, we love you.

I am going to end this book where really it all begins, with my family. To my parents, Jane and Don Yates, who truly are the best parents the world has ever known, you have always believed in me and given me the courage to dream and the confidence to make those dreams reality. You truly are my role models and I love you tons and tons. I will forever miss my grandparents, Bud and Helen Buehler, inveterate travelers who encouraged Paul and me to explore every corner of the world together, which we are. And to Paul's parents, Inez and Browder Holland, you taught me the value of humility, hard work, and putting family above all else. To my siblings, Brad, Sharon, Stacey, and Kim, each of you is amazing and have taught me so much. Lucky us to have such an incredibly loving, supportive, and connected family. The fact that I get to live near all of you and see you as often as I do is such a blessing.

To our girls, Kylie, Devon, and Piper, you are incredible young women, each with amazing talents you generously share with the world. You bring spirit, life, light, hope, and fun to everyone around you. Dad and I could not be more grateful to have you in our lives. Thank you for cheering me on every day and inspiring me to make the world a better place. I love you so very much!

And Paul, because of you I know pure joy and a sense of peace, belonging, and unconditional love for which I can never thank you enough. You are so right, we do have "the love for the ages." You complete me and make me better. Mach49 and *The Unicorn Within* would never have happened without your unwavering support. Yet these are merely the latest chapters in the story of our grand adventure. We share a life together that knows no bounds. So, here's to perhaps the greatest love story ever imagined, and here's to what is yet to come. I'm so excited, I thank you, and I love you!

About the Author

Linda Yates is the founder and CEO of Mach49, the growth incubator for global businesses. She is a seasoned CEO with over thirty years of experience creating global strategy, building companies, and driving innovation for large multinationals worldwide. A native of Silicon Valley, Linda has an extensive local and global network. She has been a bridge between Silicon Valley and the boardrooms and C-suites of large multinational corporations throughout her career.

She launched Mach49 as the first Silicon Valley incubator/accelerator focused on helping global enterprises leverage their talent, ideas, brands, assets, competencies, capital, and customers to drive meaningful growth. Whether disrupting inside out—launching ventures, building venture factories, and seizing the Mothership advantage—or disrupting outside in—building world-class corporate venture funds, helping senior executives operate as top-tier VCs, maximizing the partnership value of external startups, and providing M&A support—Linda helps global enterprises beat the startups at their own game. Focused 100 percent on execution, she is committed to developing clients' capability to create a pipeline and portfolio of new ventures on their own for the long term.

Linda spent a decade as a member of the board of directors for NYSE-traded Sybase Inc. (now SAP) and has been a board member and adviser to many entrepreneurs and private companies. She was CEO of Strategos, pioneering the field of corporate innovation with the cofounder and chair, professor Gary Hamel. Prior to Strategos, Linda spent six years with the Mac Group/Gemini, where she was head of the San Francisco office and co-head of the high-tech practice on the West Coast and, later, Europe (based in Amsterdam). Her career began with two years at Smith Barney in corporate finance and M&A.

Linda has extensive global experience, having lived in, worked in, or traveled to over seventy countries. She is a Henry Crown Fellow with the Aspen Institute. She is an environmental activist who, with her best friend and husband, Paul Holland, built Tah.Mah.Lah, considered the greenest home in the United States. She holds a BA in foreign affairs from the University of Virginia and an MA in international relations and comparative politics from Stanford University, where she guest lectures. She and Paul are blessed to have three amazing daughters, Kylie, Devon, and Piper.